INTERNATIONAL POLITICAL ECONOMY

International Political Economy

Miquel-Angel Galindo Martin
and
Edward Nissan
Editors

Nova Science Publishers, Inc.
New York

For permission to use material from this book please contact us:
Telephone 631-231-7269; Fax 631-231-8175
Web Site: http://www.novapublishers.com

LIBRARY OF CONGRESS CATALOGING-IN-PUBLICATION DATA

International political economy / editors, Miquel-Angel Galindo Martin, Edward Nissan.
p. cm.
Includes index.
ISBN 978-1-60876-172-2 (hardcover)
1. International economic relations. I. Galindo Martin, Miquel-Angel. II. Nissan, Edward, 1929-
HF1359.I5854 2009
337--dc22

2009042906

Published by Nova Science Publishers, Inc. ✦ New York

CONTENTS

PREFACE

During the last century most of the economic literature and approaches were developed following closed macroeconomic models. The solution of the problems were "national". Policy makers used fiscal, monetary policies or mixed fiscal-monetary policies to improve the situation. The exchange rate policy was considered as a supplement measure to use in case of necessity. During the 1980´s and especially 1990´s this view changed drastically. A policy coordination was considered as a positive condition to achieve national objectives. If there is not such coordination, the positive effects of some national policies are reduced and sometimes eliminated. On the other hand, a globalisation process had arisen. A free capital, persons and goods movement were pursued considering the fact that it is economic growth enhancing and a suitable way to solve employment and production problems. Due to this situation it was necessary to develop models including variables about trade and relations among countries. For this reason, an analysis of the international political economy is a relevant topic to be considered when it is studied in the relation to the countries. Several and different issues can be considered in these kinds of studies, as author can see in the chapters of this book.

Chapter 1 - The objective of this chapter is to critically analyze climate change policy and governance. Drawing on the history of climate change anomalies and processes author examine why there is a gap between knowledge and action. This "gap" hypothesis postulates that a number of contradictions led policy and practices to be several steps behind the degree to which greenhouse gasses have been building up. This gap is set to continue through the Coppenhagen and future climate accords as the policy-making bodies have a weak commitment to global accord, mitigation and adaptation. The chapter starts with a brief history of climate change and the policy response. Then the core contradictions precipitating increasing levels of greenhouse gasses in the atmosphere are scrutinized. Lastly, a review of current policies is undertaken to see how effective they are in addressing climate change.

Chapter 2 - Governance is not a controversial and misunderstood concept. Sometimes concepts such as corruption, institutions and democracy are used as governance's proxy. In general terms, it means how an organization is governed being the science of government performance and behavior and it refers to several processes that must include from historical, cultural, social and political determinants. For this reason it is possible to establish a relationship between governance and institutions.

Communities of persons, firms, institutions are essential ingredients of good governance and its analysis could be developed considering two possibilities. First, considering the factors under which government would more efficient in welfare terms. Second, taking into account the economic results obtained by the government. Precisely, the main goal of this paper is analyse the relationship between governance and economic growth. Author will consider the indirect effects of governance on growth through its effects on private investment, public expenditure and income distribution. An empirical analysis is developed considering the case of 48 countries, considering a multiequational model that includes a private investment, public investment, Gini and GDP equations.

Chapter 3 - Industrial concentration is broadly defined as a few firms controlling a substantial share of assets or sales of the market. In the multinational industrial sector, this chapter shows that the largest 100 in the world control substantial amounts of assets and sales, both foreign and total. Two well known indexes of concentration were used, the Herfindahl and Theil's entropy, to check the levels of concentration between 1990 and 2005. It was found that changes in concentration were not statistically significant when compared on a yearly basis.

Chapter 4 - Multinational companies investing in communications, energy, transport and financial services, can have a differentiated effect in the host economy comparing with the one attributed to manufacturing investment. These companies are characterized by generation of an intermediate input aimed at practically the totality of an economy's sectors (intermediate input as well as a final good for consumers), reason why author have denominated the matter multinational transversal services. Author have analyzed in this paper if inflow foreign direct investment in transversal services over economic growth and productivity is significantly higher to the effect caused by inflow foreign direct investment in manufacturing sector. During the period 1985-2006, the results obtained in owner analysis show a positive and very similar effect of inward manufacturing FDI (MFDI) and inward transversal FDI (TFDI) on labor productivity (LP).

Chapter 5 - Despite the strong theoretical expected linkages between financial openness and economic growth, the financial globalization has been primarily a source of economic instability. This article presents a strategy of alternative political economy to the passivity of Latin American countries´ political economy facing up to the globalization. It emphasizes the idea that a permanent tension exists between the internationalization trend in economy relationships and the search for autonomy in the political economies; that tension is developed in an unstable external environment and in a new international financial liberal order. This paper compares the Asiatic and the Latin American trajectories after the financial crisis in 1997, and it analyzes the recent reform of the international financial architecture.

Chapter 6 - Over the last three decades, Turkey implemented a series of liberalisation programmes with the objective of increasing the availability of funds to both private and public sector. The policies were also aimed at stimulating economic efficiency of various sectors and enhancing global integration. The present chapter aims at assessing the extent by which financial liberalization has contributed to financial deepening in Turkey, and the sector that has benefited most from it. It will also show that the positive impact of trade liberalization on gross fixed capital formation and the country's economic growth has been greater than that of financial liberalization.

Chapter 7 - With globalization and the concomitant appearance of new actors in international trade, competitiveness has come to play a key role in political discourse and to constitute an objective of economic policy in both developed and developing nations. The term competitiveness, however, can be interpreted in a number of ways and tends to be ambiguous. The present article focuses on international competitiveness. Its review of the chief ex-ante and ex-post indicators used to measure that concept is followed by a discussion of export base growth as an element of competitiveness, illustrated with a model applied to the Spanish economy. Finally, the competitiveness of Spanish manufacturing industries that compete with imports is shown to be related to their respective technology intensity.

Chapter 8 - Author present an assessment of net financial benefits for the U.S. and the European Monetary Union (EMU) against the rest of the world (ROW). While other assessments of regional integration in the Global economy are possible, NAFTA and EMU affects nearly 40 percent of world trade. The assessment results from Computational General Equilibrium (CGE) method using GTAP data sets. On balance, author find positive net benefits, which tend to decline in the EMU after the initial impact. A popular explanation is that the benefits for a currency union can be sourced to the saving from having a single currency. Another explanation is that profits fall as convergence takes place. Overall, globalization reflects reduction of interest rates, deficits, and unemployment rates.

Chapter 9 - A certain loss in efficient national economic policies has taken place, given that the globalization of the economy and steps towards economic integration mean that the economic policies of different countries has an effect that reaches beyond their own borders, not only positive ("locomotive effect"), but also negative ("beggar your neighbour").

In addition, taking into account the efficiency problems of fiscal policy and the effects caused by other countries, coupled with the fiscal policy effects on monetary policy in the Monetary Union, the basis for coordinating national fiscal policies and the conditions set out in order to form part of the EMU, were established in the Maastricht Treaty. This process of restricting room for manoeuvre in national fiscal policies culminated in the Stability and Growth Pact (SPG)

So, this chapter is devoted to the analysis of the evolution and theories that analyze the economic effects of the use of fiscal policy. The third section undertakes the analysis of the conditions imposed by the Stability and Growth Pact and how it conditions the possibilities of using fiscal policy on the part of member states. Section four contains an empirical analysis of the evolution of public finances for countries in the Euro zone. The chapter ends with some brief conclusions

Chapter 10 - From both the macroeconomic and microeconomic or business perspectives, innovation is a path that can lead to sustainable success on today's current scene. In other words, the way innovation policy is posed is of great relevance. The existence of a market failure is often used as a justification for innovation policies. The scope of application for innovation policy is also a key point. Here author can find the idea of Regional Innovation Systems (RIS) and their evolution. The relationship between science policy and innovation policy is therefore important and often not sufficiently examined. It is important to analyse, in turn, the role of clusters and the policies relating to them.

Chapter 11 - Sometimes environmental problems can become a business opportunity for certain companies, and more specifically, for those author can refer to as the ecoindustry. In this paper, a discussion is introduced on firms which, in their search for better environmental performance, are led to develop research activities in the area of pollution-control technologies, in order to optimize their waste management processes. This can lead to technological breakthroughs that eventually can be attractive for others. Companies adopting such a strategy could also enjoy an advantage, and even lobby governments for harder regulations.

Empirical analysis in the paper indicates that, at the mean, an increase in CO_2 emissions will present a positive effect on high technology exports. The hypothesis that improvements in water quality induce positive effects on high technology exports is rejected. Instead, a negative, although fairly small, elasticity at the mean has been estimated. The negative sign of the interaction term in the econometric model indicates that improvements in water quality and CO_2 emissions can be considered to be substitutes, rather than complements, in the high technology exports process.

Chapter 12 - The concept of economic development has different meanings; it's essentially, though, an aim for all countries in order to boost wealth and the welfare of their citizens. Nowadays, the Information and Communication Technologies (ICT) are becoming a key factor in allowing economic development to improve in the world. On the other hand, education itself contributes to development, while being the complement necessary to make good use of the ICT potential.

The main aim of this chapter is to analyze, from different points of view, the role that such important factors, like ICT and education, may play in the world's development. Throughout the chapter, the different aspects of each one of them will be assessed, as well as their relation to economic development, to conclude with a review of the situation in the European Union which, resulting from the implementation of the Lisbon strategy in 2000, started to devote attention to technological and educational factors, and regarded them as an improvement for the economy.

Chapter 13 - In the U.S., illegal immigration is a very controversial issue. One dimension of this controversy involves whether this illegal entry in the country leads to higher rates of crime. If a clear link between crime in the U.S. and illegal immigration is established, the argument for more border security and enforcement is established. Clearly, such policies could lead to political tensions between the U.S. and Mexico. That said, according to the Federal Trade Commission, identity theft constituted the most common consumer complaint in the U.S. in 2006. Using state-level data for the 50 states for 2005, author find, among other things, that the rate of reported identity theft per 100,000 population is directed related to the unemployment rate, the percent of the population residing in urban areas, and the extent of undocumented immigration. Author also find investigate the impact of undocumented migration upon "property crime" in the forms of "robbery" and "burglary" per 100,000 population is directly impacted by undocumented migration, as well as the unemployment rate and the percent of the population living in urban areas.

Chapter 14 - Using recently developed indices of fractionalization and polarization, author investigate the effects of religious diversity on corruption across countries. Author find a linear and positive relationship between religious polarization and corruption and an inverse U-shaped relationship between religious fractionalization and corruption, and thus the corruption maximizing level of religious fractionalization. According to author results, a 1 standard deviation increase in polarization index causes the corruption index to increase by 0.17 standard deviations which is almost 3 times larger than the effects of some of the control variables such as openness and education on corruption. All else constant, corruption is maximized when the fractionalization index is equal to 0.57 which falls well within the range of observed values.

Chapter 15 - The recent economic and financial crisis has led to questions about the appropriateness of State intervention in the economy and the need for greater regulation. This has increased State intervention, characteristic of the European Ordoliberal model, and clashes with the U.S. Neoliberal model. In this chapter the benefits of a greater EU-style State intervention are stated, and how ICTs can contribute to the development of Latin American and Central and Eastern European countries.

In: International Political Economy
Editors: M.A. Galindo Martin, E. Nissan

ISBN: 978-1-60876-172-2

Chapter 1

Climate Change Trends and Governance: History, Contradictions and Prospects

Phillip Anthony O'Hara
Global Political Economy Research Unit,
Curtin University, Perth, Australia

Abstract

The objective of this chapter is to critically analyze climate change policy and governance.[1] Drawing on the history of climate change anomalies and processes we examine why there is a gap between knowledge and action. This "gap" hypothesis postulates that a number of contradictions led policy and practices to be several steps behind the degree to which greenhouse gasses have been building up. This gap is set to continue through the Coppenhagen and future climate accords as the policy-making bodies have a weak commitment to global accord, mitigation and adaptation. The chapter starts with a brief history of climate change and the policy response. Then the core contradictions precipitating increasing levels of greenhouse gasses in the atmosphere are scrutinized. Lastly, a review of current policies is undertaken to see how effective they are in addressing climate change.

1. History of Climate Change and Policy

Basic knowledge of climate change trends has been quite well known for a few decades; now the evidence is what we call "overwhelming". For instance, we know that there have been waves of climate change in the past, both during and after human beings became the dominant species on Earth. Some of this data is speculative because it depends on core samples from ice in the Arctic and Antarctic regions, Oceans in the Pacific and Atlantic, and certain other geographic and geological locations. The evidence points to the existence of

[1] I wish to thank Lynne Chester and anonymous referees for comments, and Miguel-Ángel Galindo Martin for editorial assistance. Email: philohara1@yahoo.com

100-140 million year waves of heating and cooling during the Phanerozoic eon (1 million to 500 million years ago). There were 75,000 to 110,000 year waves of heating and cooling during the Pleistocene era (15,000 to 500,000 years ago). During the current Holocene period when humans have and continue to dominate Earth there have been irregular waves of heating and cooling (zero to 12,000 years ago). Overall, especially for the Holocene period, the evidence is moderately good. For instance, we know about the medieval warm period between 975 and 1425AD, the little ice age in Europe from 1440 to 1710AD, and also the warming trend since industrialization commenced around 1850 (O'Hara 2009).

The evidence for climate change since the beginning of the industrial age around 1850 is good but still subject to some uncertainty. There are different estimates based on different core samples and historical records differ depending on which areas and regions are scrutinized. For instance, the IPCC-I (2007a) report shows that in 1850 the global land surface temperature (decadal mean) was around 13.68°C, but with an uncertainty range of 0.22°C. In 2005 it was said to be around 14.47°C, with a much less uncertainty range of 0.12°C. Similarly, they cite figures for the global mean sea level in 1880 being 130mm lower than the 1961-90 mean figure, with an uncertainty range of 43mm; while in 2005 the figure is 70mm above the 19961-90 mean, with uncertainty being low (IPCC-I, 2007a). Uncertainty has thus declined through time as the figures become more reliable. Uncertainty thus does not mean there is no climate change but simply that knowledge is incomplete or lacking in some instances, or some changes are non-linear rather than being easily predicted.

On the subject of greenhouse gasses, then, while some uncertainty exists the record is still fairly plain to see. The statistics at the chosen site show an increase in the index of the stock of CO_2 emissions from 100 (1970) to 115 (2005) or from 332ppp to 379ppm (IPCC-I, 2007a, p. 138). This 15 percent expansion of GHG stocks contributed to a decline in the Living Planet Index (LPI) from 100 to 72 (WWF, 2008) over the same period as terrestrial, marine and freshwater species became extinct and declined in numbers[2]. Surprisingly, the United Nations Human Development Program (UNDP, 2007), and to a much lesser extent the IPCC (2007) and Stern (2007) Reports, pay little attention to the declining state of biodiversity as the habitats of many species of plant and animal decline through human excesses. They seem to have concluded that if they concentrate on human concerns the message of climate change will be easier to 'sell' to governments and the community. While they may be correct, many feel this to be a narrow-minded approach, lacking in true humanity and feeling for other life forms on Earth.

The evidence has supported increasing greenhouse gas emissions, warming of the environment, rising sea levels, increasing extreme events, and declining precipitation on a global scale. Despite this evidence, little has been done in the way of policy to rectify the situation. To date, much of the blame has been put on certain ideological positions associated with conservative governments, corporate vested interests and the lack of an effective international body to push for change. Optimists have come to think that new conclusive evidence, more progressive governments and a global commitment to change will reduce the

[2] The Living Planet Index is based on an analysis of 3600 populations of more than 1300 vertebrate species around the world, subdivided into 695 terrestrial species, 274 marine species and 344 freshwater species. For these purposes, the Earth's surface is divided into 14 terrestrial habit types and 8 biogeographic habitat covers. The data is from a variety of sources, including scientific journals, NGO literature and the Internet. Plants and invertebrates were excluded due to lack of data. (WWF/GFN/ZSL, 2006.) More detail is available from Loh et al (2006).

gap between knowledge and policy. But to date no real action has been taken, of a substantive nature, to address the greatest potential crisis known to the human world.

During the period 2007-2010 it is fair to say that virtually all major parties and governments have come to recognize the *magnitude* of the problem. The major reports on climate change have established beyond doubt the seriousness with which climate is changing. The IPCC Reports (2007a,b,c,d), Stern Review (2007), UNDP Report (2007) and Gaunaut Review (2008) have all basically agreed on the magnitude of the problem and what to do about it. Al Gore's (2006) film *An Inconvenient Truth* played some role in changing public opinion. The reports all agree that without mitigation and adaptation CO_2-e stocks will rise to about 700-900ppm by 2100, resulting in a rise in average global temperatures of at least 4-5°C. This will lead potentially to dozens of major cities being submerged in water, an increased incidence of drought and flooding, extreme temperatures and hurricanes, and the extinction of possibly up to 50-60 percent of animal and plant species.

Up to 2005, at least, there was considerable resistance to acknowledging this state of affairs for political and ideological reasons. More recently, there has been an almost unanimous agreement about the extent of the problem. But the gap between knowledge and action has been evident in the past and likely to continue into the foreseeable future. This gap is the main stumbling block to effective climate change governance, and may even lead to a systemic failure to prevent major threshold catastrophes from occurring. Up until now certain critical areas of Earth have been subject to extreme climate effects, but into the future as the global average temperature exceeds 2-3 degrees from preindustrial times threshold catastrophes of major concern are likely.

Without immediate action the problem is going to get deeply serious very quickly. This is because of a lag between stocks and flows of greenhouse gasses, such that it may take 50 years or more for decreasing flows to reduce stocks if the stocks rise too much over the next decade. This is the major problem proposed by the "gap" hypothesis. Some explanation here is required. The problem is that GHG emissions are continuing to increase, which leads through lags to rising stocks of Co_2-e. If nothing is done then the stock is likely to rise to something like 750ppm by 2100. Much uncertainty though exists about the relationship between stocks of GHGs and temperature changes by 2100. This doesn't mean that temperatures are unlikely to rise, only that we are not sure exactly how much they will change. For instance, Nicholas Stern (2008) shows that with a business as usual approach of no mitigation and no adaptation to climate change, when GHG stocks are 750ppm there is a 82 percent chance of temperatures exceeding 4°C, 47% chance of it exceeding 5°C, 22 percent change of exceeding 6°C, and 9 percent chance of exceeding 7°C.

It used to be thought that GHG stocks could be eventually capped at around 550ppm (Stern, 2007).[3] Lately estimates of what would be reasonable have declined to around

---

[3] As a a simple rule, one can use CO_2 rather than CO_2-e contributions to radiative forcing, since the difference between CO_2 and CO_2-e is *negative* forcing components such as aerosols and surface albedo (IPCC 2007a:4). Total CO_2 (93%) plus natural solar irradiance (7%) contributions equal total net anthropogenic radiative forcing (100%). However, the level of scientific understanding of CO_2 is much greater than most other radiative forcing elements, and they have differing impacts through time. Richardson et al (2009:18) say about CO_2 and CO_2–e that: "Today, the Co_2 concentration is around 385ppm, and is rising by 2ppm per year, The 2007 concentration of all greenhouse gasses, [CO_2-e]… was 463ppm. … Adjusting this concentration for the cooling effects of aerosols yields a CO_2-equivalent concentration of 396ppm." (As a crude approximation, one could assume that 350ppm $CO_2 \approx$ 450ppm Co_2-e, ignoring the negative elements associated with aerosols etc. and uncertainty levels.) (see O'Hara 2009.)

450ppm (Garnaut, 2008, p. 46), even though some are still arguing that 450-550ppm would be all right (Hepburn and Stern, 2008, p. 260), while some are reducing this estimate to 400ppm (O'Hara 2009). The lower level of 400ppm GHG (equivalent to about 300ppm CO_2) is better because one estimate shows that at the 450ppm GHG level (≈350ppm CO_2) there is a 78 percent chance of temperatures rising by *more* than 2°C, 18 percent chance of more than 3°C, and 3 percent chance of more than 4°C. At the 550ppm level there is a 69 percent chance of temperatures rising more than 3°C, 24 percent chance of more than 4°C, and 7 percent chance of more than 5°C (Stern 2008). So while there is considerable uncertainty about the precise relationship between GHG stocks, temperature increases and climate change more generally, we can be moderately certain that the business as usual approach will lead to more than a 5°C increase in global temperatures. Very probably temperature increases should be kept below 2°C above preindustrial levels, which would indicate that GHG stocks should be kept below 450ppm, possibly as low as 400ppm.

The major concern about uncertainty is not so much how much GHGs will rise, or what the temperatures will be in future, but what effect these rising GHG and temperatures will have on the nature of climate more broadly speaking. A warming trend is one thing, but changes in the nature of sea levels, wind speeds, currents, rainfall, droughts, hurricanes, floods and the like are another thing. Related to this, but more critical, is at what points will the crucial tipping points or threshold effects start to come into play. These include coral bleaching, the melting of Arctic sea ice, thinning of the Greenland ice sheet, separation of ice sheet from bedrock in the Western Antarctic, collapse of the Gulf Stream, intensification of the El-Nino effect, and the destruction of the Amazon rainforest. Here uncertainty really comes into play, not so much because tipping points are uncertain per se, but increasingly because many of them are looking less uncertain about happening sooner rather than later. It is the *uncertainty about how early certain tipping points may start to magnify* that is the worry.

A critical factor generating much of the uncertainty is the likelihood of non-linear changes in the climate. Uncertainty would be lower if things happened linearly, in a stable progressive fashion. But these major climate events and especially the threshold effects tend to have transformational dynamics that lead them to escalate beyond a certain temperature; most say around 2°C, other effects may escalate around 3°C above pre-industrial (1850) levels, with some of them happening much later. Since some of them are thought to start impacting at around 2° C, this is of major concern because this is the level at which responsible governance is committed to reducing temperature increases. For the policy-maker this is the most depressing news possible, because it indicates nothing much can be done, even if temperatures are moderated at reasonable levels through effectively capping GHG emissions.

2. Political Economy Contradictions of Climate Change

Contradictions are complex processes that instigate change and motion. They are the dynamic factors that lead also to conflict and metamorphosis. Centering on contradictions is a way of getting to the source of the major elements at work affecting the phenomena in question. Contradictions concern opportunity costs and trade-offs concerning various elements in the equation, and one needs to have a balance in order to solve most problems. Contradictions abound in the area of climate change due to the non-linear relationship between many variables, conflict between major stakeholders, instability in the parameters, and vested interests who have a stake in the payoffs.

The *core (first) contradiction* at play is that between the *knowledge* we have of climate change and the *lack of policy activism* to address the problem. We now have a relatively good knowledge of the patterns and processes linking greenhouse gas emissions (GHGE) with changes in temperature and rising sea levels. There may be much uncertainty about the tipping points but this uncertainty seems to lie in the tendency to think they are happening sooner than later. Broadly speaking we have agreement about the urgency of the problem. But policy lags behind, partly due to the late emergence of broad agreement, 2007 being a crucial year in this respect; and partly due to free rider or prisoner dilemma problems. Everyone wants to reduce GHGE, but nobody wants to put in the effort, regardless of whether others are acting proactively to reduce the problem. Most parties would prefer others to incur the costs of action. The investment share of GDP required to reduce the major costs of climate change are likely to be greater than the 1 percent estimate made in the Stern Report (2007) and 2 percent of later studies (e.g., Stern 2008).

Because climate change is a global phenomena, although there are regional variations, the same result can be made if some parties act while others don't. Business doesn't want to incur the costs of mitigation and adaptation. Governments don't want to act in the light of short political cycles. Consumers don't want to reduce their levels of conspicuous consumption and waste. Developing nations recognize the problem emanating from the advanced world and want to leave it to them to sort out. Advanced nations want China and India to play a role even though they argue the core problem is consumption rather than production. Perhaps at the core of this problem of lack of action is that humans tend to act on these sort of problems only when an emergency arises. But because there are long lags between GHG flows and stocks, any changes in the flows due to perceived emergency will not affect rising stocks for perhaps half a century, if we wait too long into the future. In the meantime much of the ecological capital may have already been in the process of being destroyed. This contradiction between knowledge and lack of action is perhaps unlikely to be solved in the near future.

This is linked to research showing a negative relationship between concern for climate change and the degree of wealth of a nation. Sandvik (2008), for instance, indicated that people resist climate change if they are going to have to pay for its mitigation. Populations with high levels of wealth and consumption, would have to majorly reduce their addiction to gluttonous lifestyles of waste and obesity that are the causes of GGHG emissions. Most people who have to change their lifestyles will resist science that indicates the need for much action on global warming (both mitigation and adaptation). They will tend to assume that quick technological or tax solutions exist, and they are positive about the future even though they have more information at their disposal than poorer nations. Exceptions are some nations which have experienced extreme weather events lately, such as France and the Czech Republic.

A *second contradiction*, although a more fundamental one, is that between *ecological capital and human durable fixed capital*. Clearly in an historical sense there has been a negative relationship between the buildup of durable fixed capital such as machinery, equipment, buildings, consumer durables, and infrastructure (on the one hand) and ecological capital such as populations of species, habitat, current and wind patterns (on the other hand).

Industrialisation and the associated later rise of consumerism are the main culprits that have led to a decline in plant and animal populations and genetic stock, and disrupted global and regional geo-physical patterns. The higher the stock of such durable fixed capital, the greater the flow and also stock of greenhouse gasses. In like measure, the lower also is population numbers and genetic stock of plant and (non-human) animal species.

When this contradiction is played out on the world stage the debate becomes one of who is the culprit, producers or consumers, or both. The Stern (2007) and IPCC (2007) Reports place the emphasis on production, while China and some scholars (such as Helm, 2008, Trainer, 2008) put the blame on consumption. China argues it has low per capita emissions and that it is only producing to satisfy the consumer demand of advanced nations, such as the US and the EU. It is difficult to put blame on anyone or leave anyone out of the equation, for the important thing is to recognize that production and consumption are both important. One cannot exist without the other. Whereas producers need to be more cognizant of reducing emissions consumers need to moderate their ceremonial consumption oriented to waste and emulation. Especially advanced and emerging nations thus need to act to reduce emissions from all major sources.

The rate of growth of GDP is the proximate cause of GHG emissions, since GDP includes all the major elements of production and consumption generating emissions. It is perhaps ironical that we have become convinced of the state of play of the science of climate change at a time when historically global GDP growth has been declining. The long boom of the 1950s and 1960s saw very high GDP rates in most nations. But since the 1970s global rates of growth have declined. The increases of the 2000s moderated in 2008-2010 during the global subprime crisis. For some emerging nations economic growth rates had been halved; with many nations suffering the worst recession since the Depression of the 1930s. Certainly the latter is the situation for Iceland, Northern Europe, parts of Latin America, the US, and UK, as well as for the world as a whole. Most nations have shown declining rates in recent decades. Eastern and Central Europe in the 1990s experienced a decrease in net ecological footprint because growth became negative. Van Vuuren (2008) expects lower rates into the foreseeable future which may help GHGE. However, lower global growth due to crisis often results in less action on the environment. Indeed, this is precisely what is happening at present. The subprime crisis has led many governments and oppositions to reduce their commitment to tackling climate change, due to job losses and reduced budgets.

The *third contradiction* relevant to climate change is *uneven development* in the world economy. Different nations contribute to greenhouse gasses at different rates, mainly due to differential rates of growth, and partly standard of living differences. The advanced nations of the US, EU, Australia and Canada have high per capita contributions. The underdeveloped nations of sub-Saharan Africa, Asia and some Latin American nations have low per capita emissions. There is a complex relationship between aggregate and per capita emissions and the adverse effects imposed by climate change. Most developing or underdeveloped areas (with low per capita and aggregate emissions), especially in the tropics and sub-tropics, are being and are likely to be affected the most by climate change. They are experiencing many more floods, droughts and other extreme events, and these are likely to continue to increase markedly as global GHGEs rise.

Sociological political economists have been developing the notion of ecologically unequal exchange to help explain these global contradictions and injustices. Jorgenson et al (2009:263), for instance, demonstrate that the "vertical flow of exports is a structural mechanism allowing for more-developed countries to partially externalize their consumption-based environmental impacts to lesser-developed countries." The terms of trade plays a role here in tending to undervalue minerals, agricultural output and to some degree mass production manufactures from the periphery while enhancing the value of high-technology goods and high-skill output from the core and semi-periphery. What has been called the 'ecological Prebisch-Singer hypothesis' postulates that the periphery provides materials, labor power and energy to support the development of the core and semi-periphery. In the process the periphery suffers the negative social and ecological costs of soil degradation, deforestation, and the entropic unavailability of resources. This also negatively impacts on industrial development potential, standard of living and quality of life. The core is simultaneously saved many of these social and environmental costs through cheap resources from overseas, lower levels of domestic ecological waste, and being able to protect their own environmental space (see O'Hara 2009).

Advanced areas that contribute more to climate change thus tend to have fewer effects from it than those who contribute less to GHGE. The result of this is that not only are advanced nations going to have to pay the price for reducing their high levels of emissions, but they are also going to have to provide enormous resources to underdeveloped nations to help them overcome problems generated elsewhere. Plus, especially in or near the advanced nations that are less affected, there are areas that will actually benefit from climate change. Many areas of the US, EU, Arctic Circle and even Antarctica will have warmer temperatures which will stimulate agricultural productivity, with the GHGEs providing a critical source of CO_2 fertilization that reinforces this trend (Cline 2007). Nevertheless, most areas will be worse off in advanced nations, such as especially south-western United States, the Mediterranean basin of southern Europe, and south-west Australia, which will experience especially declining rainfall and more extreme heat in summer (Solomon et al 2009); plus areas that will suffer from rising sea levels, such as Manhattan, coastal areas of north-west Europe, and so forth.

The *fourth contradiction* is that between *present and future generations.* Clearly it is primarily future generations that are going to have to experience the hotter weather and the more extreme climates. Current populations are having some impact from the problems emerging, but they are nothing like what is likely in the future. This is related to the question of an appropriate discount rate. Some economists argue we should have a high discount rate to value present generations greater than future ones. Others such as the Stern Review (2007) argue the opposite, that on moral grounds we should have a low or zero discount rate. The problem of multiple generations is an important one, if we just concentrate for the moment on human beings.

There is no doubt in my mind that the Stern Review is correct in positing a moral imperative to equate present and future generations. Indeed this moral argument is the prime source of action for many environmental scholars. It is argued that we need to equalize the concerns of present and future generations because future populations cannot speak for themselves. Due to the present bias in favor of human beings currently living, we need to counter that by positing a zero discount rate. While this is the case, or at least supported by many scholars and practitioners, it is unlikely to be supported by most people and states. The gap between knowledge and action is due to indifference to the future, not wanting to impose costs on the presently living, and exaggerating uncertainty about the long term. Policy-makers, consumers and business have a myopic view of reality, being unlikely to act unless they are directly affected. This is a major cause for pessimism, for the unlikelihood of action by actors, and for predicting high temperatures into the future, seriously rising sea levels, and major tipping points occurring early.

The *fifth contradiction,* which is linked to the fourth, is that policy-makers and their constituents are affected by *multiple crises* that affect them in every major decade, and which reduce the importance of climate change. At any point in time, policy makers are trying to moderate certain crises that impinge on the social, political and economic performance of their economies. These multiple crises are difficult to prioritize, demand heavy resources for their resolution, and have a circular and cumulative impact on the political economies. Climate change policies may be a permanent feature of the landscape, but they are always being affected by other developments in the world. Every time a crisis emerges it reduces the significance of climate change, and diverts resources away from its resolution.

These are what Ren (2000) calls "linked crisis events". Drawing on more critical crisis events than he, it is significant that climate change is affected by other crises. These include terrorism and the war on terrorism, recession and corporate crises, and the current global subprime crisis. There is little doubt that 9/11 impacted on climate change policies by reinforcing (initially) the popularity of President George W. Bush, and diverting resources to armaments and the military. Similarly, the corporate crises in the US in the early 2000s stimulated the inception of the Sarbanes-Oxley Act to reduce corporate irregularities and unethical accounting practices. The Afghan and Iraqi wars of the 2000s directed much of the world towards terrorism and the war on terrorism while reducing resources towards climate change efforts. The current global subprime crisis similarly directs many policy-makers toward issues associated with jobs and growth rather than the environment.

The *sixth contradiction* is *ignorance* (or asymmetric information) about the science of climate change. Most politicians, business people and the lay community have not studied the climate change literature in any real depth. As a result, they possibly think that major policy changes could be made when the catastrophes are nearly upon us. The history of humanity has seen major policy shifts when voters are experiencing depression, deep recession, war, terrorism, and/or financial crisis. At present most of the population of the world is not being affected by greenhouse gas emissions significantly enough to show much interest in change. Even if they know GHGE are relatively high, and that some of the changes are starting to appear, many probably still think change can come later rather than earlier.

This is a serious mistake, made plain by all the major climate change reports to date. Many agents are not sufficiently cognizant of the relationship between greenhouse stocks and flows. Solomon et al (2009) demonstrate very clearly that these climate changes are irreversible. For instance, they demonstrate how if CO_2 stocks reach 1200ppm by 2100 and then flows immediately decline to zero, by 3000 stocks will have declined only to around 750ppm. Similarly if Co_2 stocks reach 850 by 2100 and then flows decline to zero, by 3000 stocks will decline to around 525ppm ('quasi-equilibrium'). In both these cases, the thermal expansion of oceans has been increasing, while global warming itself remains relatively constant. This is evidence to support the proposition that climate change is closely related to the highest absolute levels of CO_2 stocks experienced.

Currently global GHG *stocks* are at about 455ppm, while human-generated *flows* are about 30Gt CO_2-e (per annum). 60 percent of the flows are from CO_2 industrial emissions, 17 percent from CO_2 land-use and forestry sources, 14 percent from methane, 7 percent from nitrous oxide, while the remaining 2 percent are from a range of other industrial gasses (Garnaut, 2008, pp. 45,53). Non-CO_2 positive emissions approximately equal cloud albedo negative emissions (IPCC-1:205). Garnaut (2008) mentions that the albedo effect should be discounted since it is likely to disappear in the long-term; while many authors mention that methane can be reduced in a short time period. To reduce GHGE to 450ppp (by 2050) will eventually require CO_2-e flows of between 3.1 and 6.7 GtC; 550ppm will require 6.7-12.6 GtC; 650 requires 14.1-15.4 GtC; 750 requires 14.1-15.4 GtC; and 1000ppm requires 15.4-15.8. Major declines in flows are thus needed even for the more extreme levels of GHGE.

These multiple contradictions are very powerful. The conflicts between science and policy, ecological and durable fixed capitals, core and periphery, present and future generations, multiple crises and ignorance are all reducing the ability of human beings to prevent further climate change. Indeed, policy making has been so poor in this area as to lead understandably to pessimism about the future. The United States has not been a leader of proactive policies. The European Union has tended to have pollution caps above likely levels. China wants to develop and is expanding its coal-fired power stations. Underdeveloped nations lack the resources to adapt to climate change. Advanced nations are unlikely to provide the resources necessary for change. The contractions have been too strong for resolution at the 2009 Copenhagen conference and into the foreseeable future.

3. Policy Plans and Priorities

This section looks more specifically at policies that have been proposed or that are currently in motion, with a view to assessing the likelihood of success into the future. It is generally agreed that the Kyoto Protocol was a good start but generally a weak agreement to develop the necessary measures to reduce greenhouse gasses by 2050 or 2100. The Kyoto Protocol included three main aspects: agreed reductions in GHGE by developed nations; flexible processes such as emission trading and the clean development mechanism; and national or regional bodies to administer the protocol. Advanced nations agreed to reduce their GHGE by an average of 5.2 percent by 2012 compared with 1990, with deviations from this for specific nations according to their special cases. Developing nations had no binding limits or rules. Kyoto was a good start because it did finally get ratified in 2005 thanks to Russia accepting the agreement, and it did direct the world towards environmental issues. However, it was weak because it concentrated on production rather than including consumption; failed to adequately include developing nations in binding agreements; and also since greenhouse gas stocks have continued to build up rather than decline.

The IPCC-III (2007c, p. 776) report, for instance, argued that consistent with trends towards 450ppm CO_2-e levels developed nations would have to reduce their emissions by between 25-40 percent by 2020, and by 80-90 percent by 2050; with *substantia*l deviations from baseline for developing nations. Alternatively, for trends to move towards 550ppm CO_2-e levels advanced nations need to reduce their GHGE by 10-30 percent by 2020 and 40-90 percent by 2050; with deviations from baseline operating for developing nations. Elzen and Hohne (2008), who illustrated these results in the IPCC report, argue that these emission reduction ranges are still operational. The trouble is the world is not keeping in line with required reductions in GHGE. Compared with 1990, for instance, advanced nations have experienced no change in emissions to 2006, developing nations have increased their emissions by 68%, while for the world as a whole emissions have increased by 25%. Most studies also show emissions likely to expand considerably through to 2020. Sheehan (2008), for instance, presents estimates of 20 percent higher emissions for advanced nations, 216 percent higher for developing countries, and 97 percent higher for the world as a whole.

Etzen and Hohne (2008) therefore conclude that "it is very likely that global emissions will continue to rise until 2012 [and beyond] when a new international climate agreement can start to become effective." UN climate change groups, representing all the major players and others, have been meeting on an almost annual basis since the Kyoto framework was devised in 1992 (UN 1992). Much depended on the *Copenhagen COP 2009* when it was hoped that a new agreement would emerge. The contradictions discussed in this paper explain most of the failures of Copenhagen. What is needed is a climate change accord (or 'deal') that resolves most of the contradictions. But the contradictions are very deeply embedded in the institutions of the current system of governance and practices as to necessitate major systemic change.

Hepburn and Stern argue that the following core components of such a deal are likely needed. The first is appropriate global emissions reductions targets for achieving the 450 to 550ppm targets, including a 50 percent reduction by 2050, three quarters of it coming from advanced nations. The second, in order to achieve this target, includes advancing global emissions trading, the clean development mechanism, research and development especially for carbon capture and sequestration, plus deforestation clauses and finance for adaptation especially for developing nations. Further down the line it is argued that developing nations will need to adopt binding national targets by 2020. This new accord is likely to represent, if successful, a type of social structure of accumulation whereby emissions may begin to decline while an environment of relatively less uncertainty can stimulate sustainable investment and growth.

Many argue that suitable emission reductions will not be possible without immediate and ongoing radical technological change. Hasselmann and Barker (2008), for instance, indicate in broad terms how this might arise through a three-phase form of technological transformation. In the first instance, improving energy efficiency immediately can in the longer term contribute to a radical lowering of GHG emissions. In the intermediate term, with benefits especially emerging through 2040 to 2100, advances through biomass, wind, hydro and geothermal energy can contribute moderately. By themselves, however, these first two advances are seen as only eventually achieving 2000 flows of emissions by 2100, with efficiency advances being four times greater than the alternative energies. The third type of innovation, solar energy, is said to likely contribute to declining emissions on the back of the other advances. This takes the form of solar thermal or photovoltaic on a massive scale. These combined are hoped to reduce emissions from 28 GTC/yr (2000) to the required 1.7 GTC/yr (2100).

Dieter Helm argues against both the Stern proposals for a new accord and the likelihood of ongoing innovation starting in the present. His argument against Kyoto and Stern (and by extension the Copenhagen agenda) is multidimensional. In the first place, they are said to concentrate on production rather than also consumption, they assume the policy costs of adjustment are minimal (possibly 1-2 percent of GDP), and they ignore the critical role of China and India in mitigation strategies. Secondly, they ignore aviation and shipping, free rider problems, and include no effective enforcement mechanisms. Helm implies that some success will need to be made to reduce advanced nations' extraordinary high levels of consumption, and that it is going to be very difficult to reconstruct stocks of ecological capital once they have been destroyed, due to the principle of strong sustainability (path dependence) that substitutability is relatively low between human and non-human capitals (especially beyond a certain point or areas).

Other core problems, according to Helm, are that the climate change industry includes a lot of pork barreling which will likely increase costs of mitigation from 1 to perhaps 6 percent of GDP. Consumers are unlikely to reduce their discounting of future utility, while advanced nations are unlikely to sufficiently compensate developing areas such as China and India for reducing their coal fired power stations. Technologically the solutions are said to be problematic. Biomass will adversely impact on agriculture and food production. Nuclear has the well-known problems of capacity shortfall, waste, safety and possible nuclear proliferation. And while carbon sequestration and solar potential are extensive, the real technological problem is that of capital investment. The energy capital stock (for e.g., electricity) has a life of about 30 years, and much of it is already in place for use until 2030. Coal sequestration and other alternatives will likely need to wait decades to substitute sufficiently for current technologies. Similarly, trends for automobiles are unlikely to lead to substitutes, even though this capital stock life is shorter. China's coal fired power stations are on the rise long term.

In short, even with the new regime in Washington, and especially in the light of financial crises, wars in Afghanistan and Iraq, and other problems likely in the future, nothing much is going to change in the short-to-intermediate-term future. Copenhagen and ongoing institutions are likely to continue to ignore the inclusion of conspicuous consumption, massive financial redistribution to developing nations for lower carbon alternatives, existing regimes of accumulation, and the recognition that capital stock questions will emerge more in the 2020s and 2030s. The costs of abatement and adaption are much higher than the major reports and agreements acknowledge, and it is very difficult to turn around core path dependent processes when the ideologies and habits are changing only marginally. A sea change is required among policy-makers, consumers and producers.

CONCLUSION

This paper has examined in some detail the historical backgound in which the climate change issues should be situated. We explored several waves of climate change through the millennia, and more recently the wave of global warming, precipitated by the forces of industrialization and consumerism. The activities associated with production and consumption anomalies that lead to problematic levels and amplitudes of greenhouse gasses need to be severely moderated. The speed of action, however, needs to be much greater than the current systems of governance and accumulation advocate. The question arises as to how effective policy and governance are in stimulating social processes leading to lower levels of greenhouse gasses in the atmosphere.

The current paper argues that there is a major gap between knowledge and action. We have the academic and practical knowledge that climate change is happening faster than we are currently acting on the problem. There is likely to be a series of tipping points of a nonlinear nature that will start to impact mostly suddenly at different global and regional temperatures. For instance, some of them may kick in at 2 degrees centigrade above preindustrial levels, others at 3 degrees, and still others at 4 and possibly again 5 degrees above preindustrial levels. These threshold effects will thus likely stimulate non-linear increases in the *impact* of climate change, including many more heatwaves, floods, droughts, and hurricanes.

There will also be considerable differentials in the extent to which different areas are likely to be affected. The developing or underdeveloped nations of the tropics and sub-tropics are likely to get hotter and dryer, while many cold and temperate climates are likely to be less adversely affected due to higher agricultural productivity (in some microcosms) and less snowcover. The areas that pollute more absolutely and relatively are thus likely to be less affected and also better able to adapt to climate change. Human development levels are also likely to become more uneven between core and periphery as a result. Hence the advanced capitalist economies are less likely to be willing to reduce their levels of consumption and production as well as assist developing or underdeveloped nations with their mitigation and adaptation practices.

Due to the slowness with which governance and other practices have reacted to the threat of climate change it is likely that humanity will fail at the task of sufficiently reducing emissions of greenhouse gasses into the environment. The major tendencies point in this direction. The gap between knowledge and action is large due to a number of core contradictions at play. Vested interests will likely dominate over the common good due to the differential impact of climate change, the short political cycle, unequal resources between core and periphery, conflict between current and future generations, the role of multiple crises, and some degree of asymmetric information between specialists, politicians and the general population.

The policies that have been introduced are not up to the task of reducing greenhouse gas emissions. Recent studies point to an increasing level of emissions and rising stocks of greenhouse gasses. The future depends on going far beyond the Copenhagen agenda towards solving the core contradictions. The probability of resolution anytime soon is low due to the powerful forces enhancing such emissions. Alternative technologies may take several decades to be institutionalized into world-system norms and practices. Lifestyle decisions to reduce consumption will likely be too weak to impact the system. Major challenges exist for policymakers and analysts as changes are due almost immediately to reduce the flows of greenhouse gasses to moderate climate change in the long-run.

References

Cline, William R. (2007). *Global Warming and Agriculture: Impact Estimates by Country.* Washington DC: Peterson Institute for International Economics.

den Elzen, Michel. (2008). Reductions of Greenhouse Gas Emissions in Annex 1 and Non-Annex 1 Countries for Meeting Concentration Stabilisation Targets. *Climatic Change,* Volume 91, 249-274.

Garnaut, Ross. (2008). *The Gaunaut Climate Change Review,* Cambridge, UK: Cambridge University Press.

Gaunaut, Ross, Howes, Stephen, Jotszo, Frank and Sheehan, Peter (2008). Emissions in the Platinum Age: The Implications of Rapid Development for Climate Change Mitigation. *Oxford Review of Economic Policy*, Volume 24, Number 2, 377-401.

Hasselmann, Klaus and Baker, Terry (2008). The Stern Review and the IPCC Assessment Report: Implications for Interaction between Policymakers and Climate Experts: An Editorial Essay. *Climatic Change,* Volume 89, 219-229.

Helm, Dieter (2008). Climate-Change Policy: Why Has So Little been Achieved?. *Oxford Review of Economic Policy*, Volume 24, Number 2, 211-238.

Hepburn, Cameron and Stern, Nicholas (2008). A New Global Deal on Climate Change. *Oxford Review of Economic Policy*, Volume 24, Number 2, 259-279.

IPCC-I. (Intergovernmental Panel on Climate Change) (2007a) Solomon, Susan, Qin, Dahe, Manning, Martin, Marquis, Melinda, Averyt, Kristen, Tignor, Melinda, Miller Jr., Henry and Chen. Zhenlini (Editors). *Climate Change 2007—The Physical Science Basis.* Contribution of Working Group I to Fourth Assessment Report. New York: Cambridge University Press.

IPCC-II. (2007b) Parry, Martin; Canziani, Osvaldo; Palutikof, Jean; van der Linden, Paul and Hanson, Clair. (Eds), *Climate Change 2007—Impacts, Adaptation and Vulnerability. Contribution of Working Group II to Fourth Assessment Report.* New York: Cambridge University Press.

IPCC-III (2007c) Metz, Bert, Davidson, Ogunlade, Bosch, Peter, Dave, Rutu and Meyer, Leo (Editors). *Climate Change 2007—Mitigation of Climate Change.* Contribution of Working Group III to Fourth Assessment Report. New York: Cambridge University Press.

IPCC-IV. (2007d) *Climate Change 2007: Synthesis Report.* IPCC: London. 73pp.

Jorgenson, A.K., Austin, K., Dick, C. (2009) Ecologically Unequal Exchange and the Resource Consumption/Environmental Degradation Paradox: A Panel Study of Less-Developed Countries, 1970-2000. *International Journal of Comparative Sociology,* Volume 50, 263-284.

Loh, J., Green, R.E., Ricketts, T., Lamoreux, T., Jenkins, J., Kapos, M. and Randers, J. (2005). The Living Planet Index: Using species population time series to track trends in biodiversity. *Philosophical Transactions of the Royal Society*, 360, 289-295.

O'Hara, Phillip Anthony. (2009) Political Economy of Climate Change, Ecological Destruction and Uneven Development. *Ecological Economics,* Volume 69, Number 2, 223-234.

Richardson, K; Steffen, W.; Schellnhuber, H.J.; Clcamo, J.; Barker, T. et al. (2009) *Synthesis Report: Climate Change: Global Risks, Challenges and Decisions.* Copenhagen: IARU (International Alliance of Research Universities), 10-12 March. 39pp. Available Online.

Sandvik, Hanno (2008). Public Concern over Global Warming Correlates Negatively with National Wealth. *Climatic Change,* Volume 90, 333-341.

Solomon, Susan, Plattner, Gian-Kaspar, Knutti, Reto and Friedlingstein, Pierre (2009). Irreversible Climate Change Due to Carbon Dioxide Emissions. *Proceedings of the National Academy of Science*, Volume 106, Number 6, 1704-1709.

Stern, Nicholas (2007). T*he Economics of Climate Change: The Stern Review.* Cambridge, UK: Cambridge University Press.

Stern, Nicholas (2008). The Economics of Climate Change. *American Economic Review: Papers and Proceedings,* Volume 98, Number 2, 1-37. (Richard T. Ely Lecture)

Trainer, Ted (2008). A Short Critique of the Stern Review. *Real-World Economics Review*, Number 45, 54-58.

UNDP. (United Nations Development Program) (2007). *Human Development Report 2007/2008: Fighting Climate Change: Human Solidarity in a Divided World.* New York City: Palgrave Macmillan. Available on the Internet.

USCCSP. (US Climate Change Science Program) (2009). *Global Climate Change Impacts in the United States.* Washington DC: USCCSP.

WWF/GFN/ZSL. (World Wildlife Fund/Global Footprint Network/Institute of Zoology) (2006). *Living Planet Report 2006*, Gland, Switz, WWF; Oakland, Calif: GFN; London, ZSL.

van Vuurens, Detlef P. (2008). Do Recent Emissions Imply Higher Emissions Forever?. *Climatic Change,* Volume 91, 237-248.

In: International Political Economy
Editors: M.A. Galindo Martin, E. Nissan
ISBN: 978-1-60876-172-2

Chapter 2

GOVERNANCE, FISCAL POLICY AND ECONOMIC GROWTH

***Miguel-Angel Galindo Martin*[1] *and María Teresa Méndez Picazo*[2]**
[1]University of Castilla-La Mancha, Spain
[2]University Complutense, Spain

ABSTRACT

Governance is not a controversial and misunderstood concept. Sometimes concepts such as corruption, institutions and democracy are used as governance's proxy. In general terms, it means how an organization is governed being the science of government performance and behavior and it refers to several processes that must include from historical, cultural, social and political determinants. For this reason it is possible to establish a relationship between governance and institutions.

Communities of persons, firms, institutions are essential ingredients of good governance and its analysis could be developed considering two possibilities. First, considering the factors under which government would more efficient in welfare terms. Second, taking into account the economic results obtained by the government. Precisely, the main goal of this paper is analyse the relationship between governance and economic growth. We will consider the indirect effects of governance on growth through its effects on private investment, public expenditure and income distribution. An empirical analysis is developed considering the case of 48 countries, considering a multiequational model that includes a private investment, public investment, Gini and GDP equations.

1. INTRODUCTION

Governance is a term that has a higher priority in certain circles, especially between economists and corporate sector. A wide literature has come out in the last decades considering different relationships and elements connected with governance from theoretical as well as empirical points of view. However, is a concept that remains controversial and misunderstood. There is not a single definition of governance and sometimes is related to concepts such as democracy, corruption, institutions…

Governance means in a broad sense how an organization is governed. Communities of persons, firms, institutions, etc. are essential ingredients of good governance. However it is not a new concept. As Bowles (2004, pp. 474-478) states, different classical thinkers, Aristotle, Aquinas, Burke, Rousseau, among others, recognized communities behavior as government ingredients. Mandeville's *Fable of the Bees* stressed that governing social interactions could encourage selfish motives that would enhance social welfare. Classical economists in their analysis of the selfish *Homo Economicus*, stressed that the ingredients of governance are the role of competitive markets, property rights and well intentioned states. During the nineteenth and twentieth centuries the economists and political thinkers were interested in the controversy state intervention versus laissez faire.

In this paper we will consider the public governance and the channels through which it affects economic growth. Not only fiscal resources are the only factor to improve economic performance but also the quality of government. Laws, decisions made by policy makers and public officials, institutions, create incentives for economic agents affecting the allocation of investment and public expenditure that have relevant effects on economic growth. From this point of view the analysis of governance can carry out from two perspectives. First, establishing the conditions and factors under which the government activity can be more efficient in terms of welfare. Second, considering the outcomes which are expected from a government. We will mainly consider the latter.

One of the most relevant economic policy goals is economic growth. Nowadays, the effectiveness of economic policy is tested on economic growth results. Countries that show better growth rates are considered as good governed. In the controversy state versus market the economic result obtained is the best way to decide between both. It is relevant to know if governance is growth enhancing.

This is the main objective of this paper. In section 2 we will briefly considered the governance concept. Section 3 the relationship between governance and economic growth is analysed. In section 4 the empirical study is developed. Section 5 contains the main conclusions.

2. GOVERNANCE

Different governance definitions can be considered. In general terms, governance is the science of government performance and behavior and it refers to several processes that must include from historical, cultural, social and political determinants.

In this sense it is possible to establish a relationship between governance and institutions. Good governance can be considered as the existence of an appropriate set of institutions in a country. North (1990) states that these institutions play an important role in the economic performance. Institutions introduce rules that determine the conduct of the economic agents in the different areas of the economic activity.

The nexus between markets and government is one of the most relevant elements in the analysis of the economic performance. Both are interdependent at least in several ways (Dréze and Sen, 1995). First, government facilitates economic growth due to its education policies that improve skill formation in the labor force. Government also generates economies of scale and technological externalities. Second, in many cases market mechanism is dependent on government economic policy. For example, government can play an important role designing measures that modify income distribution and introducing taxation policies that would have relevant effects on market dynamics. Third, markets need legal enforcement to develop their activity. They hardly can work if there are not property rights, for example.

All these reasons show the interdependence between markets and government. However the main point is to determine their respective domains and their efficiency to achieve the objectives. Developed countries, especially European Union countries, considered that the main economic objective is to achieve a certain inflation rate, more or less 2%, considering that this inflation target would contribute to obtain adequate economic growth levels. Markets flexibility, especially labor market, fiscal discipline and the interest rate modifications would be the main elements to achieve such objective. In this case, institutions would play a secondary role in the process: they must help to the markets to be more flexible. In the case of the developing countries the story is quite different. Several institutional questions must be considered: the role of corruption, the political and institutional stability, the protection of private property.

The answer to the controversy market versus government will depend on the results obtained. Economic theories emphasize efficiency and it is necessary to test if governance would help to achieve the economic goals. From a theoretical point of view and in the case of economic growth, the literature shows that there is a relationship between both. In a broad sense, economic growth rests on the following key variables: efficiency, the saving rate and the depreciation of capital. And these variables depend, in turn on governance among other variables (Gylfason, 1999, 14). The relationship between economic growth and governance is developed in the next section.

3. Governance and Economic Growth

As it is well known two main economic growth models have been developed since 1950s: exogenous and endogenous growth models[1]. Former assumes, among other questions, the existence of appropriate institutions for markets and they don't introduce any price distortions and there are no resources misallocations. All at all, exogenous growth models assume that the institutions operate in an appropriate way. There are not possibilities to create monopolies and the efficiency of the system prevents the existence of corruption. Therefore it is not possible the existence of bad governance and for this reason it is not necessary to take it into account in the analysis.

Endogenous growth models on the other way, introduces the factor accumulation from R&D expenditure, the spillovers from introduction of new technology, the development of human capital… that have relevant effects on productivity that enhances economic growth. In this sense, it is possible to incorporate the effects of governance on the capital-augmenting effects as well as on the efforts of individuals.

In this kind of analysis it is also necessary to take into account the role of fiscal policy. The empirical literature doesn't show a unique conclusion showing different results depending on the data, methodology used and the set of countries.

[1] Demand side growth models have also developed (see e.g., Lavoie, 1992, McCombie and Thirlwall, 1994). However the main economic growth literature has mainly focused on these two approaches.

If we consider the standard Keynesian analysis, fiscal policy through increases public consumption and/or reducing taxes, enhances private investment increasing domestic demand. Higher private investment has positive effect on economic growth. However it doesn't take into account the negative effects derived from this measure, such as, "crowding-out" effect, inflationary pressures, and modifications on exchange rate... that discourage the investment decisions and reduce economic growth. Other effects can also be considered, such as, wealth effect, wages...To avoid these negative effects on investment the opposite measure is recommended, that is, reduce public deficits. These reductions have also the positive effect on investors' expectatives because deficit reduction is considered as a signal of political stability (Drazen, 2001)

The previous mechanisms mainly work in the case of high-income countries. In the case of low-income countries there are some restrictions that could reduce their efficiency. For example, the existence of financial repression and not adequately developed financial markets eliminate or reduce the interest rates and wealth effect responses to public deficit. It is also necessary to consider the existence of a restricted economic freedom that discourages the investment process, especially if the property rights are not defended.[2] For all these reasons, the analysis of the relationship between governance, fiscal policy and economic growth is developed considering the investment function.

However, from our point of view we consider that there are also other channels that must be taken into account. Of course private investment is one of them but also public investment and income distribution. Good governance improves the public investment in the case of high-income countries due to the better allocation and use of the resources independently of the negative effects on economic growth derived from its financing. Low-income countries will obtain easily and more resources if they have a good governance. These relationships are showed in figure-1.

Income distribution has also effects on economic growth. Economists have not had a unanimous position on the sign of this relationship. In the literature of the 1950s and 1960s it was accepted that higher inequality would enhance economic growth (e.g. Kaldor, 1956; Kelly and Williamson, 1968; Cook, 1995).

They considered the hypothesis that the savings is related to income and play a relevant role in the economic growth process. In this case it was necessary to shift the income from consumers to savers.

This implied to use a redistribute fiscal policy that shifts income from poorer to richer, who have a higher propensity to save. A higher savings will increase capital accumulation and economic growth[3].

[2] On the other hand, private investment tends to be insensitive to price stability due to mainly to the fact that in many countries the investment process is mainly undertaken by the public sector that obtains their funds from loans provided by internationally agencies.

[3] The possibility that inequality is growth-enhancing is also supported by the stage of economic development. Countries in early stage of economic development need physical capital accumulation to improve the economic growth process. In this case, inequality is growth-enhancing, because higher savings is necessary to finance such capital accumulation. In later stages of economic development, on the contrary, equality is growth-enhancing. If inequality is maintained, with credit market imperfections, there would be lower human capital accumulation that leads to a lower economic growth. This later channel could explain why empirical evidence with a wide range of countries, shows a positive effect of inequality on growth.

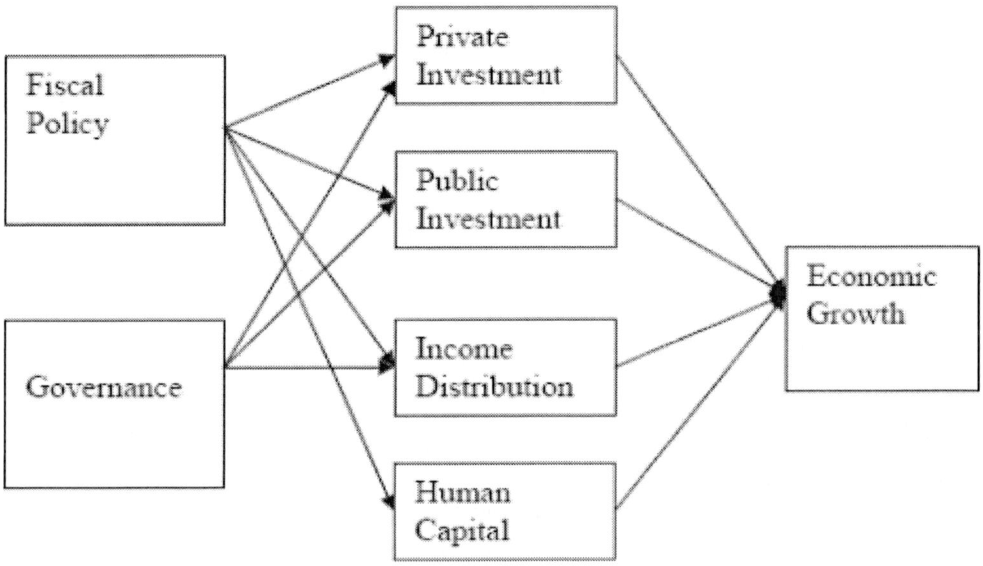

Source: Own elaboration.

Figure 1. Relationship between fiscal policy, governance and economic growth.

This view has been criticised and changed during the last decades. The introduction of endogenous growth models implied to consider again that relationship but introducing new factors and variables. The empirical literature showed from this new position that could be a negative relationship between inequality and economic growth. Different channels could explain this new view (Perotti, 1996, pp. 150-154; Aghion, Caroli and García-Peñalosa, 1999, pp. 1621-1630):

1. Fiscal channel. In an unequal society, poor voter will vote for those fiscal programs that promise a better income distribution through taxation or public expenditure. That implies the fiscal redistribution must be financed by distortionary taxation that distorts economic decisions, and discourages investment and finally economic growth (Alesina and Rodrick, 1994; Bertola, 1993. On the public capital effects, see Alfranca and Galindo, 2002, 2003).
2. Socio-political problem. Some literature (Alesina and Perotti, 1996; Benabou, 1996a, b) has stressed the impact of income inequality on political instability and social tensions. These problems will increase uncertainty that leads to a lower investment and economic growth.
3. Education. As it is well known, the empirical evidence shows that there is a positive effect of education on economic growth. In the case of income inequality, there are different mechanisms in the relationship between both variables. On the one hand, higher inequality implies higher underinvestment in the education when credit markets are imperfect. In the developing countries poor households are constraint for cash and unable to borrow, so they have many difficulties to keep their children in school. This situation leads to a vicious circle where initial poverty leads to underinvestment in education among poor which further will increase inequality. On the other hand, with the introduction of news technologies in the production process,

demand for technologically skilled workers will increase. The demand for unskilled workers will contract. The gap between poor and rich will be widening, and it will be reduced when poor keep their children in school and increase the supply of new graduates.

4. There are also other channels that consider the relationship between income distribution and growth, including democratization (Bourguignon and Verdier, 2000), property rights (Svensson, 1998; Keefer and Knack, 2000), economic volatility (Alesina and Perotti, 1996; Aghion, Banerjee and Piketty, 1997), among others.

If we accepted the modern relationship between equality and economic growth, it is necessary to introduce adequate policies that reduce inequality. In this case good governance would improve the efficacy of these measures. Therefore, a positive relationship between governance and equality is expected and indirectly on economic growth.

Governance is expected that have some influence on these factors and through them, indirectly, on economic growth. We have seen that governance would be related with fiscal policy through it effects on public investment. Also, an adequate fiscal policy designed by good institutions that are connected with good governance will also have relevant effects on private investment and income distribution. We will consider both possibilities in our empirical analysis.

4. Empirical Analysis

To carry out our analysis we are going to consider a multiequational model, three equations, using panel data for 1996-2003 period and considering two kinds of estimations. In the first one we will consider the case 48 countries[4] (Galindo, Alvarez and Mendez, 2006).

The econometric estimation method that we are going to use is fix effects panel data for the countries chosen and for the period 1996-2006.

The equations to be estimated are:

$$\ln(y)_{it} = \beta_0 + \beta_1 \ln(G)_{it} + \beta_2 \ln(I)_{it} + \beta_3 \ln(Gini)_{it} + \beta_4 \ln(KH)_{it} + \varepsilon_{it} \quad (1)$$

$$\ln(I)_{it} = \beta 5 + \beta_6 \ln(ti)_{it} + \beta_7 \ln(\tau)_{it} + \beta_8 \ln(GOV)_{it} + \beta_9 \ln(GOV * \tau)_{it} + \varepsilon_{it} \quad (2)$$

$$\ln(G)_{it} = \beta 10 + \beta 11 \ln(GOV)_{it} + \varepsilon_{it} \quad (3)$$

$$\ln(Gini)_{it} = \beta_{12} + \beta_{13} \ln(\tau)_{it} + \beta_{14} \ln(GOV)_{it} + \varepsilon_{it} \quad (4)$$

[4] These countries are: Argentina, Belgium, Bolivia, Brazil, China, Colombia, Costa,Rica, Czech Republic, Denmark, Dominican Republic, El Ecuador, Salvador, Estonia, Finland, France, Germany, Greece, Guatemala, Iceland, India, Indonesia, Iran, Islamic, Rep.Ireland, Italy, Kazakhstan, Kenya, Latvia, Lithuania, Luxembourg, Mexico, Morocco, Namibia, Netherlands, Nicaragua, Panama, Paraguay, Peru, Philippines, Poland, Romania, Slovak Republic, Spain, St. Lucia, Sweden, Thailand, Trinidad and Tobago, United Kingdom, Uruguay.

Equation (1) is GDP equation, where, y is Gross Domestic Product, IP is Public Investment, I is Private Investment, Gini is Gini index measuring income distribution and KHU is Human Capital.

The sign of public investment is ambiguous. Some authors state that fiscal policy has negative on private investment, thanks to crowding-out effect, and finally on economic growth (e.g. Bertola, 1993, Perotti, 1993, Alesina and Rodrik, 1994 and Persson and Tabellini, 1994, among others). However, the opposite studies (Bénabou, 1996a, 1996b and Bourguignon and Verdier, 2000), conclude that a redistributive policy will have positive effects on investment by different ways: increasing public investment (Saint-Paul and Verdier, 1993) or reducing credit markets imperfections or liquidity restrictions that affects negatively on investment in physical and human capitals (Galor and Zeira, 1993, Perotti, 1993, Banerjee and Newman, 1991, Piketty, 1997 and Aghion and Bolton, 1998).

Gini expected sign is also ambiguous. There are studies that state a negative relationship between income inequality and economic growth, using cross-section (Persson and Tabellini, 1994, Alesina and Rodrik, 1994, among others) or Less Ordinary Square (Clarke, 1995, for instance). Perotti (1996) reaches the same conclusion taking into account structural aspects and Alesina and Perotti (1996) and Alesina et al. (1996) considering the role of socio political instability. Barro (1999) states that there is a scarce relation between income distribution and economic growth and investment, considering that inequality slow down economic growth in poor countries and accelerate it in the richer ones. Deininger and Squire (1998) consider that initial inequality is not a robust determinant of future economic growth. There are also some empirical works that show a positive relationship between inequality and growth, for example, Zou and Li (1998), in the case of the United States. In the case of education, Sylwester (2000) shows that a higher income inequality is associated to a higher public consumption in education that at short-term has a negative effect on economic growth and positive at long-term.

In the case of private investment and human capital expected sign is positive.

Equation (2) is the private investment equation where, ti is interest rate, τ is tax rate and GOV is governance index. In this case the expected signs of interest rate and tax rate are negatives. The latter is a "proxy" variable of fiscal policy and shows the negative effect of an expansionary fiscal policy on investment decisions although there are also several literature that states the opposite. The expected sign of GOV is positive. The last term $GOV*\tau$ indicates if governance and fiscal policy interact on investment.

Equation (3) is the public investment equation. The expected sign of governance is positive because is expected that the government will increase public investment in those moments that it is considered, although they can have a negative effect on economic growth at short-term that could be compensated at long-term thanks to externalities. It is also possible to consider that in developed countries public investment is not so necessary, so good governance could control and reduce this kind of expenditure.

Equation (4) is income distribution equation. The expected sign in all the variables included in the equation is negative. Therefore, the relationship between governance and economic growth is undirected, mainly through its effects on public capital, private capital, social capital and income distribution. It is also expected that there would be an interaction between governance and fiscal policy that would affect income distribution and private investment. Governance index is calculated using principal components method considering the following four key dimensions of institutional quality supplied by the World Bank (Kaufman, Kraay and Mastruzzi, 2005):

1. Voice and accountability, that measures political, civil and human rights.
2. Government effectiveness, measuring the competence of bureaucracy.
3. Rule of law, measuring the quality of contract enforcement, the police and the courts.
4. Control of corruption, measuring the exercise of public power for private gain.

Finally, Gini index is own estimation following the data supplied by the World Bank.

The results of the estimation are showed in the tables 1-4. The signs are the expected and all the variables are significant. However, two relevant differences must be considered. In the case of public investment the sign is now positive and the interaction fiscal policy and government has a positive effect on private investment.

Table 1.

Dependent Variable: y				
Variable	Coefficient	Std. Error	t-Statistic	Prob.
G	0.092687	0.006874	13.50778	0.0000
IP	0.035119	0.004735	7.428314	0.0000
KH	0.042439	0.006915	6.225983	0.0000
GINI	-0.001873	0.000392	-4.679256	0.0000
R-squared	0.593990	Mean dependent var		0.024091
Sum squared resid	0.194346	Durbin-Watson stat		2.140120

Sources: The World Bank, Gini own estimation from the World Bank data.

Table 2.

Dependent Variable: I				
Variable	Coefficient	Std. Error	t-Statistic	Prob.
τ	-0.084566	0.017413	-4.824000	0.0000
GOVERN	0.457000	0.012319	37.55421	0.0000
ti	-0.002413	0.000511	-5.94000	0.0000
τ*IGOVERN	0.161000	0.028000	5.766506	0.0000
R-squared	0.981995	Mean dependent var		7.385453
Sum squared resid	5.930060	Durbin-Watson stat		0.935739

Source: The World Bank.

Table 3.

Dependent Variable: G				
Variable	Coefficient	Std. Error	t-Statistic	Prob.
GOVERN	0.278126	0.02758	9.998953	0.0000
R-squared	0.944726	Mean dependent var		5.937599
Sum squared resid	16.28524	Durbin-Watson stat		0.937960

Source: The World Bank.

Table 4.

Dependent Variable: GINI				
Variable	Coefficient	Std. Error	t-Statistic	Prob.
τ	-0.228969	0.042407	-5.488277	0.0000
GOVERN	-0.7492212	0.0875646	-8.486729	0.0000
R-squared	0.989895	Mean dependent var		39.42790
Sum squared resid	417.6790	Durbin-Watson stat		0.783636

Source: The World Bank and own estimations.

Table-2 shows the private investment estimation. In this case too the signs are the expected and all the variables are significant. Governance has a positive effect on private investment as well as the interaction factor, that mixes governance and fiscal policy.

Table-3 includes the public investment estimation and again the sign of the variable is the expected and significant. Governance has a positive effect on public investment.

Finally, table- 4 includes the Gini estimation. The signs are the expected and are significant. Governance has a positive effect on income distribution as well as fiscal policy and indirectly to economic growth.

Therefore, te estimation shows that governance has an indirect positive effect on economic growth through public investment and income distribution. On the other hand, fiscal policy with a good governance would have also an indirect positive effect on economic growth due to the fact that it would enhance private investment.

CONCLUSION

Governance is a concept that has been included in the economic analysis during the last decades. However, is a concept that remains controversial and misunderstood. There is not a single definition of governance and sometimes is related to concepts such as democracy, corruption, institutions… There is also some literature that analyse the controversy market versus government. The election between both will depend on the efficiency terms and their possibility to achieve economic goals. We have also developed an empirical analysis for the case of 48.

The main goal of the European Union Countries is to achieve price stability and due to this stability it is possible to enhance economic growth. This inflation target could be obtained through market labor flexibility and modifying interest rates, among other possibilities. Fiscal policy and institutions play a secondary role. The results show that there is a positive relationship between governance and private investment and inequality reduction. Both factors are economic growth enhancing. There is also a positive relationship between governance and public investment, and the latter has also a positive impact on economic growth. The interaction fiscal policy-governance shows also a positive sign in the private investment equation.

This analysis could be improved considering other factors in the equations. One of them could be social capital that in the modern literature plays a relevant role from the socioeconomic point of view. There would also be interesting to analyse the factors that would have some effects on governance.

References

Aghion, P., Banerjee, A. and Piketty, T. (1997). Dualism and macroeconomic volatility. University College, London, mimeo, 1997.

Aghion, P. and Bolton, P. (1992). Distribution and growth in models of imperfect capital markets. *European Economic Review*, 36, 1992, 603-611.

Aghion, P., Caroli, E. and Garcia-Peñalosa, C. (1999). Inequality and economic growth: The perspective of the new growth theories. *Journal of Economic Literature*, Vol. XXXVII, December, 1615-1660.

Alesina, Alberto and Perotti, Roberto (1996). Income distribution, political instability, and investment. *European Economic Review*, 40, 1203-1228.

Alesina, Alberto and Rodrick, Dani (1994). Distributive politics and economic growth. *Quarterly Journal of Economics*, 436, 465-490.

Alfranca, Oscar and Galindo, Miguel-Angel (2002). Public expenditure, Income Distribution and growth in OECD Countries. In Georgakopoulos T., Paraskevopoulos, C. and Smithin, J. (Eds.), *Globalization and economic growth. A critical evaluation*, (pp. 123-134). Canada: APF Press.

Alfranca, Oscar and Galindo, Miguel-Angel (2003). Public capital, income distribution, and growth in OECD countries. *International Advances in Economic Research*, 9, May, 133-139.

Banarjee, A. V. and Newman, A. F. (1993). Occupational choice and the process of development. *Journal of Political Economy*, 101, 274-298.

Barro, Robert J. (1999). Inequality, growth, and investment. NBER Working Paper, 7038.

Bénabou, Roland (1996a). Unequal societies. NBER Working Paper 5583.

Bénabou, Roland (1996b). Inequality and growth. *NBER Macroeconomic Anual 1996*, MIT Press, Cambridge, MA., 11-74.

Bertola, G. (1993). Market structure and income distribution in endogenous growth models. *American Economic Review*, 83, 1184-1199.

Bourguignon, F. and Verdier, T. (2000). Oligarchy, democracy, inequality, and growth. *Journal of Development Economics*, 62, 285-313.

Bowles, Samuel (2004). *Microeconomics. Behavior, Institutions and Evolution*. Princeton: Princeton University Press.

Clarke, G. R. C. (1995). More evidence on income distribution and growth. *Journal of Development Economics*, 47, 403-427.

Cook, C. J. (1995). Saving rates and income distribution: further evidence from LDCs. *Applied Economics*, 27, 71-82.

Deininger, K. and Squire, L. (1996). A New Data Set Measuring Income Inequality. *The World Bank Economic Review*, vol. 10, 3, 565-591.

Drazen, Allan (2001). *Political Economy in Macroeconomics*. Cambridge: The MIT Press.

Dréze, Jean and Sen, Amartya (1995). *India: Economic Development and Social Opportunity*. Oxford: Oxford University Press.

Galindo, Miguel-Ángel, Álvarez, Agustin and Méndez, María Teresa (2006). Governance, fiscal policy and economic growth. mimeo.

Galor, Oded and Zeira, Joseph (1993). Income distribution and macroeconomics. *Review of Economic Studies*, 60: 1, 35-52.

Gylfason, Thorvaldur (1999). *Principles of Economic Growth*. oxford: Oxford University Press.

Kaldor, Nicholas (1956). Alternative theories of distribution. *Review of Economic Studies*, 23 (2). 83-100.

Kaufmann, Daniel, Kraay, Aart and Mastruzzi, Massimo (2005). Governance Matters IV: Governance Indicators for 1996-2004. The World Bank, mimeo, May.

Keefer, P. and Knack, S. (2000). *Polarization, politics and property rights: Links between inequality and growth*. World Bank, Working Paper, 2418.

Kelly, A. C. and Williamson, J. G. (1968). Household savings behaviour in developing country: The Indonesian case. *Economic Development and Cultural Change*, 16(3), 385-403.

Lavoie, Marc (1992). *Foundations of Post-Keynesian Economic Analysis*. Aldershot: Edward Elgar.

Mankiw, N. G., Romer, D. and Weil, D. N. (1992). A Contribution to the Empirics of Economic Growth. *Quarterly Journal of Economics*, May, 407-437.

McCombie, J. S. L. and Thirlwall, A. P. (1994). *Economic Growth and the Balance of Payments Constraint*. London: MacMillan, London.

North, Douglass (1990). *Institutions, Institutional Change and Economic Performance*. Cambridge, Mass.: Cambridge University Press.

Perotti, Roberto (1993). Political equilibrium, income distribution and growth. *Review of Economic Studies*, 60, 755-776.

Perotti, Roberto (1996). Growth, income distribution and democracy: What the data say. *Journal of Economic Growth*, vol. 1, 149-187.

Persson, Torsten and Tabellini, Guido (1994). Is inequality harmful for growth?. *American Economic Review*, 84, 600-621.

Piketty, T. (1997). The dynamics of wealth distribution and the interest rate with credit rationing. *Review of Economic Studies*, 64 (2), 173-189.

Saint-Paul, G. and Verdier, T. (1993). Education, democracy and growth. *Journal of Development Economics*, 42 (2), 399-407.

Svensson, J. (1998). Investment, property rights and political instability: theory and evidence. *European Economic Review*, 42, 1317-1341.

Sylwester, K. (2000). Income inequality, education expenditures, and growth. *Journal of Developmente Economics*, 63, 379-398.

Zou, H. and Li, H. (1998). Income inequality is not harmful for growth: theory and evidence. *Journal of Development Economics*, 2 (3), 318-334.

In: International Political Economy
Editors: M.A. Galindo Martin, E. Nissan
ISBN: 978-1-60876-172-2

Chapter 3

SIZE DISTRIBUTION OF THE LARGEST 100 NON-FINANCIAL MULTINATIONALS

Edward Nissan and George Carter
University of Southern Mississippi, USA

ABSTRACT

Industrial concentration is broadly defined as a few firms controlling a substantial share of assets or sales of the market. In the multinational industrial sector, this chapter shows that the largest 100 in the world control substantial amounts of assets and sales, both foreign and total. Two well known indexes of concentration were used, the Herfindahl and Theil's entropy, to check the levels of concentration between 1990 and 2005. It was found that changes in concentration were not statistically significant when compared on a yearly basis.

1. INTRODUCTION

Helleiner (1990) declares that the word "interdependence" has become a cliché in the aftermath of the Great Depression and the Second World War. The interdependence beneficial to many nations was brought about by changes in transport and communications systems, liberal trade arrangements, and relaxed exchange controls. The consequence was the growth of international trade in goods, services, and capital. Helleiner thinks that rather than approaching world trade in terms of international trade, the emphasis now should be in terms of global industrial organization.

The actors in investment and trade are governments and transnational firms. In particular, a large portion of global trading activity is made by transnational cartels, prompting fear of conspiracy among them, as was expressed by Adam Smith in 1776 in the *Wealth of Nations* and quoted by Helleiner (page 23). "People of the same trade seldom meet together, even for merriment and diversion, but the conversation ends in a conspiracy against the public, or in some contrivance to raise prices."

Adams and Brock (1990) explain that there are two schools of thought regarding corporate size and industry concentration. The first school, identified with University of Chicago economists, contends that bigness of business and industrial concentration are dictated by economic efficiency and superior management. Concentration brings progress at lower costs to consumers. In alliance with these views, the neoliberal left believes that corporate size and business concentration are essential for competitiveness in the global market. The second school takes issue with these assessments, arguing that bigness of business and industrial concentration imply that fewer players in the market place have greater control over economic decision making.

An important tenet in industrial organization, as explained by Leach (1997), is the fear that when an industry is highly concentrated, collusion among major players becomes easy, leading to monopoly pricing. A report by the Organization for Economic Cooperation and Development [OECD (1979)] viewed asset concentration as an indicator of the power structure and power positions in an economy. Unconcentrated industries, on the other hand, are competitive, which promotes efficient pricing. Demsetz (1973) turns this argument upside down by presuming that corporate bigness and high industry concentration are consequences of efficiency in production at the lowest unit cost. Jovanovic and Braguinsky (2004) also abide by this view, showing that takeovers in businesses are efficient both privately and socially and that they are not driven by managerial empire building and the quest for market power.

A parallel to these two opposing opinions is amply present, for instance, for the banking industry. Cetorelli and Gambera (2001) side with those who believe concentration in the banking industry can have a depressing effect on growth even though it may be a key element in providing growth to other industries. Berger (1995) shares the opinions of the other side, pointing out that large market shares in banking lower the costs of operations and increase social welfare. Focarelli and Panetta (2003) explain why market power or concentration in the banking industry can increase efficiency. They enumerate for this purpose the gain in access to cost-sharing technologies, the spread of fixed costs over a larger base, exploitation of economies of scope, and improvement in managerial efficiency. The academic literature is therefore, as pointed out by Duncan and Langrin (2004), not without debate at both the theoretical and empirical levels concerning the follies or virtues of concentration.

The bigness of firms and concentration takes place, according to Graham and Krugman (1989), through investment in new facilities or through mergers and acquisitions. They show in the United States, for instance, that acquisitions constitute a larger share of growth in foreign control in terms of number of acquisitions and total expenditure on new plants and equipment. Krugman and Obstfeld (2005) refer to multinational investment as direct foreign investment (FDI).

The purpose of this chapter pertains to the levels of business concentration among the largest 100 multinationals. Hannah and Kay (1977) and White (1981) enumerate assets and sales among employment, profits or value added as units of measurement. The emphasis in this chapter will be on aggregate assets and sales for both foreign and total investments. Two measures of concentration are used, the Herfindahl index and the Entropy index. The rationale for using more than one measure of concentration, as explained by O'Neill (1996), is that there is no single measure accepted as completely correct. The data are obtained from the World Investment Report (2007) developed by the United Nations Conference on Trade and Development. The chapter is organized after this section to include a section on methodology followed by a results section. The conclusion follows.

2. METHODOLOGY

For purposes of contrast, shares of assets and sales for the largest 100 multinationals are subjected to two statistical measures in order to determine the degree of concentration. The two measures chosen are the Herfindahl (H) and Theil's Entropy (E), found by Hannah and Kay (1977) and Jacquemin and Berry (1979) to be the most reliable among the many available measures. Both measures take the form $I=\Sigma_i P_i W_i$ where $P_i(\Sigma_i P_i=1.00)$ is the share of the ith multinational, $i = 1,...,n$, and W_i is an assigned weight.

The Herfindahl (H) Index weighs each company share P_i by itself

$$H=\Sigma_i P_i P_i \qquad (1)$$

$$= \Sigma_i P_i^2.$$

when one company holds all shares, H=1.0; when shares are held equally, H=1/n.

Thus, $1/n \leq H \leq 1.0$. Note that H gives larger weights to larger companies, making it a meaningful measure of concentration, perhaps the reason it is used in merger guidelines by the U.S. Department of Justice-Federal Trade Commission in horizontal merger and monopolization cases [Rhoades (1997)]. Note also that the Federal Reserve uses the index as a first step in deciding the likely competitive impact of mergers. As an example, suppose five companies in the system have market shares of 0.50, 0.30, 0.15, and 0.05. By equation (3), $H=(.50)^2 +(.30)^2 +(.15)^2+ (.05)^2 = 0.365$. If the latter three companies merged, $H=(.5)^2+(.3)^2+(.20)^2=0.380$, indicating an increase in concentration. Therefore, the larger the H, the more concentrated the market is. In other words, fewer firms control a larger share of the market. The underlying hypothesis is that as multinationals become more concentrated through mergers and acquisitions, the more the multinationals tend to collude, acting in the process as monopolies. Prices are then set above the competitive levels which undermines consumer welfare.

It can be shown [Clarke (1985)] that the coefficient of variation,

$$V = S / \overline{P}, \qquad (2)$$

where

$$\overline{P} = 1/n$$

and

$$S = [\Sigma(P_i - \overline{P})^2 /(n)]^{1/2}$$

and where $\overline{P}$ and S are the mean and the standard deviation, is related to H by the relationship

$$V^2 = nH - 1. \qquad (3)$$

Equation (3) can be derived from the definitions above of V, $\overline{P}$ and S and the definition of H (equation 1) as follows

$$V = S/\overline{P}.$$

Substituting for $\overline{P} = 1/n,\ S = [\Sigma(P_i - \overline{P})^2/(n)]^{1/2}$, and $H = \Sigma P_i^2$, then

$$V = nS = n[\Sigma(P_i - \overline{P})^2/n]^{1/2}.$$

Therefore,

$$V^2 = n^2(\Sigma P_i - n\overline{P}^2)/n$$

$$= n(\Sigma P_i^2 - n\overline{P}^2)$$

$$= n(H - 1/n)$$

$$= n[(nH - 1)/n$$

and finally obtaining equation (3)

$$V^2 = nH - 1.$$

As a measure of relative dispersion, the coefficient of variation is smallest when dispersion is least.

The second measure of concentration is based on information theory, the Theil's (1967)

$$E = \Sigma_i P_i \log 1/P_i$$

$$= -\Sigma_i P_i \log Pi \qquad (4)$$

where P_i refers to the share of the ith multinational. If all the n multinationals have an equal share, then E=log n, and concentration is at a minimum, in contrast to E=0 when one multinational controls all shares. Thus, $0 \le E \le \log n$. For n=100, the maximum value of E is 2.00.

The entropy index E is derived from the notion of entropy in information theory. Cowell (1977) explains that in information theory, the interest is in valuing the information that a certain event from a large number of possible events has occurred. Assume that there are n possible events designated by 1,2,3,…,n with probabilities of occurrences P_1, P_2, P_3,…, P_n. Assume that event "i" has occurred and it is desired to attach a value $h(P_i)$ for the information content. If the probability P_i is close to certainty, the occurrences of event "i" carries little information, so therefore, the number $h(P_i)$ should be small. On the other hand, if event i has a small probability of occurrence, $h(P_i)$ should be large. The logical consequence, therefore, is to have a function $h(P_i)$ which decreases as the probability P_i increases, and vice-versa.

Furthermore, to accommodate the multiplication rule of probability independence of two events and simultaneously accommodate a desire for additivity of information associated with the occurrence of the two events, that is

$$h(P_iP_j) = h(P_i) + h(P_j),$$

a functional form that satisfies this condition is

$$h(P_i) = -\log P_i.$$

In order to deal with n events and their associated probabilities P_i and associated information h(Pi), a weighted average using the probabilities as weights is the entropy of equation (4)

$$E = - \sum P_i \log P_i.$$

In terms of the use of E as a measure of concentration, reinterpret the n events as n = 100 multinationals and reinterpret P_i as the share of multinational i in total assets and log P_i is the amount of information associated with share P_i. It should be noted that the smaller the value of E, the larger is the concentration. Note that E, unlike H, is more sensitive to very small companies.

Another measure of concentration is numbers-equivalent. The number of firms "m" which would yield H or E if all firms were of equal size is called "numbers-equivalent." Given an H or E and n firms, m provides the number of equalized companies necessary to generate a level of concentration comparable to that obtained in the industry [Miller (1972)].

For the H index, by equation (1), when all companies have equal shares,

$$H=\sum(1/n)^2$$

$$=n(1/n^2)$$

$$=1/n.$$

Solving for n and calling it m,

$$m=1/H. \tag{5}$$

For the E index, the numbers-equivalent of equal-sized companies with the same value of E is

$E=-\sum(1/n) \log (1/n)$

$=-(1/n) \sum \log (1/n)$

$=-(1/n)n \log(1/n)$

$=-[\log 1-\log n].$

$=\log n.$

Solving for n and calling it m,

m=antilogarithms of E. (6)

3. RESULTS

Table 1 shows aggregates of assets and sales in billions of dollars from 1990 to 2005 for both foreign and total investments of the largest 100 multinationals. Between these two periods, their foreign assets increased five fold from \$943 billion to approximately \$4.7 trillion. Total asset investments of these companies for the same period increased from approximately \$3.2 trillion to approximately \$8.7 trillion, a 2.7 fold jump. Noticeable here is the magnitude of the increase in foreign investment as compared to the total, with the indication of the heightened interest in foreign investments.

Table 1 also provides the magnitudes in billions of dollars of the aggregate sales for both foreign and totals. For the former, the change between 1990 and 2005 was from approximately \$1.5 trillion to approximately \$3.7 trillion, a 2.5 fold jump. For the latter, the jump of about 2 fold was from approximately \$3.1 trillion to approximately \$6.6 trillion.

Table 2 reports for every year between 1990 and 2005 the mean in column C1, the coefficient of variation (V) in column C2, the minimum (C3) and the maximum (C4) assets for both foreign and total for the largest 100 multinationals. Mean foreign assets in 1990 were approximately \$12.2 billion, increasing to approximately \$47.3 billion in 2005, while total assets for the same period increased from a mean of approximately \$32 billion to a mean of approximately \$87 billion. An interesting observation here is the ratio of foreign to total assets investments. In 1990, the ratio was about 38 percent (12.2 ÷ 32.0). In 2005, the ratio was about 54 percent (47.3 ÷ 86.8), which, again, provides strong evidence for foreign investments.

The coefficient of variation in Table 1 for both foreign and total assets hover around 1.00 for most of the years, indicating slight changes in dispersion among the largest 100 multinationals, which could give an early indication of slight changes in concentration along the years.

Table 1. Aggregate Assets and Sales ($ billion): 100 Largest Multinationals

	Assets		Sales	
Year	Foreign	Total	Foreign	Total
1990	943	3,198	1,499	3,115
1992	830	3,377	1,512	3,449
1993	759	3,649	1,602	3,711
1994	900	4,231	1,827	4,002
1995	1,588	4,164	2,045	4,178
1996	1,494	4,200	2,149	4,128
1997	1,393	4,212	2,088	3,984
1998	1,444	4,610	2,057	4,099
1999	1,640	5,092	2,092	4,294
2000	2,554	6,293	2,441	4,797
2001	2,982	6,061	2,273	4,470
2002	3,317	6,891	2,446	4,749
2003	3,993	8,023	3,003	5,551
2004	4,728	8,852	3,407	6,102
2005	4,732	8,683	3,742	6,623

Source: World Investment Report (2007).

Table 2. Foreign and Total Assets Shares ($ billion): 100 Largest Multinationals

Foreign				Total			
Year	C2	C3	C4	C1	C2	C3	C4
1990	1.04	4.2	69.2	32.0	0.98	5.5	180.2
1992	0.93	4.5	69.4	33.8	1.01	6.3	192.9
1993	0.90	4.0	69.4	36.9	1.02	6.8	251.5
1994	0.89	4.7	63.7	42.3	0.99	6.9	251.5
1995	0.87	5.8	79.7	41.6	0.97	8.9	238.5
1996	0.88	6.8	82.8	42.0	1.03	8.8	272.4
1997	0.85	6.8	97.4	42.1	1.09	8.5	304.0
1998	0.93	6.8	128.6	46.1	1.07	9.7	355.9
1999	0.99	7.0	141.1	50.9	1.11	8.0	405.2
2000	1.17	7.4	221.2	62.9	1.24	9.5	487.8
2001	1.02	9.5	187.8	60.6	1.15	11.6	495.2
2002	1.10	10.4	229.0	68.9	1.14	11.1	575.2
2003	1.08	12.1	258.9	80.2	1.10	13.4	647.5
2004	1.21	13.7	448.9	88.5	1.11	16.2	750.5
2005	1.11	15.6	412.7	86.8	1.06	18.3	673.3

Note: C1 = mean, C2 = coefficient of variation, C3 = minimum, and C4 = maximum.

Source: World Investment Report (2007).

Finally to be observed in Table 2 are the minimum and maximum among the largest 100. For instance, in 1990, the smallest company had foreign assets of $4.2 billion as compared to the largest of $69.2 billion, which is 16 times as large. In 2005, a similar comparison gives $15.6 billion as compared to $412.7 billion, which is 26 times as large. Similar comparisons are found for total assets, whereby the corresponding comparisons were from $5.5 billion and $180.2 billion for 1990 to $18.3 billion and $673.3 billion in 2005. In the interim period, therefore, the largest company in 1990 had total assets 33 times as large as the smallest company; this changed a bit to 37 times as large in 2005.

Table 3 has a similar format as Table 2, this time for sales of the largest 100 multinationals. The table provides the mean, the coefficient of variation, the minimum and the maximum. Again, there is a noticeable change when comparing the largest and the smallest companies between 1990 and 2005 where for foreign sales the ratio in 1990 was 35 percent and 61 percent in 2005. For total sales, the corresponding ratios were 41 percent and 69 percent.

Table 3. Foreign and Total Sales Shares ($ billion): 100 Largest Multinationals

	Foreign				Total			
Year	C1	C2	C3	C4	C1	C2	C3	C4
1990	15.0	0.95	2.6	90.5	31.1	1.03	3.7	151.1
1992	15.4	0.88	2.4	93.1	34.5	0.95	5.5	165.8
1993	16.0	0.93	2.2	87.7	37.1	1.05	5.1	172.9
1994	18.3	0.84	2.5	72.3	40.0	1.01	5.0	175.8
1995	20.5	0.85	2.6	96.9	41.8	0.94	6.9	186.6
1996	21.5	0.79	2.8	102.0	41.3	0.86	6.5	158.0
1997	21.8	0.76	3.5	104.8	39.8	0.86	6.6	178.2
1998	20.8	0.89	1.6	125.4	41.0	0.87	6.2	155.5
1999	21.3	0.94	1.0	122.4	42.9	0.91	3.3	176.6
2000	24.4	0.92	0.6	143.0	48.0	0.94	3.8	206.1
2001	22.7	1.02	1.4	145.8	44.7	1.00	3.7	217.8
2002	24.5	1.03	0.3	146.0	47.5	1.00	2.8	244.5
2003	30.0	1.01	2.4	192.9	55.5	0.93	4.9	256.3
2004	34.1	1.10	1.7	232.4	61.0	1.00	6.4	291.3
2005	37.4	1.06	4.1	248.4	66.2	1.03	5.2	359.0

Note: C1 = mean, C2 = coefficient of variation, C3 = minimum, and C4 = maximum.
Source: World Investment Report (2007).

Table 4 shows results of the concentration measures, Herfindahl (H) by equation (1) and Theil's index E, by equation (4) with their corresponding numbers-equivalent, m, by equation (5) and equation (6), respectively, for foreign and total assets. For both measures the numbers-equivalent increased for foreign assets, implying lessening of concentration from 1990 to 2005, decreasing slightly in the early 1990s, and reaching its lowest level in 1993.

Table 4. Foreign and Total Asset Concentration: 100 Largest Multinationals

	Foreign				Total			
Year	H	m	E	m	H	m	E	m
1990	0.0268	37.34	1.7347	54.29	0.0195	51.24	1.8543	71.49
1992	0.0289	34.60	1.6754	47.36	0.0200	49.98	1.8514	71.02
1993	0.0334	29.98	1.6008	39.89	0.0202	49.58	1.8491	70.65
1994	0.0295	33.88	1.6524	44.91	0.0197	50.72	1.8483	70.51
1995	0.0189	53.04	1.8496	70.72	0.0192	51.98	1.8653	73.33
1996	0.0214	46.64	1.7971	62.68	0.0205	48.75	1.8567	71.90
1997	0.0228	43.80	1.7665	58.41	0.0217	45.98	1.8488	70.59
1998	0.0253	39.53	1.7449	55.57	0.0213	46.97	1.8533	71.33
1999	0.0258	38.81	1.7461	55.73	0.0222	44.96	1.8413	69.39
2000	0.0235	42.47	1.8315	67.85	0.0253	39.46	1.7959	62.50
2001	0.0204	49.14	1.8544	71.51	0.0230	43.50	1.8243	66.73
2002	0.0221	45.34	1.8393	69.07	0.0228	43.90	1.8258	66.96
2003	0.0215	46.46	1.8381	68.88	0.0220	45.42	1.8366	68.65
2004	0.0245	40.89	1.8197	66.02	0.0222	45.05	1.8356	68.48
2005	0.0222	45.03	1.8396	69.12	0.0212	47.16	1.8412	69.37

Note: H is the Herfendahl index and m its numbers-equivalent by equations (1) and (5). E is the entropy index and m its numbers-equivalent by equations (4) and (6).

Source: World Investment Report (2007).

For H, m increased from 37.34 in 1990 to 53.04 in 1995, and declined to 45.03 in 2005. For E, the corresponding numbers were 54.29 to 70.72 to 69.12. The striking observations for both H and E for foreign assets investments in Table 4 are the overall continual reductions in concentration from 1990 to 2005. For H, the decrease was from H=0.0268 to H=0.0222. For E, where a larger number indicates a smaller concentration, the increase was from 1.7347 to 1.8396.

For total assets concentration in Table 4, the picture is slightly different than for foreign assets. For both measures, the numbers-equivalent decreased slightly, implying increase in concentration from 1990 to 2005. For H, m decreased from m=51.24 to m=47.16, while for E, m decreased from m=71.49 to m=69.73. For both H and E, there was an overall increase in concentration throughout the period. The H index increased from H=0.0195 in 1990 to H=0.0212 in 2005. For the E index, where a smaller number indicates larger concentration, the decrease was from E=1.8543 to E=1.8412.

Table 5 shows results of the concentration measures, Herfindahl (H) by equation (1) and Theil's index E, by equation (4), with their corresponding numbers-equivalent, m, by equation (5) and equation (6), respectively for foreign and total sales. For both measures, the numbers-equivalent decreased, implying increase in concentration. For H, m decreased from m=52.73 in 1990 to m=47.57 in 2005. For E, the decrease for the same period was from m=71.46 to m=68.40. Correspondingly, the index H increased from H=0.0190 to H=0.210 and E index decreased from E=1.8540 to E=1.8350.

Table 5. Foreign and Total Sales Concentration: 100 Largest Multinationals

	Foreign				Total			
Year	H	m	E	m	H	m	E	m
1990	0.0190	52.74	1.8540	71.46	0.0206	48.61	1.8272	67.17
1992	0.0179	55.75	1.8653	73.33	0.0189	52.94	1.8512	70.99
1993	0.0186	53.86	1.8531	71.31	0.0209	47.91	1.8231	66.54
1994	0.0170	58.97	1.8695	74.05	0.0200	49.94	1.8332	68.11
1995	0.0172	58.29	1.8721	74.50	0.0187	53.60	1.8528	71.26
1996	0.0163	61.53	1.8852	76.77	0.0173	57.70	1.8676	73.73
1997	0.0164	61.12	1.8778	75.47	0.0174	57.56	1.8693	74.01
1998	0.0180	55.58	1.8684	73.86	0.0174	57.41	1.8659	73.44
1999	0.0191	52.37	1.8499	70.78	0.0183	54.77	1.8524	71.18
2000	0.0184	54.39	1.8575	72.03	0.0187	53.42	1.8436	69.75
2001	0.0203	49.17	1.8427	69.62	0.0198	50.49	1.8350	68.40
2002	0.0206	48.58	1.8334	68.14	0.0198	50.39	1.8331	68.09
2003	0.0202	49.52	1.8441	69.84	0.0186	53.80	1.8537	71.40
2004	0.0221	45.32	1.8205	66.14	0.0199	50.18	1.8384	68.92
2005	0.0210	47.57	1.8350	68.40	0.0205	48.74	1.8284	67.36

Note: H is the Herfendahl index and m its numbers-equivalent by equations (1) and (5). E is the entropy index and m its numbers-equivalent by equations (4) and (6).

Source: World Investment Report (2007).

In Table 5 for total sales, there was hardly any change for the numbers-equivalent for both indexes. For the H index, m=48.60 in 1990 and m=48.73 in 2005, even though there were some changes between the two dates. Similar observations are noticed for the E index where m=67.17 in 1990 and changed a bit to m=67.36 in 2005. For the indexes between the two periods, the H changed from H=0.0206 to H=0.0205 and the E index changed from E=1.8272 to E=1.8284.

Even though the results of Tables 4 and 5 seem surprising, there are explanations as to why the changes in concentration among the top 100 companies for the 15-year period were slight. The explanations follow logically that the top 100 multinationals comprise an exclusive club of the largest companies in the handful of countries in which they operate. Duncan and Langrin (2004) forward an explanation for the banking industry, using the case of Jamaican banking. Analysis of market shares owned by the top 50 banks showed that after mergers, there were relatively small changes in relative asset share ownership during the period even though mergers and acquisitions were highly common. Banks' market shares of the most dominant players kept the relative patterns and movements of ownership of their shares almost intact over the period under consideration in the sense that the increases in shares were diffused throughout the banking system proportionally.

In table 4, the increase in concentration as observed by the H index for the years 1990 and 2005 was for total assets from H=0.0195 to H=0.0212 and foreign sales in Table 5 moving from H=0.0190 to H=0.0210. To test whether the increase in Herfindahl is statistically significant, a device connecting H of equation (1) with the square of V–(V^2) of equation (3) is used. This is done by testing for equality of variances and, by implication, the equality of V^2. This is so because with a fixed number of companies throughout the period, testing for V^2 is identical to simply testing for S^2 as the mean (1/n) in equation (2), where n=100, is the same for each year. In turn, this leads to an implied test statistic for equality of H for pairs of years j and k by the F-distribution,

$$F^{*}=S^2_j/S^2_k. \qquad (7)$$

The rationale for equation (7) is justified on the grounds that the ratio of the square of two coefficients of variation, say V_1 and V_2 from equation (2) is

$$V_1^2/V_2^2 = (S_1/\overline{P}_1)^2/(S_2/\overline{P}_2)^2.$$

Since $\overline{P}_1 = \overline{P}_2 = 1/n$ for all years under consideration, the cancellation results in

$$V_1^2/V_2^2=S_1^2/S_2^2,$$

with a generalization reached in equation (7).

The test statistic F* of equation (7) for the two cases mentioned above is compared for significance with critical point $F(\alpha/2, n_j-1, n_k-1)$. Since n_j and n_k are the same at 100 companies, the critical F at α=.05 is F(.025,99,99)≈1.43. Inspecting the results of the calculations yields for total assets from Table 2, $F^{*}=(1.06)^2/(0.98)^2=1.17$ and for foreign sales from Table 3, $F^{*}=(1.06)^2/(0.95)^2=1.24$, both of which are less than tabular 1.43. The overall conclusion gained from Tables 4 and 5 is that concentration among the largest 100 multinationals did not change much during the period 1990 to 2005. The important finding of the paper is that the fear of increase in concentration among the largest 100 multinationals is not warranted.

Conclusion

Sagafi-nejad (2008) is full of information about the rise of multinationals, and the roles that many United Nations agencies played in our understanding of the multinationals impact on the post-World War II global political economy. The United Nations contributed by making suggestions for regulations through host country policies as well as thorough corporate structure. Sagafi-nejad explains that multinationals provide dynamism in furthering the process of globalization, which often is a target of criticism. Multinationals are viewed by some as driven by the profit motive at any cost. Others view the multinationals as a means of economic transformation. There is no doubt, however, that multinationals were able to upgrade productivity and enhance economic development in emerging economies. Yet, there is a wave of unfriendly opinion regarding the concentration of economic power in the hands of a few large corporations. With excessive concentration, there is the fear of harm to competition and increase in power of monopolists as explained by Baker (2003). However, as Barth, Nolle, and Rice (1997) point out for the banking industry, for instance, as large multinationals compete with one another as well as with other multinationals domestically and internationally, these multinationals make every effort to operate efficiently. Furthermore, as Vossen (1999) has pointed out, RandD spending is higher in more concentrated industries.

In somewhat similar interest for this chapter; Dosi, et.al. (2008) were concerned with changes in the size distribution and degrees of concentration of industries due, in their opinion, to the emerging presence of information-centered technology. The assumption was that the advances in the new technologies in manufacturing, services and life sciences could have strong influence in shaping anew the structure of industries vertically and horizontally. The results of this chapter are in conformity with their results in that during the recent decades, there was no hint of detectable changes in the size distribution and concentration of the largest firms, even though the aggregate distribution of firms remains skewed. In particular, the trend towards globalization did not produce greater oligopolistic concentration of industries worldwide.

To determine the extent of the increase in the economic power, if any, in the hands of fewer and fewer multinationals, this chapter investigated the relative concentration of both foreign and total assets and sales of the top 100 multinationals in the world. Two indexes were employed, the Herfindahl H and Theil's entropy E for this purpose. A variety of statistical techniques were used to detect whether concentration increased among the multinationals in recent years. The important conclusion can be summarized as there was no significant statistical support for the hypothesis that concentration increased during 1990 to 2005. In some years during the fifteen-year period, there were modest decreases in concentration.

References

Adams, W. and Brock, J.W. (1990). Efficiency, Corporate Power, and the Bigness Complex. *Journal of Economic Education*, 21, 30-50.

Baker, J.B. (2003). The Case for Antitrust Enforcement. *Journal of Economic Perspectives*, 17, 27-50.

Barth, J.R., Nolle, D.E. and Rice, T.N. (1997). *Commercial Banking Structure, Regulation and Performance: An International Comparison.* Washington, DC: Controller of the Currency.

Berger, A.N. (1995). The Profit-Structure Relationship in Banking-Tests of market-Power and Efficient-Structure Hypothesis. *Journal of Money, Credit and Banking*, 27, 404-431.

Cetorelli, N. and Gambera, M. (2001). Banking Market Structure, Financial Dependence and Growth: International Evidence from Industry Data. *The Journal of Finance*, LVI, 617-648.

Clarke, R. (1985). *Industrial Economics*. New York: Basil Blackwell.

Cowell, F.A. (1977). *Measuring Inequality.* Oxford, UK: Philip Allan Publishers Limited.

Demsetz, H. (1973). Industry Structure, Market Rivalry, and Public Policy. *Journal of Law and Economics*, 16, 1-9.

Dosi, G., Gambardella, A., Grazzi, M. and Orsenigo, L. (2008). Technological Revolutions and the Evolution of Industrial Structures: Assessing the Impact of New Technologies upon the Size and Boundaries of Firms. *Capitalism and Society*, 3, 1-47.

Duncan, D. and Langrin, R.B. (2004). Testing for Competition in the Jamaican Banking Sector: Evidence from Bank Level Data. *Southwestern Journal of Economics*, VI, 97-120.

Focarelli, D. and Panetta, F. (2003). Are Mergers Beneficial to Consumers? Evidence from the Market for Bank Deposits. *The American Economic* Review, 93, 1152-1172.

Graham, E.M. and Krugman, P.R. (1989). *Foreign Direct Investment in the United States.* Washington, D.C.: Institute for International Economics.

Hannah, L. and Kay, J.A. (1977). *Concentration in Modern Industry: Theory, Measurement and the U.K. Experience.* London: The Macmillan Press Ltd.

Helleiner, G.K. (1990). *The New Global Economy and the Developing Countries: Essays in International Economics and Development*. Hants, England: Edward Elgar.

Jacquemin, A. P. and Berry, C.H. (1979). Entropy Measure of Diversification and Corporate Growth. *The Journal of Industrial Economics,* 27, 359-369.

Jovanovic, B. and Braguinsky, S. (2004). Bidder discounts and Target Premia in Takeovers. *The American Economic Review*, 94, 46-56.

Krugman, P.R. and Obstfeld, M. (2005). *International Economics: Theory and Policy.* Boston, MA: Pearson-Addison Wesley.

Leach, D.F. (1997). Concentration-Profits Monopoly vs. Efficiency Debate: South African Evidence. *Contemporary Economic Policy*, 15, 12-23.

Miller, R.A. (1972). Numbers Equivalents, Relative Entropy, and Concentration Ratios: A Comparison Using Market Performance. *Southern Economic Journal*, 39, 107-112.

OECD (1979) *Concentration and Competition Parity*, Paris: Organization for Economic Cooperation and Development.

O'Neill, P.B. (1996). The Trends of Aggregate Concentration in the United States: Problems of Scope and Measurement. *American Journal of Economics and Sociology*, 55, 197-211.

Sagafi-nejad, T. (2008). *The UN and Transnational Corporations: From Code of Conduct to Global Compact*. Bloomington and Indianapolis, Indiana University Press.

Rhoades, S.A. (1997). Research on 10 Topics in Banking: An Introduction and Overview. *Review of Industrial Organization,* 12, 1-8.

Theil, H. (1967). *Economics and Information Theory,* Amsterdam: North-Holland Publishing Company.

Vossen, R.W. (1999). Market Power, Industrial Concentration and Innovative Activity. *Review of Industrial Organization*, 15, 367-378.

White, L.J. (1981). What Has Been Happening to Aggregate Concentration in the United States? *The Journal of Industrial Economics*, 29, 223-230.

World Investment Report. (2007). *Transnational Corporations, Extractive Industries and Development*. New York and Geneva, United Nations.

In: International Political Economy
Editors: M.A. Galindo Martin, E. Nissan
ISBN: 978-1-60876-172-2

Chapter 4

EFFECTS OF THE TRANSVERSAL FOREIGN DIRECT INVESTMENT ON THE PRODUCTIVITY OF THE MEXICAN ECONOMY

Juan J. Durán and Fernando Úbeda
Centro Internacional Carlos V
Universidad Autónoma de Madrid, Spain

ABSTRACT

Multinational companies investing in communications, energy, transport and financial services, can have a differentiated effect in the host economy comparing with the one attributed to manufacturing investment. These companies are characterized by generation of an intermediate input aimed at practically the totality of an economy's sectors (intermediate input as well as a final good for consumers), reason why we have denominated the matter multinational transversal services. We have analyzed in this paper if inflow foreign direct investment in transversal services over economic growth and productivity is significantly higher to the effect caused by inflow foreign direct investment in manufacturing sector. During the period 1985-2006, the results obtained in owner analysis show a positive and very similar effect of inward manufacturing FDI (MFDI) and inward transversal FDI (TFDI) on labor productivity (LP).

1. INTRODUCTION

It had been assumed that inward direct investment would constitute a determining factor for economic growth; however, empirical evidence leads to contradictory results. Despite the fact that the Blomström and Kokko (1998, 2003) appear to confirm this hypothesis, there is evidence that contradicts it (Hanson 2001, Kumar 1996). Given this controversy it has been studied the structural factors that might determine the nature of the effect caused by inward FDI over economic growth and productivity.

The multinationalization of utilities and financial services were a reality of the nineties, due mostly to institutional changes and technological progress. The multinational companies in this type of service (communication, energy, transportation, financial services) are characterized by generation of an intermediate input aimed at practically the totality of an economy's sectors, as well as to the final consumer, reason why we used the term transversal foreign direct investment (TFDI) to label this type of output.

Little attention has been paid to the effects of inflow transversal service FDI have over economic growth and productivity of host countries. The main contribution of the paper is to analyze if inward foreign direct investment in transversal services (financial, communications, transport and energy) has a greater impact over productivity than the effect derived from inward FDI in manufacturing sector.

We will test the hypothesis put forward for the Mexican economy. Mexico was one of the earliest countries in Latin America to undertake macroeconomic and institutional reforms. After the debt crisis as the early 1980s Mexico adopt an open market oriented model. Important reforms were: privatizations, deregulation, national treatment of FDI, bilateral treaties and NAFTA (Ramirez, 2001). Macroeconomic and institutional changes have affected FDI decision in Mexico (Treviño and Mixon Jr., 2004, Treviño, Thomas and Cullen 2008). Mexico is the second receiver of FDI in Latin America. For the period 1986-2006 the 70% of inward in Mexico was concentrated in manufacturing sectors (of which different stages of the maquiladoras system played a relevant role) while about 20% in transversal sector.

With the object of resolving endogeneity, simultaneity and non-stationary problems of the time series, Granger's causality analysis has been carried out. The results obtained in owner analysis, show a positive and very similar effect of inward manufacturing FDI (MFDI) and inward transversal FDI (TFDI) on labor productivity (LP). May be the tradition over a long period of time of inward MFDI as well weight over total FDI (70%), together with heterogeneity of institutional framework of the transversal services can be explain the result obtained.

The rest of the chapter is structured into four parts. In the first place we proceed to justify the reasons by which inward FDI in transversal services in less developed countries should have a more pronounced effect over growth and productivity than inward FDI in manufacturing sectors. In the second place we describe the variables we have used and justify the verification tools employed. Finally we put forward the results reached and propose conclusions.

2. Theory Development

The services in finance, telecommunication, energy and transport have two main characteristics. They are intermediate goods for the whole economic activity and at the same times are final goods. Because of this reason we use the term transversal services to denominate this sector.

Given the nature of transversal services we could expect a higher positive impact on productivity and growth over those explained by the manufacturing sector. Then, we have to explain why these types of services are significant for the economy and through which channels they generate spillovers with different impact comparing to those from the manufacturing industry.

The financial sector of an economy determines efficient transformation of savings into investment, generating the necessary confidence to reduce transaction costs, diversify the supply of financial products and manage the financial risks[1]. In like manner communications, and more specifically telecommunications, are essential intermediate input for business; it also constitutes a strategic coordination and corporate management tool, an internal and external integration instrument of an economy, and also a knowledge transmission network. At the same time improvements on transportation systems and in energy supply are essential for competitiveness of domestic companies and as well as advantages for localization of FDI. Therefore, inefficient production of transversal services constitutes an important barrier for economic growth. From which what emerges is that gains of efficiency of these sectors must have a direct effect on economic growth and productivity.

If the economic activity derived from direct investment abroad in financial services, energy, transport and communications is more efficient than domestic investment, it could be consider a crucial intermediate input for the economic activity. Thus due to these circumstances we have denominated this type as *"transversal"* foreign direct investment (TFDI).

Inward FDI has a direct effect over gross capital formation of the host economy. Its impact over economic growth and productivity is essentially due to its capacity to transfer technological knowledge and new management capabilities. In this sense the literature review made by Blomström and Kokko (1998, 2003), Hanson (2001), Lipsey (2002), de Mello (1997) and Kumar (1996) amongst others, put forward mechanisms for transfer of knowledge that can be articulated between the MNCs and domestic companies. Empirical evidence reveals that the impact of inward of FDI over the economic growth of the less developed economies cannot be generalized, as in many cases it was even inferior to what was expected[2].

The activity developed by a foreign subsidiary of a Multinational firm (MNC) can bring a spillover effect on the host economy. The analysis mode by Blomström and Kokko (1998) identify four ways of externalities: a better qualification of local workers; increases in competition together with a demonstration effect, customer-suppliers relationship and finally the impact on the industrial structure of the host economy. The last two reasons are the more likely forces to have a positive impact of TFDI on productivity and economic growth (See Figure 1).

[1] Evidence on the impact of development of the financial system over economic growth is to be found in Pagano (1993).

[2] Empirical evidence reveals that the impact of inward of FDI over the economic growth of the less developed economies cannot be generalized, as in many cases it was even inferior to what was expected. In these sense, studies at a country level, such as Mexico (Blomström and Persson 1983, Cuadros, Orts and Alguacil 2004, Jordaan 2005), Malaysia and Thailand (Chowdhury and Mavrotas 2006), China (Chen et al., 1995), Colombia (Kugler 2006), Morocco (Haddad and Harrison 1993), Indonesia (Takii 2005) verify that presence of multinational companies has a positive effect over productivity and/or economic growth. However, said results are not extendable to countries such as Brazil, Argentina (Cuadros, Orts and Alguacil 2004), Chile (Chowdhury and Mavrotas 2006) and Venezuela (Aitken and Harrison 1999). In like manner the analysis made by Hsiao and Hsiao (2006) over the effects of inward FDI in a group of eight Southeast Asian economies is not conclusive either. Likewise, works published by Fry (1993) and Hein (1992) for different samples of less developed countries, put on display scarce or nil impact of inward FDI over economic growth

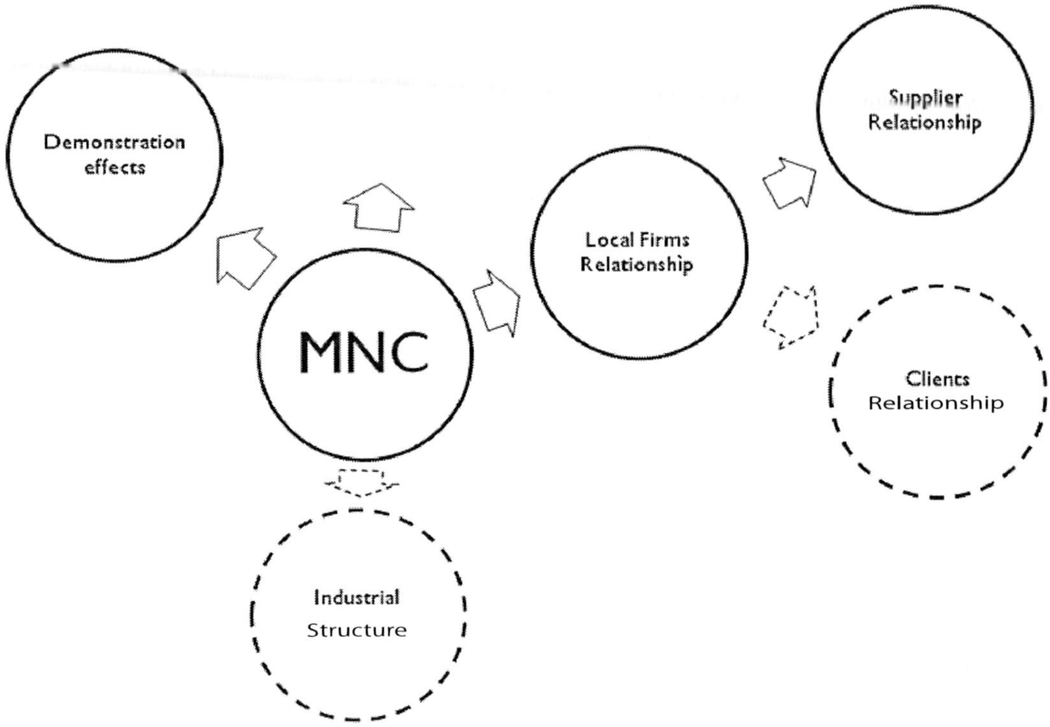

Based in Blomström and Kokko (1998), Rodríguez-Clare (1996).

Figure 1. Spillover sources.

The type of interaction between MNCs and local suppliers and clients constitutes an essential element in the externalities generation. This type of spillover occur when local firms benefit from MNC affiliate´s superior knowledge of product, process, technologies or markets, without incurring a cost that exhaust the whole gain from the improvement (Findlay 1978, Blomström and Kokko, 1998). This is named by vertical spillover as opposed to horizontal spillover[3] (Caves 1999). It is precisely the essential differentiating element that exists between transversal services and the manufacturing industry. Despite the fact that both can indeed generate vertical spillover, the real difference between both sectors has to be found in the number of sectors to which there are transaction relationships which clearly are higher in the transversal services case. For this reason the externalization must be far more intense in the inward transversal FDI than in manufacturing FDI.

The transversal services can lead the establishment of a close and long-lasting relationship with domestic companies (clients and suppliers). This reality will favor generation of spillover, given that this relationship facilitates adaptation of the products to the client's needs, as well as possible transfer of technology (telecommunications sector) or good corporate practices (financial sector).

Our hypothesis is based on the variety of differentiated inputs within the supplier-customer relationship in the host economy (Rodríguez-Clare, 1996) and overall based on the

[3] Kugler (2006), using a sample of Columbian companies, has verified that transfer of knowledge essentially takes place between the MNCs and their suppliers.

higher number of economic agents involved in transactions explained by transversal services comparing to those explained by manufacturing sector.

Finally, the effects of inward FDI are conditioned by the institutional environment and the competitive structure of markets. We are aware that transversal services are provided for regulated sectors, with a monopoly or oligopoly structure, then the competitive structure and institutional development will be the determining factor in the intensity and sign of inward FDI effect over the host economy (Mattoo et al. 2006), which would in itself constitute a distinctive element of this type of FDI as opposed to the manufacturing sectors subsidiaries.

3. Methodology

The economy of Mexico has been selected since it is one of the earliest countries in Latin America to undertake macroeconomic and institutional reforms, after the debt crisis as the early 1980s Mexico adopt an open market oriented model. Important reforms were: privatizations, deregulation, national treatment of FDI, bilateral treaties and NAFTA (Ramirez, 2001). Macroeconomic and institutional changes have affected FDI decision in Mexico (Treviño and Mixon Jr., 2004, Treviño, Thomas and Cullen 2008). Mexico is the second receiver of FDI in Latin America. Although in the case of Mexico, empirical evidence that is available confirms that entry of direct investment has had a positive effect over economic growth (Cuadro, Orts and Alguacil 2004) and productivity (Jordaan 2005). There is no evidence available on the effects of inward FDI in the transversal services sectors on growth and productivity, which constitute our main contribution.

The period of analysis goes from 1985 to 2006. The Labor productivity (LP) is defined by the growth rate of GDP (in constant 2006 dollars) divided by the number of workers. The rate offered by the Groningen Growth and Development Centre. The inflows FDI have been estimated with the data offered by the OECD (Organization for Economic Co-operation and Development). The GDP deflator proposed by the Groningen Growth and Development Centre has been applied with the object of expressing the figures in real terms.

The analysis about the effects of inward FDI bring a endogeneity problem since the inward FDI can be itself an economic growth factor, and at the same time it is accepted that the productivity growth constitutes a localization factor. In this type of analysis we face a problem of simultaneity, since the evolution of both variables is conditioned by the tendency of the international economy, which can generate spurious relations. It is with the object of avoiding endogeneity and simultaneity problems we have done a Granger Causality analysis.

The bias associated to the non-stationary and cointegration in the time series analysis in the Granger Causality perspective could be the explanation why there are a lag of conclusive empirical evidence about the causality relationship among inward direct investment, economic growth and productivity. When the variables of a regression are not stationary and cointegrated the traditional tests (F-test and Wald test) in a Granger causality analysis they are not valid (useful), given that distributions are not the usual ones (Zapata and Rambaldi, 1997). These are the reason why regressions that incorporate integrated variables can make spurious relations explicit (Granger and Newbold, 1974). Furthermore, Giles and Mirza (1999) explained that the non-stationary and the cointegration it can lead to severe overrejection of a non-causal null, leaving open the possibility of distortion in the inference procedure.

For the specification of Granger Causality test we have done the following analysis (Cuadros, Orts and Alguacil 2001):

a) We use the Augmented Dickey-Fulller Statistic for stationarity analysis of the time series.
b) The Johansen cointegracion test allowed as analyzing the level of cointegration.
c) One of the methodological problems of the VAR system is to determine the optimal number of lags (k). In this sense, when work takes place with reduced samples the Schwarzt statistic is recommended by Kukertpohl (1993).
d) If the series are not cointegrated it is not possible to establish a long term relationship among the variables. In this case, the Granger causality analysis will identify the short term relationships. When the series were cointegrated we will consider the Error Correction Term in the VAR System in order to determine the nature of the long term causality.
e) The weakness of the test that determine the optimal number of lags and the degree of cointegration represent the main problems in the Granger Causality analysis. Hence, Toda and Yamamoto (1995), Dolado and Luketerpohl (1996) propose a methodology that can be applied independently of the model's integration or co-integration properties. In this context, a Modified Wald Test is used in this method, the same based on an extended VAR model, of which order is determined by the number of optimal length lags (k) and the maximum number of times that the variables are to be differentiated. However, this approach is inefficient and suffers some loss of power since over-fit VAR's. For this reason this approach could be considered as a complementary tool (Toda and Yamamoto 1995).

4. RESULTS

As can be seeing in Figure 1, the Mexican economy has been growing since 1988 in real terms, with the exception of the 1994 and 2001 crisis. The inflow FDI showed a different behavior (see Figure 2) especially relevant is the growth from 1995 to 2005. More than 70% of the inward FDI was concentrated in the manufacturing sector. The inward FDI in transversal sectors that start to acquire special relevance since 1992, account for 20% of the total FDI received between 1986 and 2006. Also, despite the manufacturing sector maintaining a constant rate of inflow FDI, in the case of transversal services were heavily concentrated between the years 2000 and 2002, and the 87.3% of it have been concentrated in the financial sector (see Figure 2 and Figure 3).

Source: The Conference Board and Groningen Growth and Development Centre, Total Economy Database.

Figure 2. Mexican labor productivity in 2006 constant dollars (1985-2006) (expressed in logarithmic terms).

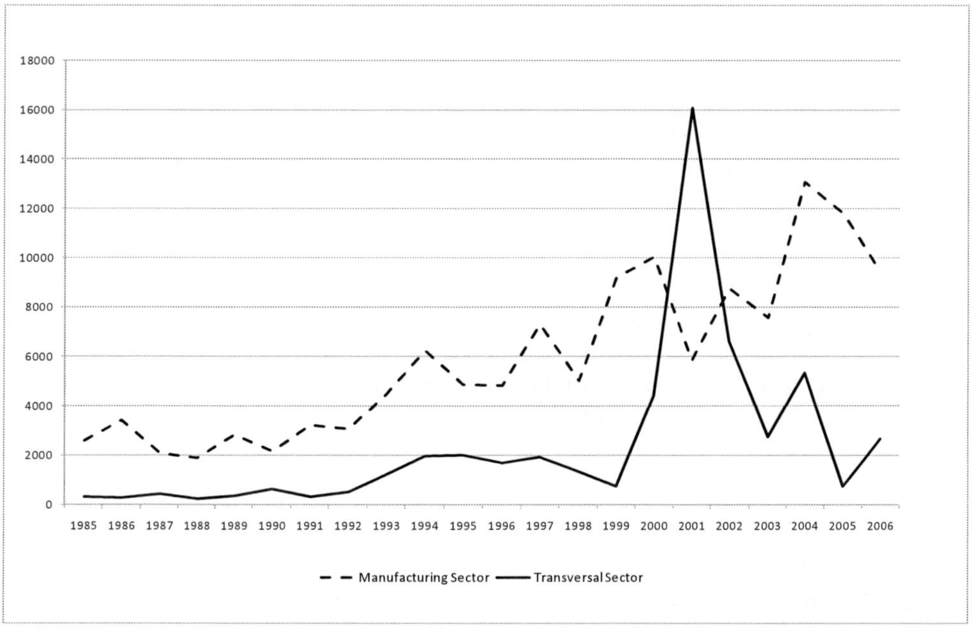

Source: OCDE and the GDP deflator estimated by the Groningen Growth and Development Centre.

Figure 3. Sector break-down of FDI inflows in Mexico in 2006 constant dollars (1985-2006).

To determine the order of integration of variables incorporated in the model we apply the Dickey-Fuller statistic. The results evidence that all variables are I(1) (see Table 1). One of the methodological problems of the Granger causality test is to determine the optimal number of lags *(k)*. In this sense, when work takes place with small samples, use the Schwarzt statistic is recommended by Kukertpohl (1993). The results obtained are outlined in Annex I, Table 2, where it can be observed that the lack of freedom does not allow us to develop any of the models in which productivity, inflow FDI in manufacturing and transversal sector are simultaneously included.

Table 1. Analysis of unit roots

	Augmented Dickey-Fulller Statistic		
	(1)	(2)	(3)
MFDI	-0.591	-3.988*	1.103
TFDI	-1.696	-2.754	0.371
LP	-2.366	-3.260**	-2.472*
First Difference			
ΔMFDI	-5.164	-4.893	-4.371
ΔTFDI	-4.086	-4.019	-4.057
Δ LP	-5.731	-5.571	-5.744

MFDI: inflow FDI in manufacturing sectors, TFDI: inflow FDI in transversal services sectors. LP1: labor productivity (growth rate of GDP divided by the number of workers).

Notes: (1), (2) and (3) respectively correspond to the statistical model with constant, with constant and tendency and without any of the above.

* The nil hypothesis for a level of confidence of 99% is rejected, ** rejects the nil hypothesis for a level of confidence of 95%,

The Johansen co-integration tests confirm existence of at least one co-integration vector between labor productivity (LP) and the manufacturing FDI as well as transversal services FDI, which are similar to the results obtained by Cuadro, Orts and Alguacil (2004) for a different time period, using quarterly data and for the total Mexican inward FDI (Annex I, Table 5). This imply that in the Temporal Granger Causality Test on ECM we should consider one error correction vector (s=1). The absences of error autocorrelation allow us to assure that VAR systems are adequate (See Annex I, Table 7).

In Table 2 we show the results of the Temporal Granger-Causality test on ECM it is possible to observe the intensity and nature of causality relations. As a summary we can observe that:

a) The inflow manufacturing FDI (MFDI) has a positive and long term impact on labor productivity. Said result is coherent with that presented by Jordaan (2006), which is based on a sample of manufacturing Mexican companies.
b) The FDI in transversal services has a positive and long term impact on labor productivity and productivity.
c) The coefficient of Granger Causality Test and the impulse analysis evidence a very similar impact of both types of inflow FDI on labor productivity. In these sense, we do not verify the main hypothesis of this paper.

d) We have observed a short term negative effect on labor productivity by the inflow FDI in transversal services, probably by a crowed-out effect.
e) The results do not clearly show a positive effect on productivity due to inflow manufacturing FDI. This result does not permit confirm that the search for efficiency, fundamentally based on a lower cost of the work factor, constitutes a localization advantage offered by the Mexican economy, conclusions of the previous research by Love and Lage-Hidalgo (2000) and García-Herrero and Santabárbara (2007)

Table 2. Temporal Granger-Causality test on ECM

	Causality Source		
Lags: 2	ΔLP	ΔMFDI	ECT
	$\sum coeff$ (χ^2)	$\sum coeff$ (χ^2)	Coef (t)
ΔLP	0,097 (0.171)	0,020 (1.738)	-1.077** (-2.506)
ΔMFDI	-6,557 (1.414)	-1,253* (6.006)	8.515 (1.216)
ECT=LP(-1) -0.01xMFDI(-1)* + 0.115*			
	Causality Source		
Lags: 2	ΔLP	ΔTFDI	ECT
	$\sum coeff$ (χ^2)	$\sum coeff$ (χ^2)	Coef (t)
ΔLP	-0,594** (7.035)	-0,04208* (14.381)	-0.122*** (-1.954)
ΔTFDI	-9,574 (1.084)	0,105** (9.085)	6.550* (3.476)
ECT=LP(-1) -0.130xTFDI(-1)*+ 0.027x@TREND(85)* + 0.608			

MFDI: inflow FDI in manufacturing sectors, TFDI: inflow FDI in transversal services sectors. LP: labor productivity (growth rate of GDP divided by the number of worked hours). ECT: error correction term. Δ first diference. OLS regressions. Temporal period: 1985-2006.
*, **, *** indicate significance levels at 10 per cent, 5 per cent, and 1 percent respectively.

The Granger Non-Causality Test applying the Toda and Yamamoto Modified Wald, does not allow to confirm the results obtained. There is not a causality relation between inward manufacturing FDI and labor productivity.

At the same time, it is showed a negative relation between inward FDI in transversal services and labor productivity (See Annex I Table 6).

Conclusion

The transversal services (energy, transport, communications and financial services) are suppliers of intermediate goods for the whole economy as well as of final goods for consumers (final demand of the economy).This features are a support in of our main hypothesis: the inward FDI in transversal services has a greater spillover capacity over manufacturing FDI. For this reason we should expect a greater effect on productivity by the transversal services.

The results obtained in the analysis show a positive and a greater effect of inward manufacturing FDI (MFDI) on labor productivity (LP) that the one obtained from inward transversal FDI (TFDI). Probably, the relative short time series used (1985-2006) and the concentration of inflow transversal FDI in few years can explain the no verification of the hypothesis.

For future research agenda it is necessary to study the institutional framework of these type of services since it could be a determinant factor for transfer of knowledge (Matoo et al.2006). The competitive structure and the quality of supervision among the transversal services advise to do a disaggregated analysis to test the relationship between inward FDI and economic growth.

The relative small size of the time series and the necessary to do a causality analysis are without any don't the main weak point of the research, since we do not have enough degree of freedom to run the models and control for the omitted variables, in other words, factors that could explaine the increases in productivity were not taken into account.

References

Aitken, B.J. 6 Harrison, A.E. (1999). Do Domestic Firms Benefit from Direct Foreign Investment?. *American Economic Review,* 89(3), 605-618.

Blomström, M. and Kokko, A. (1998). Multinational Corporations and Spillovers. *Journal of Economic Surveys,* 12(3), 247-277.

Blomström, M. and Kokko, A. (2003). 'The Economics of Foreign Direct Investment Incentives', *CEPR. Discussion Paper Series,* 3775.

Blomström, M. and Persson, H. (1983). Foreign Direct Investment and Spillover Efficiency in Undeveloped Economy: Evidence from the Mexican Manufacturing Industry. *World Development,* 11, 115-135.

Caves (1999). Spillover from Multinational in Developing Countries: the Mechanisms at Work, *Working Paper William Davidson Institute 247.*

Chen, C., Chang, L. and Zhang, Y. (1995). The Role of Foreign Direct Investment in China's Post-1978 Economic Development. *World Development,* 23(4), 691-703.

Chowdhury, A. and Mavrotas, G. (2006). FDI and Growth: What Causes what?. *World Economy,* 59(1), 121-129.

Cuadros, A., Orts, V. and Alguacil, M. (2004). Openness and Growth: Re-Examining Foreign Direct Investment, Trade and Output Linkages in Latin America. *The Journal of Developing Studies,* 40(4):167-192.

De Mello, Luiz R. (1997). Foreign Direct Investment in Developing Countries and Growth: A Selective Survey. *The Journal of Development Studies,* 34(1), 1-34.

De Mello, Luiz R. (1999). Foreign Direct Investment-Led Gorwth: Evidence from Time Series and Panel Data. *Oxford Economic Papers,* 51, 133-151.

Dolado, J.J. and Lutkepohl, H. (1996). Making Wald Test Work for Cointegrated VAR Systems. *Econometrics Reviews,* 15, 369-386.

Findlay, R. (1978). Relative Backwardness, Direct Foreign Investment, and the Transfer of Technology: A Simple Dynamic Model. *Quaterly Journal of Economics,* XCII(1), 1-15.

Fry, M. J. (1993). Foreign Direct Investment in a Macroeconomic Framework. *Working Paper. International Economics Department The World Bank,* WPS 1141.

García-Herrero, A. and Santabárbara, D. (2007). Does China Have an Impact on Foreign Direct Investment to Latin America?. *China Economic Review,* 18, 266-286.

Giles, J.A. and Mirza, S. (1999). Some Pretesting Issues on Testing for Granger Causality. *Econometrics Working Paper, University of Victoria,* EWP9914.

Granger, C. W. J. and Newbold, P. (1974). Spurious Regressions in Econometrics', *Journal of Econometrics,* 2, 111-120.

Haddad, M. and Harrison, A. (1993). Are there Positive Spillovers Form Direct Foreign Investment? Evidencia from Panel Data for Morocco. *Journal of Development Economics,* 12, 51-74.

Hanson, G.H. (2001). Should Countries Promote Foreign Direct Investment?. *G-24 Discussion Paper Series,* 9.

Hein, S. (1992). Trade Strategy and the Dependency Hypothesis: A Comparison of Policy, Foreign Investment. *Economic Development and Cultural Change,* 40(3), 495.

Hsiao, F.S.T. and Hsiao, M.W. (2006). FDI, Exports and GDP in East and Southeast Asia-Panel Data Versus Time-Series Causality Analyses. *Journal of Asian Economics,* 17, 1082-1106.

Jordaan, J.A. (2005). Determinants of FDI-Induced Externalities: New Empirical Evidence for Mexican Manufacturing Plants. *World Development,* 33(12), 2103-2118.

Kugler, M. (2006). Spillover Form Foreign Direct Investment: Within Or between Industries?. *Journal of Development Economics,* 80, 444-477.

Kumar, N. (1996). Foreign Direct Investment and Technology Transfer in Development: A Perspective on Recent Literature. *INTECH Discussion Paper Series,* 9606.

Lipsey, R.E. (2002). Home and Host Country Effect of FDI. *NBER Working Paper,* 9293.

Love, J.H. and Lage-Hidalgo, F. (2000). Analysing the Determinants of US Direct Investment in Mexico. *Applied Economics,* 32, 1295-1267.

Lutkepohl, H. (1993). *Introduction to Multiple Time Series Analysis*. Springer:Guilford UK.

Mattoo, A., Rathindran, R. and Subramanian, A. (2006). Measuring Services Trade Liberalization and its Impact on Economic Growth: An Illustration. *Journal of Economic Integration,* 21(1), 64-98.

Pagano, M. (1993). Financial Markets and Growth: An Overview. *European Economic Review,* 37(2-3), 613-622.

Ramirez, M.D. (2000). Foreign Direct Investment in Mexico: A Cointegration Analysis. *Journal of Development Studies,* 37(1), 138-162.

Rodríguez-Clare, A. (1996). Multinationals, Linkages, and Economic Development. *American Economic Review,* 86(4), 852-873.

Takii, S. (2005). Productivity Spillovers and Characteristics of Foreign Multinational Plants in Indonesian Manufacturing 1990–1995. *Journal of Development Economics,* 76(2), 521-542.

Toda, H.Y. and Yamamoto, H. (1998). Statiscal Inference in Vector Autoregressions with Possibly Integrated Processes. *Journal of Econometrics,* 66, 225-250.

Treviño, L.J. and Mixon, F.G. (2004). Strategic Factors Affecting Foreign Direct Investment Decisions by Multi-National Enterprises in Latin America. *Journal of World Business,* 39(3), 233-243.

Treviño, L.J., Thomas, D.E. and Cullen, J. (2008). The Three Pillars of Institutional Theory and FDI in Latin America: An Institutionalization Process. *International Business Review,* 17(1), 118-133.

Yamada, H. and Toda, H.Y. (1998). Inference in Possibly Integrated Vector Autorregresive Models: Some Finite Sample Evidence. *Journal of Econometrics,* 86, 55-95.

Zapata, H.O. and Rambaldi, A.N. (1997). Monte Carlo Evidence and Cointegration and Causation. *Oxford Bulletin of Economics and Statistics,* 59(2), 285-298.

ANNEX I

Table 3. Schwarzt Test

Own lags	1	2	3
LP, MFDI	-3.741	-3.903*	-3.790
LP, TFDI	-2.479	-2.561*	-2.322

MFDI: inflow FDI in manufacturing sectors, TFDI: inflow FDI in transversal services sectors. LP: growth rate of GDP divided by the number of workers.

Table 4. Outliers

LP,	1994, 2000
MFDI	2004
TFDI	1999, 2005

MFDI: inflow FDI in manufacturing sectors, TFDI: inflow FDI in transversal services sectors. LP: growth rate of GDP divided by the number of workers.

Table 5. Johansen cointegración test

H_0:	Mod, 1	$\lambda(0,95)$	Mod, 2	$\lambda(0,95)$	Mod, 3	$\lambda(0,95)$
	LP, MFDI-Manufacturing					
λ_{max}						
0	29.480*	20.261	33.972*	25.872	33.227*	18.397
1	6.235	9.164	9.004	12.517	8.261*	3.841
	TFP1, TFDI-Trans					
λ_{max}						
0	26.212*	20.261	28.246*	25.872	20.247*	18.397
1	4.065	9.164	5.502	12.517	4.093*	3.8414

MFDI: inflow FDI in manufacturing sectors, TFDI: inflow FDI in transversal services sectors. LP: growth rate of GDP divided by the number of workers.

Mod (1), (2) and (3) respectively correspond to the statistical model with constant, with constant and tendency and with not linear tendency.

*, **, *** indicate significance levels at 10 per cent, 5 per cent, and 1 percent respectively.

Table 6. Test for Granger Non-Causality applying the Toda and Yamamoto Modified Wald Test

	Causality Source	
Lags	LP	MFDI
2+1	$\sum coeff$ (χ^2)	$\sum coeff$ (χ^2)
LP	-0,078 (0.310)	0,008 (3.460)
MFDI	8,507 (1.720)	0,754 (0.733)

	Causality Source	
Lags	LP	TFDI
2+1	$\sum coeff$ (χ^2)	$\sum coeff$ (χ^2)
LP	0,387 (2.648)	-0,002* (9.932)
TFDI	20,281 (3.999)	0,873* (10.07)

MFDI: inflow FDI in manufacturing sectors, TFDI: inflow FDI in transversal services sectors. LP: labor productivity (growth rate of GDP divided by the number of workers). Lags=3. OLS regression.

*, **, *** indicate significance levels at 10 per cent, 5 per cent, and 1 percent respectively.

Table 7. VEC Residual Serial Correlation LM Tests

LP-MFDI

Lags.	LM-Stat.	Prob.
1	2.230868	0.6934
2	1.919504	0.7506
3	5.134589	0.2738
4	5.594230	0.2316
Probs from chi-square with 4 df.		

LP-TFDI

Lags.	LM-Stat.	Prob.
1	9.016934	0.0607
2	3.027763	0.5532
3	1.921866	0.7501
4	3.359755	0.4995
Probs from chi-square with 4 df.		

In: International Political Economy
Editors: M.A. Galindo Martin, E. Nissan
ISBN: 978-1-60876-172-2

Chapter 5

FINANCIAL GLOBALIZATION AND PERIPHERAL STRATEGIES: RECENT EXPERIENCES IN LATIN AMERICA AND LESSONS FROM ASIA

Santos Miguel Ruesga Benito[1], André Moreira Cunha[2] and ***Julimar da Silva Bichara***[3]
[1]Universidad Autónoma de Madrid, Spain
[2]Universidade Federal de Rio Grande do Sul, Brasil
[3]Universidad Autónoma de Madrid, Spain

ABSTRACT

Despite the strong theoretical expected linkages between financial openness and economic growth, the financial globalization has been primarily a source of economic instability. This article presents a strategy of alternative political economy to the passivity of Latin American countries' political economy facing up to the globalization. It emphasizes the idea that a permanent tension exists between the internationalization trend in economy relationships and the search for autonomy in the political economies; that tension is developed in an unstable external environment and in a new international financial liberal order. This paper compares the Asiatic and the Latin American trajectories after the financial crisis in 1997, and it analyzes the recent reform of the international financial architecture.

1. INTRODUCTION

Financial globalization has been one of the most important dimensions of the process of international economic integration. The cycle of entry of private capital in developing countries, which began at the end of the 1980s, highlighted the permanent tension between the significant development of market forces and high instability. That movement of *boom* was fuelled by great faith in the virtues of globalized, deregulated finances. However, the Mexican crisis of 1994–95 and, most of all, the Asian crisis of 1997, revealed that the international economy was going through a period of growth shrouded in great tensions of instability. Between 1998 and 2002 there were more and more instances of financial crises. Private capital flows stagnated in the midst of contraction in the growth of the developed economies and the effects of deflation on the prices of financial assets in the United States.

Furthermore, after 2003, in an environment of very low interest rates in the major industrialised economies, of recovery of world trade and of the weakness of the dollar, international investors again acquired assets coming from emerging countries. As a whole, the latter were transformed, in recent years, into net capital exporters, largely because trade surpluses were reconverted into reserves held in convertible currencies, especially the dollar (IMF, 2005).

The surprising recovery, in the years subsequent to the financial crisis, of the Asian countries that had gone through strong depression during the periods of crisis of 1997 and 1998, as well as the dynamism of China and India, is an interesting phenomenon. That made specialists the world over look towards the East, mainly because there were strong signals indicating that the recent cycle of economic globalization, especially in its financial dimension, had not succeeded in generating a process of balanced growth within the capitalist periphery. It is, in fact, quite the opposite: empirical evidence suggests that financial globalization, with its promises of growth, led to further instability, as the latest reports elaborated by the IMF (Prasad et al., 2003, World Bank, 2006) indicate.

As in the last four decades, the performance of peripheral countries has been quite irregular and variable. In *Asia In Development*[1], even during the crisis of 1997, a higher pace of growth was maintained, which resulted in many countries using macroeconomic strategies that were not in close touch with the suggestions that emanated from Washington or Wall Street. And, on the contrary, by reproducing a pattern of management of financial flows, of the exchange rate and of official reserves — considered by some to be mercantilist (Eichgengree, 2004; Goldstein, 2005) and by others to be a reproduction of the spirit of Bretton Woods (Dooley et al., 2003 and Garber, 2005) — some Asian countries made it clear that they were not willing to passively accept the internalisation of the *feast or famine*[2] financial cycles that have been such a feature of the recent dynamics of globalized, deregulated finances.

In this context, the point of departure for this paper is a series of observations by Dooley et al. (2003) and Dooley and Garber (2005) regarding the rationality of what is termed as the Asian strategy[3], and which implies the search for ways of preserving degrees of freedom for macroeconomic management in an atmosphere of international financial volatility. For those authors, such a strategy reproduces the experiences of many developed countries in the period

---

[1] Terminology used by the IMF in its most recent publications, especially World Economic Outlook.

[2] The IMF (2003, appendix to Chapter III) the expression *feast or famine* is used to describe the cycles, shorter and shorter, of expansion and contraction of international financial liquidity. The phases of *feast* determine the massive entry of resources into the periphery. The phases of *famine* are characterised by a lesser willingness on the part of investors to take risk and buy assets in emerging markets. In both cases, there is no close relation between the decision to invest or not invest, and any solid economic bases. Speculation predominates, as in the Kindleberger models (2001).

[3] Dooley et al. (2003) do not use this terminology. They identify two groups of countries: (1) the trade account block, comprising mainly Asian countries, who adopt current account surplus strategies, the huge accumulation of reserves in strong currencies, and the active management of the exchange rate and financial flows; (2) the capital account block, characteristic of the Latin American countries, marked by floating exchange rate policies, and a high level of financial openness.

during which the Bretton Woods Agreements operated. Taking as a reference the sixty years since the celebration of that agreement, they tried to examine the differences and similarities between two historical moments of the search for the ordering of international economic relations: the construction of a post-war institutional environment, and the attempt to face the 1990s financial crises. So, rather than returning to the relevant question of alternative models of development, which would lead us back to a more structural discussion, the aim of this paper is to find the main theoretical elements that underlie the strategies of the Asian countries in the period subsequent to the crisis of 1997. Emphasis is placed on the idea that there is a permanent tension between the trend towards the internationalisation of economic relations, (which reduces the margin of manoeuvre for the development of sovereign economic policies, aimed at certain concrete objectives within national policy makers and the search for a certain degree of autonomy, in an unstable external environment which is dominated by a new international financial order that is of a decidedly liberal bent. The way Asia has fared is compared to how Latin America has fared during the recent period of financial crisis and reforms in the international, financial setup.

The questions dealt with in this paper become even more relevant in the present context of serious international financial crisis, which originated in the United States and quickly spread through financial markets across the world, plunging the global economy into the worst economic circumstances known since World War II. Now, in 2009, with increasing demands for reform in the international financial architecture, the new "Bretton Woods Agreements" is no longer simply a question of interest to peripheral countries.

2. What Has Happened to the Financial World Since Bretton Woods?

The Bretton Woods Agreements were reached over sixty years ago; they gave rise to what many consider the most satisfactory institutional international finance arrangement of the last 150 years. In the two-and- a-half decades during which it functioned, multilateral trade flows were recovered, Europe and Japan were reconstructed, industrialization in peripheral countries advanced noticeably, and a new vision of complementariness between the actions of national states and markets was consolidated. With regard to macroeconomic development, the golden age — the decades of the 50s and 60s — saw record rates of income growth, with the maintenance of relative stability, in developed economies as well as in a significant part of the periphery[4].

Mistrust of the self-regulatory properties of markets and the influence of state planning and intervention ideas in the economy — given legitimacy by the liberal crisis of the Interwar Period by the first success of the Soviet experience, of the New Deal and the war effort — gradually gave rise to the intellectual and political environment that paved the way for the Bretton Woods Agreements[5]. A new international financial order emerged from it (Block 1977), which sought to combine the stability brought by the gold standard- based regime of fixed exchange, with the flexibility required by national governments that then assumed as a

---

[4] Maddison (2001) offers a revision of the empirical evidence which upholds our argument.

[5] See Block (1977), Eichengreen (1996), Mikesell (1196), Skidelsky (2000) and Boughton (2002).

key task the maintenance of full employment, which in turn led to the need for greater autonomy in the use of the instruments of economic policy. With the establishment of the International Monetary Fund (IMF), the idea was to stabilise the processes of foreign account adjustment, to avoid a repeat of competitive devaluation and trade protectionist policies. Furthermore, it was only geopolitically logical that the fear of the spread of communism should transform the United States into the most active agent of the dissemination of favourable conditions to countries aligned with the capitalist block.

In its origins, the Agreements were marked by tensions that emerged from the clash between United States and British proposals. Keynes tried to reproduce, at an international level, an institutional architecture that translated his concerns for limiting the destabilising power of private finances (Skideslky, 2000). At the heart of his proposal was the creation of an International Clearing Union capable of issuing and managing an international currency. The role of such an institution was to regulate international liquidity, to stabilise payment patterns, by minimising the risk of excessive devaluations/revaluations of domestic currencies. Such an automatic stabiliser would increase the degree of freedom of national governments to implement the counter-cyclical policies necessary for the preservation of full employment and, thereby, ensure social and political stability, within the framework of liberal democracies and market economies. In opposition to the English proposal, the United States Treasury advocated a reduced model, in which the dollar maintained its position as the key currency. Apparently, the United States were not willing to risk its decisive autonomy in the interest of a global bureaucratic arrangement, no matter how appealing the rationality associated with the idea of an effective moneylender ultimately acting in the international sphere (Keynes 1943 and 1944) might have seemed.

The Bretton Woods System (BWS) crisis gradually created room for the return of a liberal order in international finances, marked by the expansion of financial capital in global markets and by the recurrence of episodes of financial crises (Strange, 1998; Solomon, 1999; Eatwell and Taylor, 2000). Recently, after the boom of private capital flows towards emerging markets between the late 1980s and early 1990s, the Asian crisis (1997–1998) ushered in a phase of less liquidity and greater instability[6]. There is growing evidence that financial globalization has been key to the explanation of this phenomenon, confirming the fears of the Interwar Period´s generation of reformers, the architects of BWS. Recent literature has pointed out that the domestic credit expansion associated to financial globalization (internal and external) is at the origin of the booms of the real and financial markets. An environment is created in which the appreciation of the exchange rate, inflation in the price of financial assets and external vulnerability – together with the worsening of current account balances and the reduction in liquidity (greater relation between liabilities and external assets and reduction in the periods of asset positions) – can be added to the role of endogenous (especially fiscal) factors and exogenous factors (such as an increase in international interest rates) in the rapid deepening of the crisis[7].

[6] Net private capital flows into developing countries peaked in 1996–1997 — 3.5 percent of GDP of all those countries as a whole. In 2000, however, this flow reached its lowest value since the external debt crisis of the early 1980s. This reduction must be attributed to reductions in bank credit and portfolio investment flows, which were much more volatile than direct investments. At present (2004-2006), there is a new increase in flows towards developing countries, as a result of the high liquidity at present in the international financial market. (These calculations were done by the authors, from the IMF data base — World Economic Outlook).

[7] See, Kaminsky et al. (1998), Demirgüç-kunt and Detragiache (1998) Aziz et al. (2000) and Prasad et al. (2003).

With the drop in the capital inflow in developing countries, the increase in financial instability, reflected in recurrent crises, and the questioning of the allegedly automatic links between capital account globalization and economic growth, the official establishment began to be more cautious in the way it chose to assess the costs and benefits of financial globalization. It is important to remember that at the late 1980s and early 1990s, there was great optimism about financial globalization, a posture that was reinforced by United States pressure on the opening of capital flows in several developing countries. The warning sounded by academic experts regarding the need for the establishment of an appropriate sequence for financial opening was relegated to a secondary plane. After the Mexican crisis, and, most of all, after the Asian crisis, issues such as the sequence of the opening of capital lows and the careful regulation of domestic financial systems came into vogue again. The position of the IMF and World Bank reports gradually reflected this new perspective.

Within the academic mainstream, some voices vigorously criticised the probable automatic links between financial globalization and the real expansion of the economy. Rodrik (1988) was one of the first academics to alert about the fact that, in the recent cycle of globalization, financial opening might not necessarily be linked to greater income growth. Furthermore, he criticised the imbalances between the institutional costs of the promotion of liberalising reforms and the effective results in terms of development, especially when we consider that the countries that did not follow the agenda of liberal reforms coming out of Washington and Wall Street achieved greater growth (Rodrik, 2005). Radalet and Sachs (1998) and Stiglitz (2002) questioned the asymmetry of results in the globalization process and the non-neutrality of the IMF in its policy for financial crises management.

In recent studies done within the domain of the IMF, this position has been reinforced, and there is now a more cautious approach with regard to the potential impact of capital flows on developing countries. When measures for financial openness and the indicators of economic development and domestic financial markets were related, a "weak relationship between growth and capital account liberalizations was found and, as in other studies, it was difficult to discern any significant relation between growth and globalization" (IMF 2005:143). Furthermore, the greater level of capital account globalization in many developing countries might have been accompanied by an increase in the volatility of net capital flows and a reduction in economic growth. The IMF sought to associate this unfavourable development with the institutional failings of capital-receiving countries. However, two bigger studies found no solid links between financial globalization and growth of developing countries either (Prasad et al., 2003; World Bank, 2006).

In a close analogy with the crisis of the liberal order prior to the constitution of BWS, there has been an hot debate in the academic and the private and public sectors, about what came to be called reforms in the international financial architecture. At certain moments, the feeling was that post-Cold War capitalism might be in serious danger of going back to a period of weakness similar to that of the crisis of the 1930s, when the real economy crumbled under the weight of the finance debacle[8]. Initially, the private and public establishment, with the analytical support of the theoretical models of financial crises, was quick to point to the

[8] Krugman (1999) refers to the fear of a return to the *depression economy*. Similar arguments can be found in almost all the analyses carried out in this period, from analysts aligned to the establishment (Solomon, 1999, for example) insiders (Stiglitz, 2002) or critics (Strange, 1998; Eatwell & Taylor, 2000).

institutional weaknesses of debt countries as being at the origin of the instability. This is so reflected in the aforementioned studies of the IMF.

In these terms, the IMF, the World Bank, the Bank of International Settlements (BIS) and the new Financial Stability Forum, amongst many other multilateral forums (controlled by the G7, especially by the United States) would do well to focus their efforts on the supervision of the system, through the identification of parameters for the proper functioning of financial markets, for their careful regulation by the monetary authorities, for fiscal management, for transparency in micro and macroeconomic information and corporate governance. It must be borne in mind here that in the midst of the recurrent crises and subsequent help mega-packages, the IMF was strongly questioned not only for the efficiency of its policies, but also for creating systematic moral risk, in so far as its help policies might have led new international investors to think that they would always be bailed out in the event of a liquidity and reliability crisis (Fischer, 1999, Meltzer, 2000). Without either a mandate or the financial resources to act as an effective ultimate lender, and, most of all, without the political support of its majority shareholders to do so[9], the Fund reinforced its statutory role of monitoring and supervising member countries in financial difficulties (Krueger, 2001, 2003).

Such a conservative agenda of reforms in the international financial architecture was gradually perceived as insufficient by academic experts, by the financial markets themselves, and by multilateral agencies not directly subject to the interests of the Washington Administration, such as UNCTAD[10] and ECLAC[11]. Here, the original insight of the architects of BWS, the notion that financial markets should be subject to the needs of national governments so they can implement full employment policies on the domestic front, was taken up again. However, in a context of growing interdependence in the international arena, the proposals for the strengthening of the international financial architecture in a non-conventional way lead to the idea of creating multilateral institutions, capable of ensuring balanced relations between debtors and creditors and, most of all, of regulating private finances. As in the past, such proposals would bring with them a considerable reduction in the degree of freedom of credit countries to impose their interests, as well as affect predominant demand in the private sector of a simple but effective legal structure that would place emphasis on the defence of the right to ownership and the free mobility of factors (Strange, 1999, Stiglitz, 2002). It is why they still do not have the solid, political support necessary.

On the other hand, there was a gradual movement, within the establishment, towards recognition that their own reform agenda was probably insufficient. A more cautious understanding of the effects of financial globalization led to a return to the perspective that there could be valid, systematic controls of capital flows (especially inflows), with the aim of altering the temporary profile of investments, to reduce their potential volatility or, even more so, to guarantee sufficient margin for the execution of a broader process of institutional modernisation (Ariyosh et al., 2000; Rogoff, 2002). Furthermore, it was recognised that the

---

9 The Clinton Administration (1993-2000) managed the international crises, especially the Mexican and Asian crisis, with a policy of strong financial aid, in close collaboration between the US Treasury, and the IMF. The Bush administration (2001-2008) is showing greater sensitivity towards the argument of moral risk, in line with the Republican behaviour of limiting budget allocations to IMF capital, necessary for increasing financial support to emerging countries (Stiglitz, 2002; Solomon, 1999).

10 United Nations Conference on Trade and Development.

11 Economic Commission for Latin America and the Caribbean; CEPAL (2004), Eatwell & Taylor (2000), Davidson (2003), Mikesell (1996), Strange (1998), Tobin (2000Stiglitz (2002).

origin of the debt crisis might have been the opportunistic (short-term) behaviour of private investors, so that countries of long-term solvency, that were going through temporary liquidity difficulties, could be catapulted to a crisis without being able to fall back upon mechanisms such as financial default, which are so common for the protection of companies and creditors in industrialised countries. Surprisingly, the IMF itself (Krueger, 2001) eventually placed at the heart of the debate the rather unconventional proposal, defended years ago by UNCTAD and academic economists, for the establishment, in the international sphere, of statutory mechanisms for mediation in conflicts between private creditors and sovereign debtors. That proposal was strongly criticised by the private sector and did not get the effective support of the G7 governments. Once again it is possible to draw a parallel with the atmosphere that prevailed prior to the constitution of Bretton Woods. In an initial version of his plan, Dexter White vouched for much broader statutory control of financial flows. Private sector pressure, especially from Wall Street, made him back off (Block, 1977; Broughton, 2002; Skidelsky, 2000).

3. Peripheral Strategies in the Face of Financial Instability

In the face of the clear demonstration that the of capital account liberalization is one of the major sources of international financial instability and of the exchange crises that assailed Latin American countries, an increasing number of scholars now question the so-called automatic links between financial globalization and economic growth. In this sense, Dooley et al., (2003) and Dooley and Garber (2005) suggest that the use of an economic policy strategy such as those currently adopted by some developing Asian countries, is a rational economic policy management solution for peripheral countries in an international economy characterised by financial instability. For that reason, it is referred to here as the Asian strategy or the peripheral strategy, in reference to the countries on the periphery of international capitalism, in terms of participation and capitalist development. It is a macroeconomic management standard whose aim is to reduce as much as possible the degree of vulnerability of the said countries in the face of the perverse effects of financial cycles of the feast or famine variety (IMF, 2003).

The key variable of this strategy is the management of financial flows in strong currencies. It implies the use, whether combined or not, of several monetary policy instruments such as: restriction of the free movement of capital; use of a controlled exchange rate regime; a significant export thrust; and an increase in the stock of international reserves.

These unconventional elements constitute a framework of macroeconomic management marked by fiscal and monetary conservatism. Furthermore, the management pattern of these elements has been contrary to the conventional orthodoxy. A pragmatic case is Korea, which formally adopts a floating exchange regime associated to a system that is inflationary in outlook, but which has not prevented the monetary authorities from pragmatically intervening, in the foreign exchange market with the double aim of minimising appreciation pressures on the won (the Korean currency) and, at the same time, of transforming the positive international trade balances into official reserves (ADB, 2005, IMF, 2005). As is well known, a country that adopts a floating exchange regime would not necessarily have to interfere in the exchange market or accumulate reserves.

The Asian strategy might be contributing towards the attainment of a combined situation of economic growth and reduction in the dependence on short term private finance sources held in a strong currency. In this sense, Dooley's argument (2003), as well as those by Dooley and Garber (2005), point to the non-conventional analyses, which, in the last two decades, have adopted a more critical perspective, with regard to the capacity of economic globalization, especially in its financial dimension, to create conditions for development with social inclusion and macroeconomic stability.

The economic results of Asian countries, as compared to Latin American countries, help us to explain the success of the Asian strategy. In the period between 1995 and 2003, which coincides with growth in international financial instability and with the implementation of structural reforms in the periphery, especially in countries that have IMF and World Bank financial support programmes, the macroeconomic development of Asian economies was greater. In spite of the financial crisis of 1997–98, which fully hit Asian countries, Korea, Hong Kong, Singapore and Taiwan as well as other developing countries in the region managed to grow at a pace that was significantly higher than the average of the capitalist periphery economies as a whole. In this period, per capita income grew by only 0.6 percent a year in Latin America, as opposed to 5.4 percent in Asian countries, and 3.6 percent in those Asian countries considered as developed (IMF, 2005). On the other hand, *expansionist* monetary and fiscal policies have been more frequently used in the Asian economies than in the Latin American economies, without that leading to higher inflation rates. On the contrary, inflation was higher in Latin American countries than in Asian countries (IMF, 2005).

The reduction in external vulnerability became a central element in the definition of the macroeconomic policy objectives of Latin American and Asia countries. After financial opening, which led to greater external weakness, many Asian economies began to adopt as a strategy the creation of sufficiently elastic liquidity cushions (in United States dollars) so as to avoid what was perceived as a risk that is inherent to the globalization process: financial crisis generated by capital account convertibility (ADB, 2005).

As a result of that strategy, some indicators of external vulnerability revealed substantial improvement in Asia. The ratio between international reserves and exports more than doubled, at the same time that the ratio between international reserves short term debt multiplied by four. It is important to underline that the latter indicator is used as a reference to identify problems of liquidity in a free movement of capital environment. In the comparison with Latin America, with its restrictive fiscal and monetary policy and its passive exchange rate policy, it can be observed that while the indicators of external vulnerability, between 1995 and 2003, improved in Asia, they got worse in Latin American countries. Furthermore, the financial cost of external debt is almost three times lower in Asia (2 percent) than in Latin America (6 percent).

Different external account adjustment patterns can be gleaned from the international financial cycles. If, before the Asian crisis, the advanced and developing economies in the region absorbed an excess of domestic saving, which was compensated for by structural current account deficits, after 1997 significant adjustment took place: trade surpluses allowed for the compensation of net capital outflows in the period of deepest crisis and, furthermore, allowed for the accumulation of international reserves. In 1997, at the highest point of the crisis, the current account surplus of Asian NICs[12] and of developing Asia was positive, to the tune of 670 billion dollars. In the same period, Latin America maintained a position of deficit (accumulating 340 billion dollars in debt); only in 2002, with the economic depression and the expansion of exports, did they manage to reverse that deficit. At the same time, the international reserves of Asian countries quadrupled their value, moving from 477 billion dollars to over 1.6 trillion dollars in 2005. At that same time, in Latin America, international reserves moved down from 141 billion dollars to just over 200 billion dollars, in 2005.

Another important feature of the Asian strategy is intervention in the foreign exchange market. Persistent trade surpluses and the return of private capital to the region served to push the exchange market towards currency appreciation. Although there are many different types of exchange rates regimes in Asia, such as the currency board of Hong King, the fixed exchange of Malaysia and China (both until 2005) and the floating regimes which are, de facto controlled, interventions in the exchange rates markets have been constant. Apparently, the monetary authorities try to minimise the effects of the fall of the dollar on the international market (Goldstein, 2005).

In the Asian case, in the period between 2002 and 2007, the variation in the amount of reserves as a proportion of the GDP reached the highest average level of the last two decades, around 6.8 percent, as opposed to an average of just over 1 percent for the period between 1970 and 2000[13]. Such a level is unprecedented in the recent history of developing economies. Some analysts suggest that this accumulation of reserves might be linked to a combination of three major factors: (i) the significant export dynamism, the element that best defines the development pattern of Asian countries, further strengthened by the recent recovery of the United States economy, and by the strong growth of the Chinese economy (which accounts for 30 percent of the growth of the global demand); (ii) greater international liquidity and (iii) the strategies of the local monetary authorities, aimed at minimising the appreciation pressures of national currencies. Furthermore, as Eichengreen (2004) and Dolley et al (2003) point out, there is an added rationality linked to the search for protection in a financial environment that is more and more liberalised and deregulated, and, for this reason, more volatile.

It is important to recall that the financial crisis of 1997-98 caused great trauma, given that it exposed the fragility of the strategy of financial globalization of the 1990s. The majority of the countries of the region had reduced the control mechanisms for capital inflows and outflows. Internal funding was often exchanged for external and it was often encouraged many times. The investment boom was fed and fuelled by external saving. The absence of an efficient structure of regulation for financial markets and the spread of hands off policies, in a direction contrary to the developmental policies of the recent past, contributed to the creation of an institutional environment that was hardly adequate. (Radalet and Sachs, 1998; Stiglitz, 2002).

Furthermore, aid packages from official agencies were accompanied by conditions that were, at the time, unusual: they included reforms in the financial systems, reorganisation of the patterns of corporate governance, redefinition of the scope and range of sectoral policies. The degree of interference in national policies went beyond the traditional limits of the monetary and fiscal sphere, which greatly disconcerted several national governments (Stiglitz,

[12] New Industrialized Countries.

[13] Estimations by the authors with data from the World Economic Outlook Database, available at www.imf.org.

2002 and Escap, 2002). Since then, the Asian authorities have insisted that it is not their aim to pursue passive strategies of inclusion into international financial markets. In reaction to the crisis and to the aid packages from International agencies, the Japanese government suggested the creation of an Asian Monetary Fund. Even though this initiative was aborted because of external pressure, the crisis created conditions in the region for a deeper discussion of the issue of the creation of formal channels for the exchange of information and the coordination of the actions of monetary authorities. The currency swap mechanism, officially signed into existence in 2000 by the Association or Southeast Asian Nations (ASEAN)[14] countries, along with Korea, Japan and China, which has been dubbed the Chiang Mai Initiative, and the Collective issuing of national currencies-denominate international bonds, giving rise to the Asia Bond Market Initiative, are important steps towards the promotion of greater financial integration in the region (ADB, 2005).

4. Towards the Global Financial Crisis

Throughout 2008, especially in the second half of the year, the global nature of the financial crisis originating in the United States became increasingly evident. The disruption of the credit channels occurred at the same time that many instances of default and/or restructuring of important financial institutions, with strong state intervention, mainly in the United States and Europe, started to come about. All the segments of the financial markets, in almost all the economies, were strongly affected, and there was a substantial fall in the prices of financial assets. The deflationist spiral of financial markets was materialised through a "complex process of deleveraging", in so far as it brought with it the breaking off with financial positions previously acquired in a context of high leverages levels (IMF, 2008, UNCTAD, 2008).

In addition to the appreciable reduction in the value of financial wealth, the crisis also affected the real economy side, rapidly reversing the previous environment of growth with stability. "Great moderation", as it has been called (Bernanke, 2004), and the thesis of the "decoupling" of emerging markets gave rise to a widespread perception that the real economy dimension of the crisis would eventually come to reach and affect all. The IMF, the World Bank and other official, multilateral agencies and independent scholars speak of the possibility that in 2009 the first contraction of the global economy since the Second World War could come about.

The crisis has been transmitted through two different channels, with different impacts on the main emerging markets. If it is true that the crisis now is widespread and generalised, it also seems reasonable to assume that its dynamics, its intensity, its scope and the possibilities of recovery depend, among other things, on the international insertion model structured in the period prior to economic implosion, as was analysed earlier. A study of the pattern of external trade and financial insertion that took place in the expansionist years of the global economy after 2003 will therefore help to understand its potential effects.

The contagious effect of the crisis was articulated through various channels of transmission, encompassing the current account (fall in commodity prices and global demand

---

[14] Association of South-East Asian Nations: Indonesia, Malaysia, The Philippines, Singapore, Laos, Brunei, Cambodia, Vietnam, Thailand and Burma.

and the increase in profit transfers with financial and non financial corporations) and the capital account (fewer direct investment inflows, portfolio investments, disruption of commercial credit lines and a strong contraction of bank loans). The dissimilar trade and financial insertion models of the main emerging regions, in the 2003–2007 period help to explain the channels of transmission and, consequently, the heterogeneous impact of the financial crisis on their respective currencies and economies. For that reason, even countries with solid macroeconomic bases were not immune to capital flight, when the crisis worsened.

Between 2003 and the first half of 2008, the global economy followed a period of high expansion that was exceptionally *large and long-lasting* favourable. Its extraordinary nature was due to the confluence of *three distinctive components*: high economic growth – with average annual variation rates in global GDP of around 4 percent - associated with low inflation (at least until the middle of 2007); recovery of economic dynamism in regions which, in the 1980s and 1990s, showed low levels of income growth, such as Latin America, Africa and Eastern Europe, or in mature economies such as United States and some European Union countries; substantial improvement in developing economies' external and public sectors, previously characterised by high levels of external vulnerability and fiscal weakness (Toloui, 2007, BIS, 2007 and 2008, ECLA, 2008, IMF, 2008a). These features emerged at a moment in which a new reality became evident in the organization of the global economy: emerging economies such as China, India, Russia and Brazil, among others, began to carry significant weight in world income, in trade flows, equivalent or superior to those of developed economies. According to IMF estimations (2008a), in 2007 and 2008, more than half of global GDP, in purchasing power parity, was generated in developing countries.

The central axis of this new global order revolved around the United States and China (Ferguson and Schularick, 2007, UNCTAD, 2008, BIS, 2007 and 2008). The former represented the ultimate great consumer market and the latter the new industrial factory of the world. Counter to the favourable results of former economic expansion several imbalances emerged, especially in international payments. The United States economy, with its record levels of public and private debt, showed patterns of domestic spending that exceeded — worryingly so — national income. As a consequence of that, current account deficits increased, moving from 2 percent of GDP at the late 1990s, to 4 percent, at the early of 2000s, reaching a maximum around of 7 percent in 2006 and 2007. Such levels of absorption of external savings were possible in as much as the rest of the world, especially the governments of countries with current account surpluses, began to accumulate asset reserves, also at unprecedented levels (El-Erian, 2008, UNCTAD, 2008, BIS, 2008).

The increase in private spending in the United States was made easier by the strongly expansionist fiscal and monetary policies of the early 2000s. In fact, monetary management between 2001 and 2004 was driven by the effort to moderate the effects of the stock exchange markets, in their "new" and "old" edition, on the real economy. Interest rates were reduced from 7 percent to 1 percent, bringing relief to the most heavily indebted sectors and creating an opportunity for real estate expansion and the appearance of speculative bubbles in several financial assets. Parallel to this, the fiscal policy of the Bush government (2001–2009) was such that it inverted the previous tendency of public debt reduction and balance budgets. The combination of tax cut, especially for business and very high incomes individuals, and increase in expenditure, especially in defence, contributed decisively to the return of twin deficits to the United States, fuelling a new cycle of based on consumption and debt-based growth. Such stimuli were reproduced in some European countries, where the real estate boom also represented a source of domestic demand expansion.

If, on the global demand side, the United States economy represented the main source of dynamism, fed and fuelled by cheap and easy credit and by the wealth effect, on the supply side, the global trade and production networks situated in China guaranteed the increase in manufacturing supply at low prices. In fact, China itself gradually became an increasingly important source of demand, especially in energy, food and raw. The strong increase in commodity prices did not translate into inflation, at least not until the middle of 2007, since China, ultimately responsible for that shift, guaranteed the maintenance of manufacture prices at stable or downward prices. China provides a fundamental explanation of the apparent miracle of accelerated growth with low inflation.

The combination of record increases in the prices of commodities (brought on and strengthened by speculative movements in an s liquidity and no regulation) and the stability of industrial prices led to a positive shock in the developing countries' terms of trade, particularly Latin America and Africa, because it permitted a virtuous cycle of growth with balance budgets and current accounts surpluses. In this way, the "great moderation" scenario was completed. However, the financial crisis that began in the United States was also a product of financial globalization, of easy credit and of the absence of regulatory mechanisms capable of ordering the finances world. The "exceptionally favourable" period of growth was radically transformed into the biggest economic and financial crash known since 1929.

It is important to emphasise that, unlike the crises of the late 1990s, whose epicentres were the emerging economies, the present financial crisis originated in the high risk American mortgage markets and immediately infected, in its first months, the remaining developed economies. In the first half of 2008, it started spreading towards a few emerging countries, and, from September onwards, it became a systematic phenomenon (after the Lehman Brothers´ default). It reached all countries, including those with solid macroeconomic bases, considered to have responsible economic policies.

In response to the contagious effect of the crisis, the governments of various emerging economies sought, following the example of their counterparts in advanced countries, to implement a host of initiatives to soften the effects of the depreciation of their currencies, as well as the adverse impact on the national financial systems – directly (in the case of systems more dependent on external funding or with a significant presence of foreign banks) or indirectly (due to the losses of companies with derivatives denominated in foreign currencies or because of the increase in the preference for liquidity on the part of agents in the face of great uncertainty).

The common denominator of these initiatives was, in most cases, counter-cyclical policy measures; different from the adjustment model used in previous financial and exchange rate instability periods. Thus, another unprecedented dimension of the present crisis (in addition to its origin at the heart of the system) is the change in the governments´ positions, who decided that support for economic activity would be a priority (save a few exceptions, such as Hungary, who raised its interest rate after signing an agreement with the IMF).

These two unprecedented dimensions can be linked. In the crises of the 1990s, the adoption of pro-cyclical policies (i.e., restrictive policies) defended by multilateral agencies and G7 governments, was aimed at restoring credibility to the financial markets, which would be a pre-condition for the return of capital flows from outside. In the present context, in the face of the systematic nature of the crisis, the governments of emerging countries are conscious of the fact that these policies, apart from being totally innocuous, only aggravate the perverse effects of economic recession, creating a vicious circle between exchange rate depreciation, credit contraction, assets deflation, income reduction and a slash in firm´ ability to pay.

5. Final Remarks

The analysis carried out here leads us to the conclusion that the main countries of South East Asia have attempted to reduce, especially from 1997–98 onwards, the extent to which their economies are exposed to the effects of financial cycles of the feast or famine variety. This implies the combination of macroeconomic policies not in line with the interests of the Washington-Wall Street powerhouse, with massive interventions in currency markets through the acquisition of assets in hard currencies, such as the dollar or the euro, in proportions never seen in the recent history of international finances. It is not surprising that the voices most identified with the financial establishment, such as Goldstein (2005), Eichengreen (2004) or the Institute of International Finance (IIF, 2004), to mention the most representative, have been strong critics of what has been called the Asian strategy, depreciatively called mercantilist.

The aim of such a strategy is to preserve the external competitiveness of the countries of the region, but also to function as a protection mechanism against the external environment of volatility and keep the region safe from the instability of the international financial world (IIF, 2004). In this way, by avoiding a situation of external vulnerability, which led to the 1997–98 crisis, the policies for the management of financial flows that constitute the Asian strategy are supported by empirical evidence such as that recently elaborated by the IMF itself and other authors (Prasad et al., 2003, World Bank, 2006), who point to financial liberalisation more as a source of instability than of growth.

The critics of the Asian strategy argue that massive intervention in currency markets artificially preserves the external value of currencies, which only makes it difficult to resolve the external imbalances of the United States economy. Furthermore, in the Asian perspective, the accumulation of official reserves has brought two medium and long- term consequences: the potential loss of efficiency and welfare due to the artificial reduction in the imports of capital and consumption goods, and the expansionist fiscal effect of sterilisation policies.

Davidson (2003), for his part, insists on the need for hard reforms in the international financial architecture and points to the hypothesis that the accumulation of international reserves could lead to global equilibrium with unemployment. He thinks that the conventional reform policies for international finance architecture (greater transparency, Tobin tax, legal harmonization in many areas, IMF reforms, among others) are not enough to resolve the major problem of the international economy: the trend towards a situation of structural unemployment through insufficient effective demand. His view is that the international economy can be viewed as a closed economy, in terms of the Keynesian analysis in *The General Theory*, where the overstated increase in the preference for liquidity can lead (even when prices are flexible) to a new equilibrium with unemployment. These situations tend to occur when there is a collapse in the general state of confidence on the part of the economic agents, especially businessmen, who, in a climate of radical uncertainty, seek protection in instruments that are representative of wealth in its most liquid and universal form: currency and some established derivatives of it. In such cases, as Minsky (1991) suggests, and as the practices of governments after the Second World War illustrate, it is necessary to use counter-cyclical fiscal policies (Big Government) and pursue the pragmatic management of currency, in order to minimise the negative effects of the downturns.

In this way, Davidson (2003) contends, it would be possible to show that, in recent years, the presence of governments that adopt mercantilist strategies of accumulation of reserves in hard currencies as a protection mechanism in an atmosphere of financial globalization and market deregulation, is equivalent to a situation of excess savings (or lack of demand for capital assets) determined by a high preference for liquidity.[15] The globalized economy would function, in practice, as a closed economy. He departs from the notion that the economic agents decide not to spend on goods and services that generate employment, which would give rise, potentially, to a situation of redistribution of employment and income in favour of countries capable of implementing mercantilist strategies to the detriment of the others. Of course, the country issuing the international leading-currency continues to enjoy the possibility of accumulating current account deficit, financed by those who stockpiled assets held in that currency in the form of international reserves. What is a winning individual strategy, in terms of Dooley et al. (2003), becomes something irrational for the host of economies as a whole. Inspired in Keynes, Davidson considers that the only structural solution for these asymmetries is the creation of an international currency that cannot be used as reserves for private agents and which, as well, must be administered by a supranational monetary authority. The objective, alongside the objective developed by Keynes (1943) in the period prior to The Bretton Woods Agreements, is to limit the power of private finances and increase the degree of freedom of national governments to pursue full employment policies.

In spite of the accuracy of Davidson's observations (2003), the hard fact is that the reforms in the international financial architecture, as was the case in the 1940s, are limited and marked by a conservative bias, intended to serve the interests of credit countries, or, more specifically, private finances. In these terms, Rodrik (2005) and Dooley and Garber (2005) sustain that the developing countries that have been most successful in their quest for degrees of autonomy for the implementation of growth strategies are precisely those that are managing to counter the power of globalized finances.

In conclusion, there is evidence that the developing Asian economies managed to maintain high rates of economic growth with the use of less restrictive fiscal and monetary policies, even in an atmosphere of greater instability. The majority of Latin American countries, on the other hand, succumbed to the financial crises of the second half of the 1990s. It has been argued that the active search for reduction in external vulnerability through the management of capital flows and the exchange rate is one of the elements that help to explain the recent Asian success. And, on the contrary, the structural dependence on external financing has made Latin American economies an easy target for public and private pressures for the implementation of restricted macroeconomic policies.

It is important to observe that the recent evolution of the international conditions is exceptionally favourable, generally speaking, to emerging countries, and, especially, to Latin America countries. In this paper, we have presented a summary of how Asia and Latin America have fared recently. It is clear that after the financial crisis of 1997 and 1998, the

[15] Bernanke (2005) also suggests that there is a global problem of excess savings.

Asian countries sought to reinvigorate growth based on exports and also, most of all, to reduce external vulnerability. To that end, different macroeconomic strategies were used, with regard to exchange rate management and capital flows. The presence of institutional environments relatively more open to financial capital, such as, for example, South Korea, Singapore, Indonesia and the Philippines, contrasts with those countries that adopt stricter controls on capital inflows and outflows, as is the case, notoriously, of China. All these countries sought to increase their international liquidity and even those that formally have flexible exchange rate regimes sought to avoid excessive appreciations in their currencies. These elements are the features of a broader development strategy which would be based on the financing of the American deficits.

In the most recent period, China has seen itself as the driving force in the region, to give impetus to growth originating in the West, and this is shaping a new scenario of integration of the Asian economies. This, on the one hand, increases the risk of the contagious-effect derived from a reversal of the external situation, and, on the other, opens the way to the emergence of a new and more organic geopolitical block. It has, since the financial crisis of 1997–98, made a greater effort for the institutionalisation of economic cooperation, in trade as well as in finances.

On the other hand, the favourable path followed by Latin American economies, driven by exports and with the reduction of some aspects of external vulnerability, might just possibly be the reproduction of the Asian strategies considered successful by Dooley and Garber (2005), Rodrik (2003) and Stiglitz (2002), among others. This leaves room for speculation that the external position of Latin American countries is now more solid, making them less prone to a new external scenario of reduction in liquidity. Such a scenario could lead to the correction of the financial imbalances of the United States, both external and fiscal. In this sense, the following elements can be underlined: (i) improvement of external current account, due to the favourable conditions for commodity exporters; (ii) no structural change of the Latin American economies' international insertion generated by a quantitative change in their export base, a reflection itself of deeper changes in the economic structure of their economies; (iii) in moments of enormous international liquidity, whose levels were equivalent to the boom prior to the Asian crisis, low cost rewards were noticeable; in an environment of low interest rates in the developed economies and guaranteed the absorption of external resources financed by the capital account; however, the depression of 2008–2009 marked the end of such a favourable situation; (iv) in spite of the adjustment of flows and stocks in t, Latin America's level of reliability and liquidity is lower than that of Asia and other emerging regions; (v) finally, with more flexible exchange rate regimes and less controls on capital flows (Dooley and Garber, 2005), Latin American countries are more exposed to the potentially destabilising effects of the financial cycles and the prices of commodities in spite of the difference in the strategy that has been noticeable in these last years.

The new global financial crisis has once again thrown into relief the vulnerability of the pattern of international insertion of Latin American economies, because of their dependence on the evolution of terms of trade and on the external liquidity. It has also highlighted the weakness of the export model of Asian countries because its high dependence on the export of manufacturing goods to the United States has become the main channel through which the depressive effects of the United States model of growth with debt are transmitted. Furthermore, the days of financial globalization in an era of radical market deregulation, inherited from orthodox economic theories hegemony, seem to be numbered. The global challenge can now be summarised in two salient objectives: the coordination of political interventions and the attempt to reorder private finances, departing from the base of a new regulatory framework. At the same time, the peripheral countries continue to look for alternatives to reduce the social and economic vulnerability of their development models and, consequently, their meaningful entry onto the international stage.

References

Ariyoshi, A., Habermeier, K., Laurens, B., Otker-Robe, I., Canales-Kriljenko, J. and Kirilenko, A. (2000) "Capital Controls: Country Experiences with Their Use and Liberalization". IMF Occasional Paper No. 190. Washington, DC: International Monetary Fund.

Asian Development Bank. (2005). Asian Development Outlook 2005: promoting competition for long term development. Manila.

Aziz, J., Caramazza, F. and Salgado, R. (2000). "Currency Crises: in search of common elements". IMF Working Paper, WP/00/67. Washington, DC.

Bernanke, B. (2004). "The Great Moderation", Remarks by Governor Ben S. Bernanke at the meetings of the Eastern Economic Association, Washington, DC, February 20,

Bernanke, B. (2005). The Global Saving Glut and the U.S. Current Account Deficit. Washington, DC: Federal Reserve Board.

BIS (2008) 78th Annual Report. Basle, Bank for International Settlements, (www.bis.org).

BIS (Bank International of Settlements) (2007). 77th Annual Report. Basle, Bank for International Settlements, (www.bis.org).

Block, F. (1977). *The Origins of International Economic Disorder*. Berkeley: University of California Press.

Boughton, J.M. (2002). "Why White, Not Keynes? Inventing the Postwar International Monetary System". IMF Working Paper, 02/52. Washington: International Monetary Fund.

CEPAL (2008). Panorama de la inserción internacional de la América Latina y el Caribe 2007, tendencias. Octubre. http://eclac.org

CEPAL. (2004). Desarrollo Productivo en Economías Abiertas. Santiago, Chile: CEPAL.

Davidson, P. (2003). The Future of International Financial System. *Conference on the Future of Economics*, Cambridge University, September, 18, 2003.

Dooley, M. P., Folkerts-Landau, D. and Garber, P. (2003). "An Essay on the Revived Bretton Woods System". NBER Working Paper n. 9971. Cambridge, Mass.

Dooley, M. P., Folkerts-Landau, D. and Garber, P. (2005). International Financial Stability, Deutsche Bank,. (http://econ.ucsc.edu/~mpd/).

Dooley, M. P. and Garber, P. (2005). "Is It 1958 or 1968? Three Notes on the Longevity of the Revived Bretton Woods System". Brookings Panel on Economic Activity.

Eatwell, J. and Taylor, L. (2000). *Global Finance at Risk*. New York: The New Press, 2000.

ECONOMIST, The (2008). "Into the storm", The Economist print edition, Oct. 23th.

Eichengreen, Bar.(2004). "Global Imbalances and the Lessons of Bretton Woods". NBER Working Papers 10.497.

Eichengreen, Barry (1996). *Globalizing Capital: a history of the international monetary system*. Princeton: Princeton University Press.

El-Erian, M. (2008). *When Markets Collide: investment strategies for age of global economic change*. New York, McGraw Hill.

Ferguson, N., Schularick. M. (2007). "Chimerica and Global Asset Markets", *International Finance*, Blackwell Publishing, vol. 10(3), pages 215-239, December.

Fischer, S. (1999). *On the Need of International Lender of Last Resort*. Washington, DC: IMF.

Goldstein, M. (2005). "What Might the Next Emerging-Market Financial Crisis Look Like?" IIE Working Paper 05-7 Washington, DC: Institute for International Economics.

IMF (2005). *World Economic Outlook*, September. Washington, DC: IMF, 2005.

IMF (2008a). *World Economic Outlook*, Oct. http://www.imf.org.

IMF (2008b). *Regional Economic Outlook – Western Hemisphere*, Oct.

IMF (2008c). *Regional Economic Outlook – Europe*, Oct.

IMF (International Monetary Fund) (2003). *Global Financial Stability Report*, March. Washington, DC: IMF, 2003.

Institute of International Finance (2004). *Regional Overview*: Asia. IIF.Washington, DC.

Kaminsky, G., Lizondo, S. and Reinhart, C. (1998). *Leading Indicators of Currency Crisis*. Washington, DC: International Monetary Fund.

Keynes, J. M. (1950). "The International Clearing Union, 1943". In: Harris, S.E. *The New Economics*. New York: Alfred A. Knopf.

Kim, S. and Yang, D. Y. (2008). "Managing capital flows: the case of the republic of Korea", *ADB Discussion Paper*, n.88, Tokyo: Asian Development Bank Institute.

Kindleberger, C. H. (2001). *Manias, Panics, and Crashes: A History of Financial Crises*. John Wiley and Sons; 4th edition, 2001.

Krueger, A. O. (2001). International Financial Architecture for 2002: A New Approach to Sovereign Debt Restructuring. Speech at the National Economists' Club Annual Members' Dinner American Enterprise Institute, Washington DC.

Krueger, A. O. (2003) Detecting and Preventing Financial Crises—Recent IMF Approaches. Speech at the Bretton Woods Committee Annual Meeting U.S. State Department.

Krugman, Paul (1999). *The Return of Depression Economics*. W. W. Norton and Company.

Maddison, A. (2001). *The World Economy: a millennial perspective*. Paris: OECD.

Meltzer, A. H. (2000). Report of the International Financial Institution Advisory Commission: International Financial Institution Advisory Commission, Washington, DC.

Mikesell, R.F. (1996). "Revisiting Bretton Woods". Public policy Brief, n. 24. The Jeremy Levy Econ. Institute.

Minsky, H. P. (1991). "The Financial Instability Hypothesis: a Clarification." In: Feldstein, Martin. *The Risk of Economic Crisis*. The University of Chicago Press, Chicago.

Prasad, E., Rogoff, K., Wei, S. and Kose, M.A (2003). "Effects of Financial Globalization on Developing Countries: Some Empirical Evidence". Occasional Paper n. 220, IMF, Washington, DC.

Radalet, S. y Sachs, J. D. (1998). "The East Asian Financial Crisis". Brookings Papers on Economic Activity, n.1. Brookings Institution, Washington, DC.

Rodrik, Dani (1998). "Who Needs Capital-Account Convertibility?" In: Fischer, S. and others, Should the IMF Pursue Capital-Account Convertibility? Essays in International Finance No. 207. Princeton University.

Rodrik, Dani (2005) "Growth Strategies". In: Aghion, P., DURLAUF, S. (eds.). *Handbook of Economic Growth*, North-Holland.

Rogoff, K. (2002). "Rethinking Capital Controls: When Should We Keep an Open Mind?" *Finance and Development*, v. 39, n. 4. IMF, Washington, DC.

Skidelsky, R. (2000). *John Maynard Keynes: fighting for Britain, 1937-1946.* MacMillan, London.

Solomon, R. (1999). *Money on the Move: the revolution in international finance since 1980.* Princeton University Press, Princeton.

Stiglitz, J. E. (2002). Globalization and Its Discontents, W.W. Norton and Company.

Strange, S. (1998). *Mad Money: when markets outgrow governments.* The University of Michigan Press.

Tobin, J. (2000), "Financial Globalization". *World Development*, v.28, n. 6, pp. 1101-1104.

Toloui, R. "When Capital Flows Uphill: Emerging Markets as Creditors". PIMCO, 2007. (www.pimco.com).

UNCTAD (2008). Trade and development report, Sept., (http://www.unctad.org).

World Bank (2006). *Economic Growth in the 1990s: learning from a decade of reform,* World Bank, Washington, DC.

In: International Political Economy
Editors: M.A. Galindo Martin, E. Nissan

ISBN: 978-1-60876-172-2

Chapter 6

FINANCIAL AND TRADE LIBERALIZATION AND THEIR IMPACT ON PRIVATE SECTOR INVESTMENT IN TURKEY

Sima Motamen-Samadian
Westminster Business School

ABSTRACT

Over the last three decades, Turkey implemented a series of liberalisation programmes with the objective of increasing the availability of funds to both private and public sector. The policies were also aimed at stimulating economic efficiency of various sectors and enhancing global integration. The present chapter aims at assessing the extent by which financial liberalization has contributed to financial deepening in Turkey, and the sector that has benefited most from it. It will also show that the positive impact of trade liberalization on gross fixed capital formation and the country's economic growth has been greater than that of financial liberalization.

1. INTRODUCTION

During the last three decades and in particular following the international debt crisis of the early 1980s, Turkey changed its growth strategy from import substitution to export-led growth. The main objective of the programmes was to achieve greater economic and financial integration in the global markets. Accordingly, Turkey adopted a series of structural reform programmes in the form of financial, trade and capital account liberalization. The objective was to stabilize the economy, improve the mobilization of funds by reforming the financial system, and encouraging both internal and external private sectors to engage in various economic activities. A number of earlier studies such as Tulay (2000), Ünalmiş (2002), Ulussever (2004), and Ardic and Damar (2006) had already highlighted the positive and negative effects of the liberalization policies. They had not exactly identified, however, the policy which had a greater impact on growth and capital formation of the country. The present chapter aims at filling the above gap and providing a base for comparing the contribution of each programme on Turkish economy.

The organisation of the chapter is as follows. Section two provides a brief background to economic and financial reforms that took place in Turkey in the 1980s. Section three will assess the extent of financial deepening. The next section examines the impact of financial and trade liberalization on economic growth and overall investment in the country. Here the policy that has had the more significant impact on the economy will be identified. Finally section five provides the conclusion.

2. Turkish Economic Background

Historically, the Turkish financial system has been dominated by its banking sector. According to a report by the Central Bank of the Republic of Turkey (CBRT 2006), bank assets in 2006 accounted for more than 88 percent of total assets of the financial sector. Prior to the 1980s reforms, Turkey's government exercised direct control over economic activities of various sectors. Despite such controls, the economy experienced large fluctuations in macroeconomic indicators. Most state-owned enterprises were loss making and dependent on subsidised bank loans. Accordingly, as pointed out by Ulussever (2004), banks were mostly forced to exercise credit rationing in response to government policies.

To reduce the international debt and government involvement in various sectors, throughout the 1980s the authorities implemented a series of structural reform policies. These policies began with financial and trade liberalization in the early 1980s. Financial liberalization began with relaxation of interest rate controls in 1981, and continued further in mid 1984 when banks were allowed to engage in foreign exchange transactions and accept foreign currency deposits. Shortly after, banks were allowed to determine their own reserve requirement ratios. In 1986 the stock market was re-opened[1] and for the first time an inter-bank money market was launched where banks could borrow short term funds from each other and the central bank. By 1987 the CBRT engaged in open market operations, and finally in mid 1989 the currency became fully-convertible and the capital account was completely opened up.

After the financial liberalization, the number of banks increased from 4 foreign banks that operated in Turkey prior to 1980 to 46 banks in 2008, with 7480 branches in Turkey and 50 branches abroad[2]. Currently, there are 33 commercial banks and13 non-deposit banks which specialize in funding development and investment[3]. Apart from the banking industry, there is also a growing insurance sector that includes 60 insurance companies[4]. Capital markets are still relatively small and dominated by government securities.

To provide a glimpse of how economic activities have been affected by the reform policies, Figure 1 demonstrates the pattern of change in the ratio of various sectors' share of

---

[1] The stock exchange is state-owned but autonomous.

[2] Of the above 33 commercial banks 12 are privately owned, 3 are state-owned, 10 are foreign-owned banks that were founded in Turkey, 7 are foreign owned with branches in Turkey, and one bank under the deposit insurance fund. The three state owned commercial banks control over 30 percent of banking assets. The foreign banks account for 6 percent. For more information on the name of banks see Burak Sansal(2008)

[3] Among the 13 specialised banks four are foreign owned, 6 are privately owned and 3 are state owned.

[4] Among the insurance companies 5 are foreign-owned and 2 are state-owned.

GDP over the last 40 years. As can be seen from this figure, throughout the period between 1968 and 2008, while the agricultural sector's share of GDP continuously declined, that of the service sector increased.

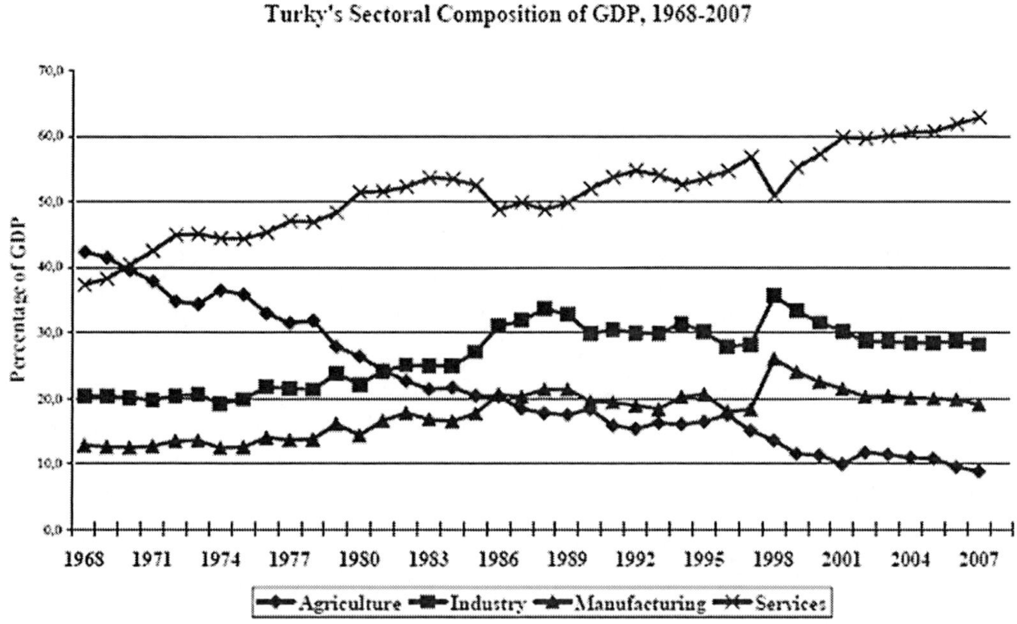

Source: Calculated and produced by the authors using the data provided in the World Development Indicators (December 2008).

Figure 1.

The industrial sector's share of GDP began to rise a bit after the financial and trade liberalization of the early 1980s, but began to decline again from the late 1980s onwards. A somewhat similar pattern was observed in the case of the manufacturing sector, where its share of GDP continued to remain below the industrial sector. Indeed, as can be seen from Figure 1, after nearly 30 years since the launch of trade and financial liberalization policies, the manufacturing sector's share of GDP is almost the same rate as it used to be before the reform policies were implemented.

3. Financial Liberalisation and Its Impact on Gross Fixed Capital Formation

Private sector investment in Turkey is predominantly financed by the banking sector. Hence liberalisation of the financial sector was expected to play an important role in the depth and breath of the financial sector and improve private sector's ability to invest. Data reveal, however, that despite implementation of financial liberalization policies, Turkey still has not experienced a significant level of financial deepening. This is evident from Figure 2 which shows that after nearly 30 years of financial liberalization, M2/GDP (one of the main measures of financial deepening), is still well below the level that is commonly observed in developed markets (usually above 100%). In practice it has moved up only slightly from around 16% in 1980 to slightly over 40% in 2008.

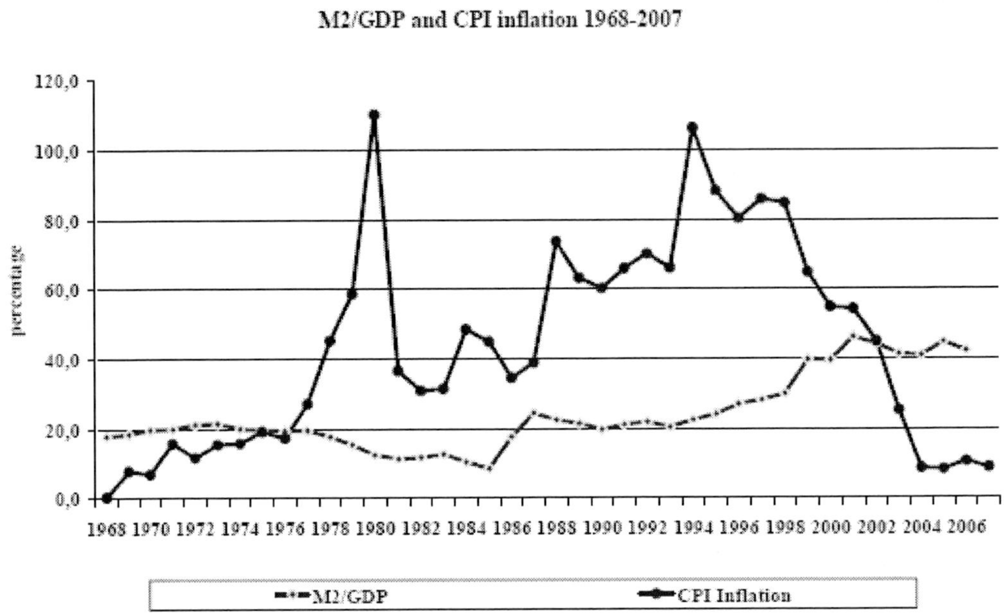

Source: Calculated and produced by the authors using the data provided in the World Development Indicators (December 2008).

Figure 2.

Figure 2 also shows that throughout the first twenty years of financial liberalization inflation continued to remain high and well above the rate of financial deepening. Thus it effectively undermined the ability of the financial liberalization policy to stimulate private sector savings and investment. This is also evident from Figure 3 which shows the path of change in the country's deposit rates and inflation between 1968 and 2007. Here it can be seen that while deposit rates increased sharply after the implementation of financial liberalisation, inflation too increased rapidly.

As can be seen from Figure 3, inflation has been consistently above deposit interest rates over 21 years and below it for only 12 years, six of which were from 2001 onwards. This is also apparent from Figure 4 which shows that real deposit rate had been negative in a number of years and fluctuated around zero for most of the period between 1980 and 2002.

To assess the contribution of financial liberalization to gross fixed capital formation, it is important to examine the extent by which banks provided credit to private and public sector. As can be seen from Figure 5, despite the fact that banks were the main source of finance for the private sector, throughout the period between 1970 and 1985, the ratio of bank credit to private sector as a proportion of GDP remained insignificant. This was mainly due to financial repression that prevailed in those years when only four banks operated in the country, and the public sector was crowding out the private sector. Following the financial liberalization of the 1980s, though the total amount of credit granted by banks continuously increased, the amount that was given to the private sector did not increase in the same proportion. In other words, while financial liberalization did provided some respite for the private sector, it did not help them as much as was expected.

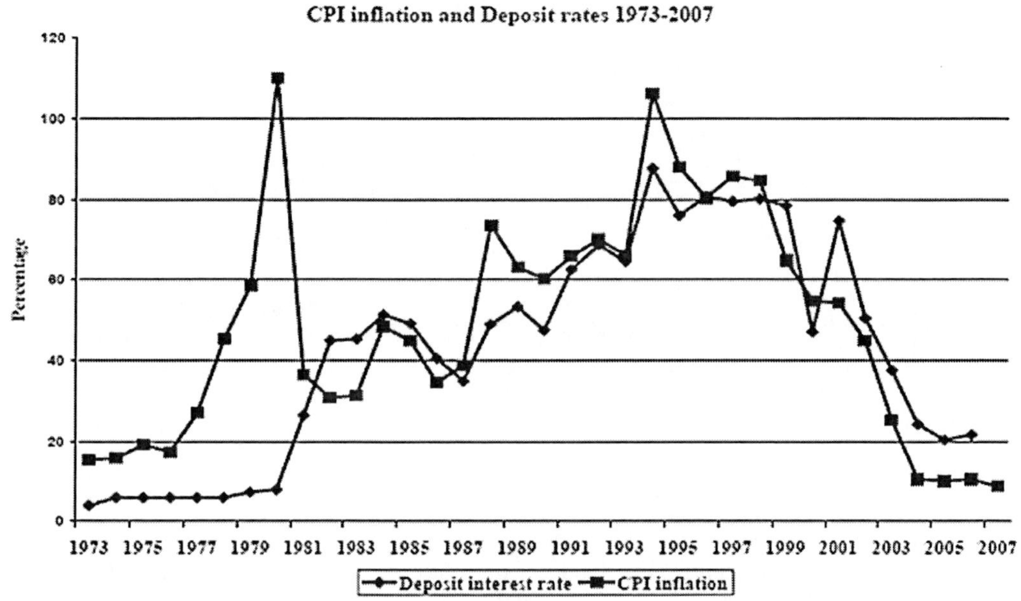

Source: Calculated and produced by the authors using the data provided in the World Development Indicators (December 2008).

Figure 3.

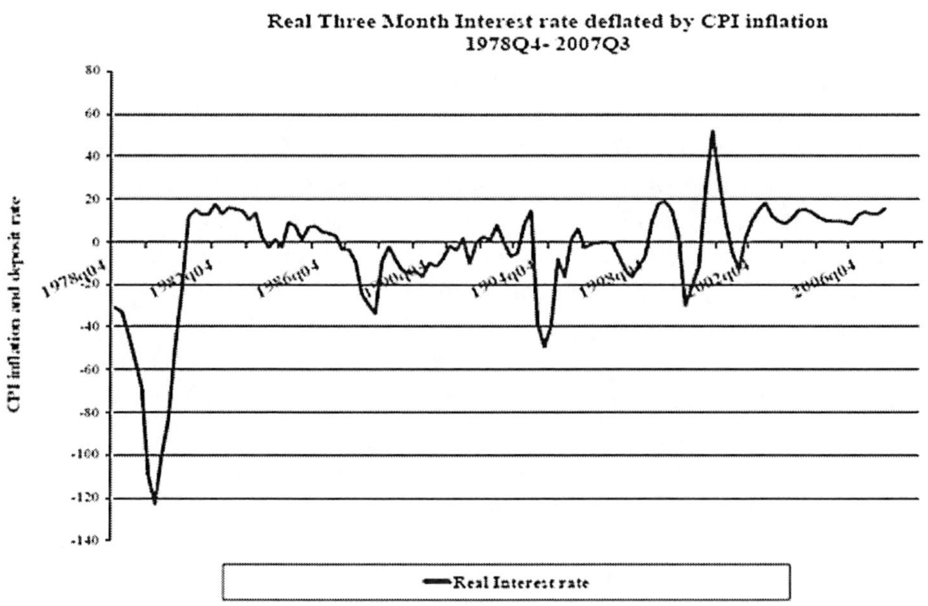

Source: Calculated and produced by the authors using the data provided in the World Development Indicators (December 2008).

Figure 4.

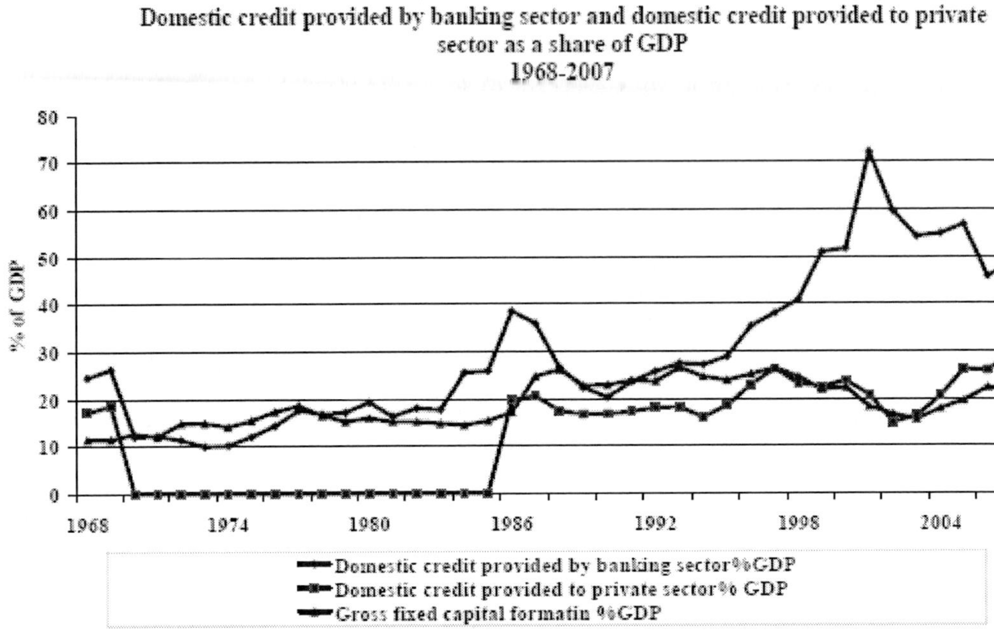

Source: Calculated and produced by the authors using the data provided in the World Development Indicators (December 2008).

Figure 5.

Figure 5 also shows how the gap between the amount of total domestic credit provided by the banking sector and that offered to the private sector had been rising over the years. The above gap represents the amount of domestic credit that had been provided to non-private sector (or public sector) as a percentage of GDP.

As can be seen from Figure 5, though in the early years after the implementation of financial liberalization policy the extent of credit to public sector had been falling, it began to rise again from the early 1990s till 2000. Such an increase clearly demonstrates the extent by which the public sector was once again crowding out the private sector and undermining the objectives of financial liberalization policy in assisting the private sector. Moreover, they suggest that most likely the government had been instructing banks to direct credit to certain priority sectors, which inevitably led to credit rationing by banks. Earlier studies such as Tulay (2000) also highlighted that financial liberalization had been mostly helping the Turkish government in covering their growing budget deficit by excessive borrowing from banks. A policy that was highly inflationary.

Figure 5 also shows that the overall gross fixed capital formation as a share of GDP did not change much in relation to the total amount of credit that had been provided by the banking sector. In other words, the credit that had been provided to the public sector had not been directed to capital investment. That had been mostly because the government had been using the credit to cover its current expenditure rather than capital expenditure. This is clearly evident from Figure 6 which shows the pattern of gross fixed capital formation by both private and public sector.

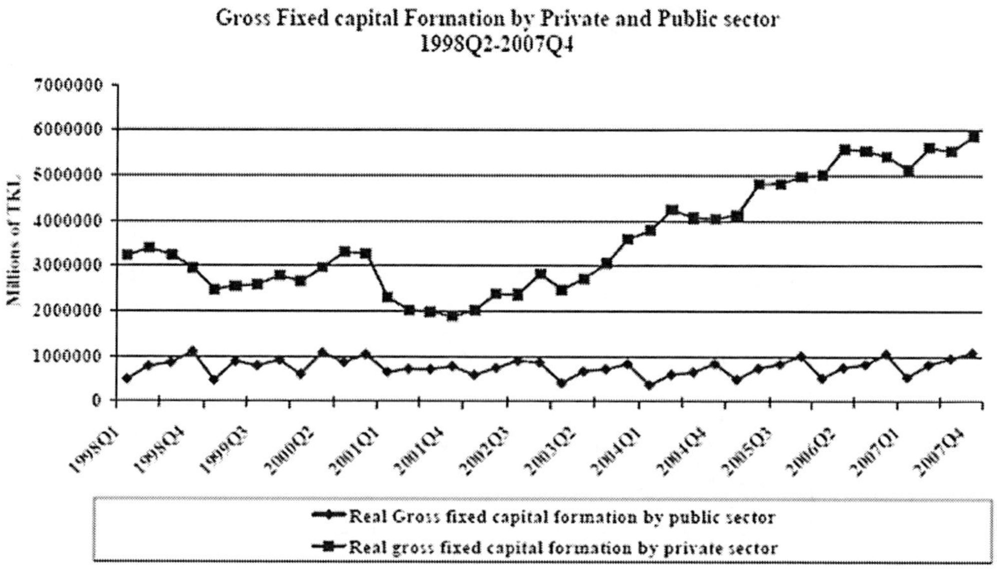

Source: Calculated and produced by the authors using the data provided by the Central bank of Turkey (December 2008).

Figure 6.

Figure 5 also shows that from mid 1990s onwards, the change in the ratio of gross fixed capital formation to GDP has been mainly influenced by the amount of domestic credit that was provided to the private sector. This explains why despite the rise in bank credit and somewhat increase in the level of financial deepening, gross fixed capital formation did not change much.

The above behaviour is contrary to the experience of developed economies such as the UK, where the change in the amount of credit provided by the banking sector as a proportion of GDP had been mostly going to the private sector, as can be seen from Figure 7 below.

Similarly, from Figure 8, we can see that while the amount of bank credit provided to the public sector had been rising in Turkey after the financial liberalization, the trend in the UK had been almost the opposite throughout the period between 1968 and 2006.

Finally, it is important to point out that after the liberalization of trade and capital account, the high level of inflation and significant increase in imports caused considerable fluctuation in the nominal exchange rate between the Turkish Lira and the US dollar. See Figure 9.

The figure shows that the exchange rate fluctuation became much more pronounced between the early 1980s and 2002. Such fluctuation was clearly causing a great deal of uncertainty for investors, and was not very conducive to capital investment. In general, when the economies suffer from high level of inflation and volatile exchange rate, private investors tend to get more involved in speculative and short term activities. That is why the service sector turned out to be the fastest growing sector of the economy, with its share of GDP increasing from 38 percent in 1970 to over 65 percent in 2007.

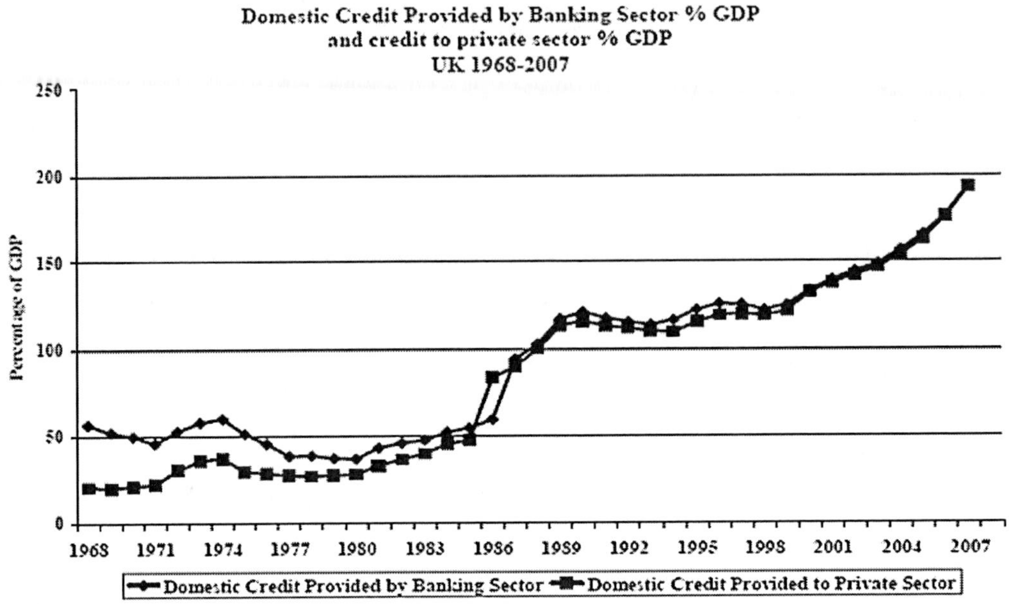

Source: Calculated and produced by the authors using the data provided in the World Development Indicators (December 2008).

Figure 7.

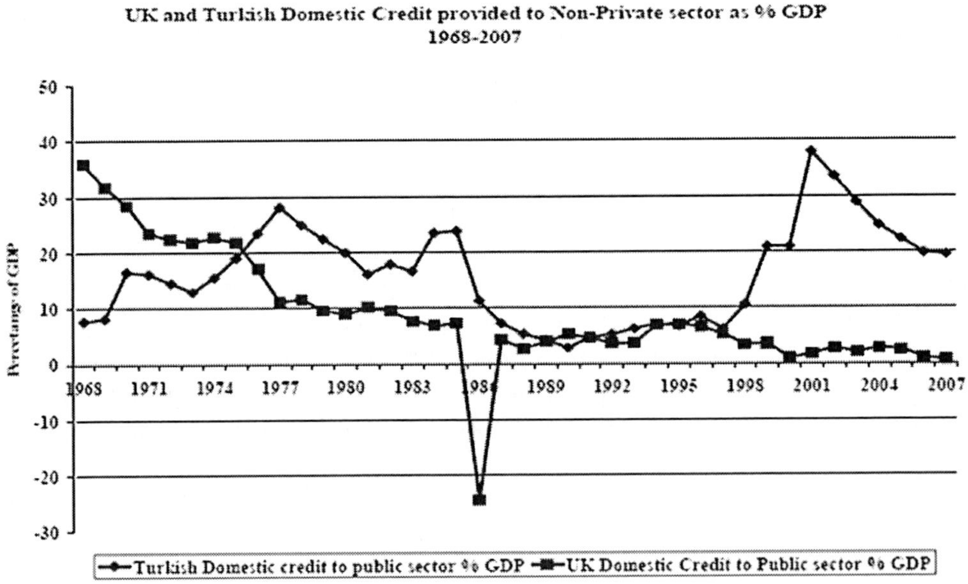

Source: Calculated and produced by the authors using the data provided in the World Development Indicators (December 2008).

Figure 8.

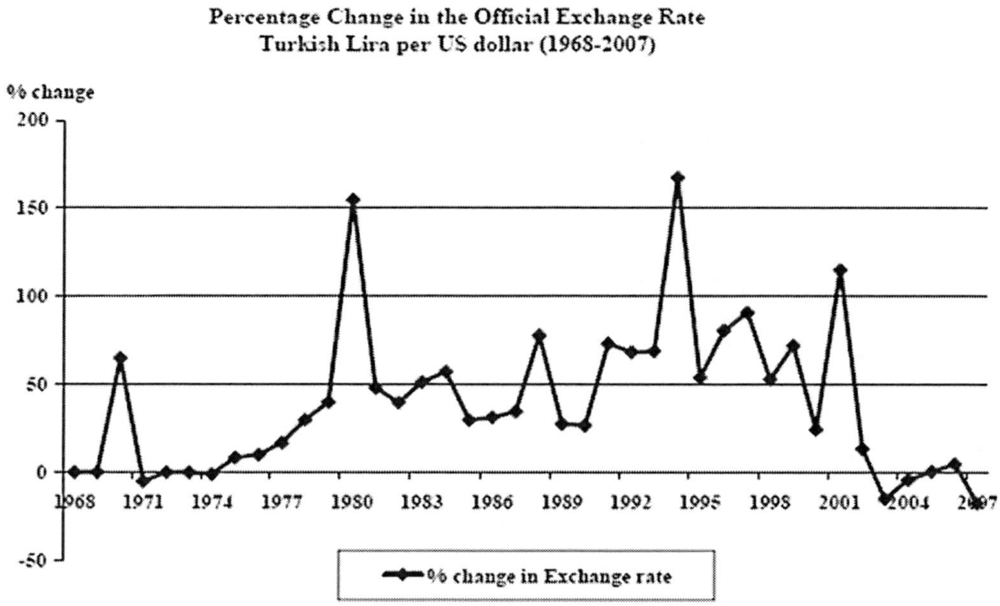

Source: Calculated and produced by the authors using the data provided in the International Financial Statistics (April 2008).

Figure 9.

4. Liberalization Programmes and Their Impact on Economic Growth and Gross Fixed Capital Formation

This section explores the impact of financial and trade liberalization on real GDP growth rate, and gross fixed capital formation share of GDP. Two models were tested to examine the relationship between the above variables using the World bank's quarterly data on Turkey and the E-view package. In the case of some of the variables, because the quarterly data for the early 1980s were not available, the tests had to be carried out for the period between 1987Q1 and 2007Q1.

The first model, examined the impact of financial and trade liberalization on real GDP growth rate and the second model assesses the impact of the two liberalization policies on gross fixed capital formation share of GDP. To determine the stationary values of the variables, the Augmented Dikey Fuller (ADF) tests had been carried out on natural log of all the variables. The tests revealed that all variables are stationary at second difference and are I(2). The only exception was the natural log of real GDP growth rate deflated by CPI, (log_RGDPCPI) which did not deliver any ADF result. That was because, the real growth rates were negative in some years and hence no log values could be obtained for RGDPGCPI. Accordingly, there were not sufficient observations for carrying out the level, first or second difference ADF tests. Subsequently the unit root tests were carried out on the level values of RGDPGCPI. These showed that the variable was stationary at all levels (0-2).

4.1. Test of Financial and Trade Liberalization on Real GDP Growth Rate

As mentioned earlier the first model assessed the impact of financial deepening and trade liberalization on real GDP growth rate. As it was not possible to check for the unit root of RGDPGCPI, an Error Correction Model (ECM) has been used to determine the short and long run elasticities of RGDPGCPI with respect to proxies of financial and trade liberalization. In line with other studies, the ratio of M2 over GDP (M2/GDP) has been used as a proxy for financial liberalization. To examine the effect of trade liberalisation on the overall trade, the sum of exports and imports has been used as a proxy for total trade (TT). The test was then carried out on the following ECM:

$$D(log\_RGDPGCPI) = C + \beta 1 D(log\_M2/GDP) + \delta 1\ D(log\_TT)$$

$$+ \mu log\_RGDPGCPI(-1) + \beta 2\ log\_M2/GDP(-1)$$

$$+ \delta 2 log\_TT(-1) \qquad \text{(Eq.1)}$$

where D(log_RGDPGCPI) is the first difference of the natural log of real GDP growth, D(Log_M2/GDP) is the first difference of the natural log of M2/GDP, D(Log_tt) is the first difference of the natural log of total trade, (log_RGDPGCPI(-1) is the natural log of real GDP growth lagged one period, log_M2/GDP(-1) is the natural log of M2/GDP lagged one period, log_TT(-1) is the natural log of total trade lagged one period, $\beta 1$ is the short term elasticity of real GDP growth rate with respect to M2/GDP, $\delta 1$ is the short term elasticity of real GDP growth rate with respect to total trade, μ is the adjustment parameter for the real GDP growth rate, and $\beta 2$ and $\delta 2$ include the long term elasticities of the real GDP growth rate with respect to M2/GDP and total trade respectively.

The regression test produced the following results:

Table 1.

Dependent Variable: D(LOG_RGDPGCPI)
Method: Least Squares
Sample (adjusted): 1987Q3 2006Q2
Included observations: 20 after adjustments

Variable	Coefficient	Std. Error	t-Statistic	Prob.
C	5.366919	1.085752	4.943045	0.0002
D(LOG_M2/GDP)	-2.113025	0.383745	-5.506324	0.0001
D(LOG_TT)	-0.329681	0.510845	-0.645363	0.5291
LOG_RGDPGCPI(-1)	-1.013988	0.140047	-7.240364	0.0000
LOG_M2/GDP(-1)	-0.123235	0.238266	-0.517215	0.6131
LOG_TT(-1)	-0.177000	0.099346	-1.781657	0.0965
R-squared	0.876085	Mean dependent var		0.937605
Adjusted R-squared	0.831829	S.D. dependent var		0.364274
S.E. of regression	0.149384	Akaike info criterion		-0.721270
Sum squared resid	0.312418	Schwarz criterion		-0.422550
Log likelihood	13.21270	Hannan-Quinn criter.		-0.662957
F-statistic	19.79609	Prob(F-statistic)		0.000007

The above results clearly demonstrate that while the coefficient of M2/GDp is significant, that of TT is not significant. It also shows that as the speed of growth of M2/GDp increases, that of RGDPGCPI decreases. In other words, a 1% increase in the rate of growth of M2/GDP, can lead to 2.113% decrease in the speed of growth of real GDP. As far as trade is concerned, the results do not support a significant relationship between the real GDP growth rate and the overall level of trade. In other words, trade liberalization does not seem to have a serious impact on the real GDP growth rate in the short run. This might be because the change in the TT variable is mostly influenced by increases in imports rather than exports. The results also do not offer statistically significant long run elasticities between either M2/GDP or TT and RGDPGCPI.

We then carried out another test on the relationship between the real GDP growth, M2/GDP and TT. This time we regressed the second difference of the natural logs of M2/GDP and TT on the level values of the natural log of RGDPGCPI. All of the above variables had been found to be stationary. Moreover, to adjust for the use of quarterly data, we included 4 lagged values of the explanatory variables.

The tests produced the following results;

Table 2.

Dependent Variable: LOG_RGDPGCPI
Method: Least Squares
Sample (adjusted): 1989Q2 2007Q1
Included observations: 37 after adjustments

Variable	Coefficient	Std. Error	t-Statistic	Prob.
C	2.760086	0.064512	42.78429	0.0000
D(LOG_M2/GDP,2)	-1.333646	0.331270	-4.025857	0.0004
D(LOG_M2/GDP(-1),2)	-2.419819	0.555304	-4.357645	0.0002
D(LOG_M2/GDP(-2),2)	-1.507368	0.706255	-2.134310	0.0424
D(LOG_M2/GDP(-3),2)	-0.303170	0.552016	-0.549204	0.5876
D(LOG_M2/GDP(-4),2)	-0.124561	0.419027	-0.297262	0.7686
D(LOG_TT,2)	0.693516	0.479169	1.447329	0.1598
D(LOG_TT(-1),2)	-0.208810	0.712601	-0.293026	0.7718
D(LOG_TT(-2),2)	0.042282	0.667745	0.063320	0.9500
D(LOG_TT(-3),2)	0.009853	0.559343	0.017615	0.9861
D(LOG_TT(-4),2)	0.284812	0.388692	0.732745	0.4703
R-squared	0.924945	Mean dependent var		2.929986
Adjusted R-squared	0.896077	S.D. dependent var		0.647404
S.E. of regression	0.208704	Akaike info criterion		-0.054027
Sum squared resid	1.132490	Schwarz criterion		0.424894
Log likelihood	11.99951	Hannan-Quinn criter.		0.114815
F-statistic	32.04112	Durbin-Watson stat		2.835927
Prob(F-statistic)	0.000000			

As can be seen from table 2, the test results once again confirmed the negative relationship between the first, second and third lagged values of M2/GDP and the real GDP growth rate. In other words, they show that an increase in the speed of growth of M2/GDP reduces the speed of growth of real GDP. As far as the trade variables are concerned, again it can be seen that they did not offer any significant coefficients.

4.2. Test of Financial and Trade Liberalization on Gross Fixed Capital Formation Share of GDP

Next the impact of financial and trade liberalization on the gross fixed capital formation share of GDP (GFCF/GDP) was tested. Here too all the stationary variables that were used were I(2). Moreover, to capture the effect of financial crisis in 2001, a dummy variable D1 was included. Its inclusion was supported by the F-test results. The model that had been tested was the following:

$$\begin{aligned} &D(LOG\_GFCFGDP, 2) = C + \beta1 D(LOG\_M2GDP, 2) + \beta2 D(LOG\_M2GDP(-1), 2) + \\ &\beta3 D(LOG\_M2GDP(-2), 2) + \beta4 D(LOG\_M2GDP(-3), 2) + \beta5 D(LOG\_M2GDP(-4), 2) + \\ &\delta1 D(LOG\_TT, 2) + \delta2 D(LOG\_TT(-1), 2) + \delta3 D(LOG\_TT(-2), 2) + \delta4 D(LOG\_TT(-3), \\ &2) + \delta5 D(LOG\_TT(-4), 2) + D1 \qquad \text{(Eq. 2)} \end{aligned}$$

where D(log_GFCF/GDP, 2) is the second difference of the natural log of the ratio of gross fixed capital formation to GDP, D(log_M2/GDP, 2) is the second difference of the natural log of M2 over GDP followed by its 4 lagged values, D(log_TT, 2) is the second difference of the natural log of total trade followed by its 4 lagged values, and D1 is a dummy variable that took values of 1 for each of the four quarters in the year 2001 and zero for all the remaining periods.

As can be seen from the above results, both coefficients of D(log_M2/GDP, 2) and D(log_TT, 2) are statistically significant. They indicate a clear positive relationship between the second difference of the natural logs of M2/GDP and TT, and the second difference of the natural log of GFCF/GDP. In other words, they indicate that a 1 percent increase in the speed of growth of M2/GDP and TT leads to 0.45 percent and 0.65 percent increase in the speed of growth of GFCF/GDP. The results also reveal that increase in the speed of growth of total trade has a greater impact on the speed of growth of GFCF/GDP. In other words, trade liberalization has a greater positive impact on formation of gross fixed capital as a share of GDP than financial liberalization. This might have been due to the fact that while financial liberalization had led to greater lending to the public sector, trade liberalization had been more useful in stimulating the private sector investment than financial liberalization.

The regression test delivered the following results:

Table 3.

Dependent Variable: D(LOG_GFCFGDP,2)				
Method: Least Squares				
Sample (adjusted): 1988Q4 2007Q1				
Included observations: 74 after adjustments				
Variable	Coefficient	Std. Error	t-Statistic	Prob.
C	-0.002632	0.012847	-0.204905	0.8383
D(LOG_M2GDP,2)	0.454864	0.126282	3.601983	0.0006
D(LOG_M2GDP(-1),2)	0.015097	0.186390	0.080998	0.9357
D(LOG_M2GDP(-2),2)	0.151854	0.223474	0.679517	0.4993
D(LOG_M2GDP(-3),2)	-0.200001	0.202744	-0.986474	0.3277
D(LOG_M2GDP(-4),2)	0.136885	0.138159	0.990778	0.3256
D(LOG_TT,2)	0.653410	0.161450	4.047145	0.0001
D(LOG_TT(-1),2)	0.125665	0.221047	0.568498	0.5718
D(LOG_TT(-2),2)	0.363144	0.231806	1.566586	0.1223
D(LOG_TT(-3),2)	0.113546	0.215373	0.527206	0.5999
D(LOG_TT(-4),2)	0.136112	0.145039	0.938453	0.3517
R-squared	0.834109	Mean dependent var		0.002252
Adjusted R-squared	0.804676	S.D. dependent var		0.242155
S.E. of regression	0.107021	Akaike info criterion		-1.484181
Sum squared resid	0.710123	Schwarz criterion		-1.110549
Log likelihood	66.91470	Hannan-Quinn criter.		-1.335135
F-statistic	28.33986	Durbin-Watson stat		3.325531
Prob(F-statistic)	0.000000			

5. Direction of Causality between Financial Development and Economic Growth

In this section two Granger-Causality tests were carried out. The first test, tried to determine the direction of causality between the natural log of real GDP growth rate and the natural log of M2/GDP. The second test, examined the relationship between the natural log of gross fixed capital formation share of GDP and M2/GDP.

For the first test an OLS regression was run on the following unrestricted and restricted models:

$$RGDPGCPI = C + \alpha 1\ RGDPGCPI(-1) + \alpha 2\ RGDPGCPI(-2) + \alpha 3 RGDPGCPI(-3) + ß1M2/GDP(-1) + ß2M2/GDP(-2) + ß3M2/GDP(-3) + D1 \quad \text{(Eq. 3)}$$

$$RGDPGCP = C + \alpha 1RGDPGCPI(-1) + \alpha 2RGDPGCPI(-2) + \alpha 3RGDPGCP(t-3) + D1 \quad \text{(Eq. 4)}$$

The first test delivered the following results:

Table 4.

Dependent Variable: RGDPGCPI
Method: Least Squares
Sample (adjusted): 1988Q1 2007Q1
Included observations: 77 after adjustments

Variable	Coefficient	Std. Error	t-Statistic	Prob.
C	26.64595	4.291691	6.208730	0.0000
RGDPGCPI(-1)	-0.830775	0.091240	-9.105350	0.0000
RGDPGCPI(-2)	-0.926462	0.068369	-13.55096	0.0000
RGDPGCPI(-3)	-0.715481	0.081616	-8.766397	0.0000
M2GDP(-1)	-0.217310	0.091119	-2.384901	0.0198
M2GDP(-2)	0.182991	0.115270	1.587506	0.1170
M2GDP(-3)	-0.115385	0.090145	-1.279989	0.2048
D1	-1.099200	4.462945	-0.246295	0.8062
R-squared	0.878791	Mean dependent var		3.501002
Adjusted R-squared	0.866495	S.D. dependent var		23.41157
S.E. of regression	8.554204	Akaike info criterion		7.228816
Sum squared resid	5049.034	Schwarz criterion		7.472328
Log likelihood	-270.3094	Hannan-Quinn criter.		7.326219
F-statistic	71.46661	Durbin-Watson stat		1.255887
Prob(F-statistic)	0.000000			

The second test produced the following results:

Table 5.

Dependent Variable: RGDPGCPI
Method: Least Squares
Sample (adjusted): 1988Q1 2007Q1
Included observations: 77 after adjustments

Variable	Coefficient	Std. Error	t-Statistic	Prob.
C	12.37197	1.275631	9.698702	0.0000
RGDPGCPI(-1)	-0.727493	0.084069	-8.653538	0.0000
RGDPGCPI(-2)	-0.924851	0.046454	-19.90901	0.0000
RGDPGCPI(-3)	-0.691437	0.082819	-8.348770	0.0000
D1	-3.639571	4.780578	-0.761325	0.4489
R-squared	0.850506	Mean dependent var		3.501002
Adjusted R-squared	0.842201	S.D. dependent var		23.41157
S.E. of regression	9.300008	Akaike info criterion		7.360638
Sum squared resid	6227.291	Schwarz criterion		7.512834
Log likelihood	-278.3846	Hannan-Quinn criter.		7.421515
F-statistic	102.4060	Durbin-Watson stat		1.214437
Prob(F-statistic)	0.000000			

To determine the direction of causality, the required F statistics was calculated. The calculations showed that the F is equal to 4.351 with (3, 69) degrees of freedom[5] was well greater than the critical F = 2.68 at 5 percent level of significance and F= 3.95 at 1 percent level of significance. Therefore, the H0: ß1+ ß2+ ß3= 0 had to be rejected, in favour of H1: ß1+ ß2+ ß3 ≠ 0. Hence the results showed that M2/GDP *does* Granger-cause real GDP growth rate (RGDPGCPI).

5.1. Causality Test between GFCF and M2/GDP

The next Granger-causality test, examined the direction of causality between the ratio of gross fixed capital formation to GDP, and the M2/GDP. Here, the unrestricted and restricted equations tested were the following:

Log_GFCFGDP = C+α1 GFCFDPG(-1) +α2 GFCFGDP(-2) +α3GFCFGDP(-3) +α4GFCFGDP(-4) + ß1M2/GDP(-1) + ß2M2/GDP(-2) + ß3M2/GDP(-3) +ß4M2/GDP(-4) + δD1 (Eq. 5)

Log_GFCFGDP = C+α1 GFCFDPG(-1) +α2 GFCFGDP(-2) +α3GFCFGDP(-3) +α4GFCFGDP(-4)+ δD1 (Eq. 6)

The results of the test on unrestricted model are as follows:

Table 6.

Dependent Variable: LOG_GFCFGDP
Method: Least Squares
Sample (adjusted): 1988Q2 2007Q1
Included observations: 76 after adjustments

Variable	Coefficient	Std. Error	t-Statistic	Prob.
C	0.576708	0.447021	1.290116	0.2015
LOG_GFCFGDP(-1)	0.677656	0.113136	5.989757	0.0000
LOG_GFCFGDP(-2)	0.413000	0.120914	3.415667	0.0011
LOG_GFCFGDP(-3)	-0.587905	0.119278	-4.928863	0.0000
LOG_GFCFGDP(-4)	0.375428	0.109783	3.419738	0.0011
LOG_M2GDP(-1)	-0.217103	0.084077	-2.582184	0.0120
LOG_M2GDP(-2)	-0.169965	0.100158	-1.696973	0.0944
LOG_M2GDP(-3)	0.119410	0.099015	1.205978	0.2321
LOG_M2GDP(-4)	0.224086	0.082105	2.729265	0.0081

[5] F = [SSRr – SSRu)/h]/[SSRu/(n-ku)] = F with (h, n-ku) = (3, 77-8)d.f. F(3, 69) d.f.
[6227.291 - 5049.034)/3]/[6227.291/(77-8)] = 392.75233/90.250594= 4.3517978
The significant F(3, 69) statistics at 5% level of significance is 2.68, and at 1% level of significance is 3.95. Therefore, as the critical test statistics of F here is greater than the statistical F statistics at 1 and 5 percent levels of significance, we reject the H0: ß1+ ß2+ ß3= 0 and accept H1: ß1+ ß2+ ß3 ≠ 0. Therefore, M2/GDP Granger-causes RGDPGPI.

Table 6. (Continued)

D1	0.003840	0.037433	0.156012	0.8765
R-squared	0.860286	Mean dependent var		3.093406
Adjusted R-squared	0.841234	S.D. dependent var		0.178366
S.E. of regression	0.071071	Akaike info criterion		-2.328205
Sum squared resid	0.333368	Schwarz criterion		-2.021530
Log likelihood	98.47180	Hannan-Quinn criter.		-2.205643
F-statistic	45.15488	Durbin-Watson stat		1.702089
Prob(F-statistic)	0.000000			

The results on the restricted model are shown in table -7.

Table 7.

Dependent Variable: LOG_GFCFGDP
Method: Least Squares
Sample (adjusted): 1988Q2 2007Q1
Included observations: 76 after adjustments

Variable	Coefficient	Std. Error	t-Statistic	Prob.
C	0.283972	0.225276	1.260550	0.2117
LOG_GFCFGDP(-1)	0.482532	0.099725	4.838612	0.0000
LOG_GFCFGDP(-2)	0.210452	0.107187	1.963410	0.0536
LOG_GFCFGDP(-3)	-0.319752	0.104985	-3.045700	0.0033
LOG_GFCFGDP(-4)	0.533490	0.097405	5.477059	0.0000
D1	0.015113	0.050752	0.297776	0.7668
R-squared	0.718517	Mean dependent var		3.093406
Adjusted R-squared	0.698411	S.D. dependent var		0.178366
S.E. of regression	0.097953	Akaike info criterion		-1.732992
Sum squared resid	0.671641	Schwarz criterion		-1.548987
Log likelihood	71.85371	Hannan-Quinn criter.		-1.659455
F-statistic	35.73652	Durbin-Watson stat		1.397099
Prob(F-statistic)	0.000000			

Here again, the calculations showed that the F test statistics is equal to 16.996451 with (4, 67) degrees of freedom[6] is clearly greater than the critical F statistics of 2.68 at 5 percent level

[6] The F test statistics can be calculated as follows:

of significance, and 3.95 at 1percent level of significance. Therefore, H0: ß1+ ß2+ ß3 + ß4 = 0, should be rejected in favour of

H1: ß1+ ß2+ ß3 + ß4 ≠ 0. In other words, here too M2/GDP *does* Granger cause GFCF/GDP.

The above results both indicated that the direction of causality is supply driven, and goes from financial deepening to both real GDP growth and gross fixed capital formation share of GDP. Indeed, while the first model showed a negative relationship between the speed of growth of M2/GDP and speed of growth of real GDP, the causality tests confirmed that the direction of causality still goes from M2/GDP to real GDP growth rate and gross fixed capital formation share of GDP. Moreover, while both financial and trade liberalization positively affected the gross fixed capital formation share of GDP, the contribution of trade liberalization had been slightly greater than that of financial liberalization. This could have been partly due to high rate of inflation that adversely affected the expenditure pattern of agents in the economy, and encouraged them to consume more rather than invest. The rise in the level of financial deepening, had been in fact mostly helping the government to fund its budget deficit, rather than helping the private sector to invest.

Conclusion

The present chapter has shown that despite some improvements, Turkey's financial sector is still rather shallow. It has also shown that while both financial and trade liberalization has had a positive impact on the ratio of gross fixed capital formation to GDP, the impact of trade liberalization had been slightly greater than that of financial liberalization. This had been partly because after the financial liberalization, the state became the main borrower from banks. Thus in practice, banks were forced to exercise some degree of credit rationing which was against the prime objective of financial liberalization. Moreover, due to high level of inflation, and large fluctuations of the exchange rate, the private sector became more involved in short term speculative activities, rather than capital investment.

References

Ardic, O.P. and Damar, H. E. (2006). Financial Sector Deepening and Economic Growth: Evidence from Turkey. Bogazici University and Pacific Lutheran University, November, mimeo.

F = [SSRr – SSRu)/h]/[SSRu/(n-ku)] = F with (h, n-ku) = (4, 76-9)d.f. F(4, 67) d.f.
[0.671641 – 0.333368)/4]/[0.333368/(76-9)] = 0.0845682/0.0049756418= 16.996451
The critical F statistics with (4, 67) degrees of freedom is 2.68 at 5% level of significance, and 3.95 at 1% level of significance. Therefore, as the F test statistics here is greater than the critical F statistics at both 1 and 5 level of significance, then we have to reject the H0 that ß1+ ß2+ ß3 + ß4 = 0 and accept
H1: ß1+ ß2+ ß3 + ß4 ≠ 0. Therefore, M2/GDP Granger-causes GFCF/GDP

Central Bank of Republic of Turkey (2006). *Financial Stability Report*. December, Volume 3, Ankara Turkey.

Central Bank of the Republic of Turkey (2008). http://evds.tcmb.gov.tr/yeni/cbt-uk.html.

Sansal B. (2007). Banks in Turkey. www.allboutturkey.com/banks.htm.

Talat Ulussever (2004). Economic Analysis of Financial Reforms in the Turkish Economy. PhD thesis, and a mimo, http://www.economics.ku.edu/documents/ grad_dissertation _abstract/ulussever.pdf.

Tulay, Arin (2000). Financial Markets and Globalisation in Turkey. University of Istanbul, *Faculty of Economics*, 254-286.

Ünalmiş, D. (2002). The Causality between financial development and Economic Growth: The case of Turkey. Research Department working paper No. 3, The Central Bank of the Republic of Turkey.

World Development Indicators (September 2006, and November 2007). http://esds. mcc.ac.uk/WDS_WB/TableViewer/tableView.aspx.

In: International Political Economy
Editors: M.A. Galindo Martin, E. Nissan
ISBN: 978-1-60876-172-2

Chapter 7

INTERNATIONAL COMPETITIVENESS: MEASUREMENT INDICATORS AND STRUCTURAL ASPECTS WITH SPECIFIC REFERENCE TO THE SITUATION IN SPAIN

Matilde Madrid Juan
Ministry of Industry, Trade and Tourism; Spain

ABSTRACT

With globalization and the concomitant appearance of new actors in international trade, competitiveness has come to play a key role in political discourse and to constitute an objective of economic policy in both developed and developing nations. The term competitiveness, however, can be interpreted in a number of ways and tends to be ambiguous. The present article focuses on international competitiveness. Its review of the chief ex-ante and ex-post indicators used to measure that concept is followed by a discussion of export base growth as an element of competitiveness, illustrated with a model applied to the Spanish economy. Finally, the competitiveness of Spanish manufacturing industries that compete with imports is shown to be related to their respective technology intensity.

1. INTRODUCTION

With globalization and the appearance of many new entrants in international trade, competitiveness has moved to the top of most governments' economic policy priorities. The Lisbon Agenda launched by the European Commission established a work plan designed to raise competitiveness in the European Union to levels that would enable it to maintain its position on world markets.

And yet, while public debate revolves around it, competitiveness has no single definition or delimited scope. From a country-wide vantage, there are two notions of competitiveness. International competitiveness is associated with the advantage that enables countries to maintain their market share on both the international and domestic markets, while aggregate competitiveness—which pursues a healthy economy—is linked to productivity.

The present discussion focuses on international competitiveness, referring exclusively to manufactured products. A description of the notion of international competitiveness and the ex-ante and ex-post indicators traditionally used to measure it is followed by an analysis of the recent behavior of these indicators and the relationship between them. Since the findings show that favorable trends in ex-ante or price indicators do not necessarily lead to gains in international market share for export majors, competitiveness would appear to be more closely associated with structural factors. The second part of the article identifies the structural factors associated, in the case of the Spanish economy, with the geographic pattern of exports, which may explain the country's fairly sustained export performance despite its loss of price competitiveness. Finally, a model introduced and applied to the Spanish economy shows that such lower price competitiveness has an adverse impact on medium to low technology industries that compete with imports.

2. International Competitiveness: Definition and Recent Trends

The globalization of international economic activity, appearance of new actors with an increasingly important role in world trade, development of new communication technologies and liberalization of many markets have obliged nations and companies to adapt to the new environment to maintain their positions in the world economy. In this regard, one of the issues that has acquired the greatest relevance in economic debates and policy priorities, in both industrialized and developing countries, is competitiveness, regarded to be economic agents' capacity to adapt and grow in a worldwide context.

Nonetheless, even though the new international environment has placed competitiveness at the hub of public debate and identified it as an objective of economic policy, its definition and interpretation and therefore its measurement with single indicators tend to be ambiguous, for want of a precise and limited definition of this term.

From the vantage of national economies[1], competitiveness studies may address one or both of the following approaches. The traditional approach associates competitiveness with an economy's capacity to sustain a growing presence on international markets, including the domestic market. This approach initially emphasized the role of relative costs and prices as determinants of competitiveness, although subsequent studies stressed the capacity to compete through product differentiation and quality and the degree of human capital and technological development[2].

Other approaches broaden this purely commercial definition to include a long-term perspective associated with welfare, giving rise to the notion of aggregate competitiveness, which associates productivity with conditioning factors and productive efficiency. In this

[1] The macro-economic approach, which covers one or several whole countries, can be distinguished from the micro-economic, i.e., industry- or company-wide approach. The macro-economic definition of competitiveness is more precise and refers to companies' capacity to expand their market. This ability may be defined by an increase in market share (Mandeng, 1991), operating income (Balassa, 1965) or by a number of variables (Porter, 1990, in Eckhard Siggel, 2007).

[2] Fagerberg and Verpagem (2000)

regard, competitiveness would be determined by questions such as the level and use of production factors, the capacity to innovate, productive specialization, market efficiency and the characteristics of business organization. These foregoing would be associated, in turn, with the quality of education, adequacy of infrastructure and corporate organization and governance, which ultimately aim to create an environment favorable to business growth. Perhaps the best known version of this concept is the one set out by the World Economic Forum, which has been releasing its Global Competitiveness Report since 1979, in which it reviews all the factors contributing to competitiveness, understood to be the set of political institutions and other conditions that determine an economy's productivity.

The focus here will be on foreign or international competitiveness, regarded to be an economy's capacity to sustain or increase its presence on the domestic and international marketplaces. Account is taken, therefore, not only of a country's export capacity, but its ability to maintain its domestic market share for goods and services produced in relation to imports. In this regard, competitive advantage and disadvantage in international trade are deduced from a countries' results in terms of trade statistics; commercial advantage is detected as upward export trends, which would reflect gains in competitiveness, while import growth would signal a loss of competitiveness.

In such a context, the essential determinants of trade outcomes and therefore economic competitiveness are reflected by "ex-post" indicators, such as the share of exports, which measures the weight of a country's total exports in total world imports, and "ex-ante" or price indicators. The two most commonly used price indicators are, first, costs and prices such as the consumer price index, unit labor costs, production costs, export costs (usually measured in terms of unit export values or export price indexes) or the GDP deflator; and second, the real exchange rate.

Both "ex-ante" or price indicators and "ex-post" indicators are used below to analyze recent trends in the major economies' international competitiveness. An attempt is likewise made to define the relationship between the two types of indicators. Only manufactured products are considered, inasmuch as the international information presently available on services is relatively scant and seldom standardized.

Consider firstly recent trends in real exchange rates which, as indicated above, take two elements into consideration: the differences in countries' production costs, which can be estimated roughly from their consumer price indexes, unit labor costs or export costs; and the variation in real exchange rates. Graph 1 shows unit labor cost-based competitiveness over time from 1999 to 2008.

Competitiveness for the euro area as a whole declined by 15 percent from 1999 to 2008, around ten percent of which would be due to the volatility of the currency since its inception and the rest to unit labor cost trends. By contrast, over the same period, Japan, the United States and to a lesser extent the United Kingdom increased their price competitiveness.

Significant differences were recorded within the euro area as a result of variations in internal labor cost trends. Whereas competitiveness rose significantly in Germany, it declined in Spain, Italy, Greece and to a lesser extent France as a result of mounting unit labor costs. As a result, the variations in this parameter diverged notably across the eurozone.

With these findings on unit labor cost trends in hand, an analysis can be conducted of their effect on the major exporters' nominal shares of world trade, according to WTO figures. The higher price competitiveness in Germany, the United States, Japan and to a lesser extent the United Kingdom did not lead to a larger share of world trade: on the contrary, these countries' shares declined.

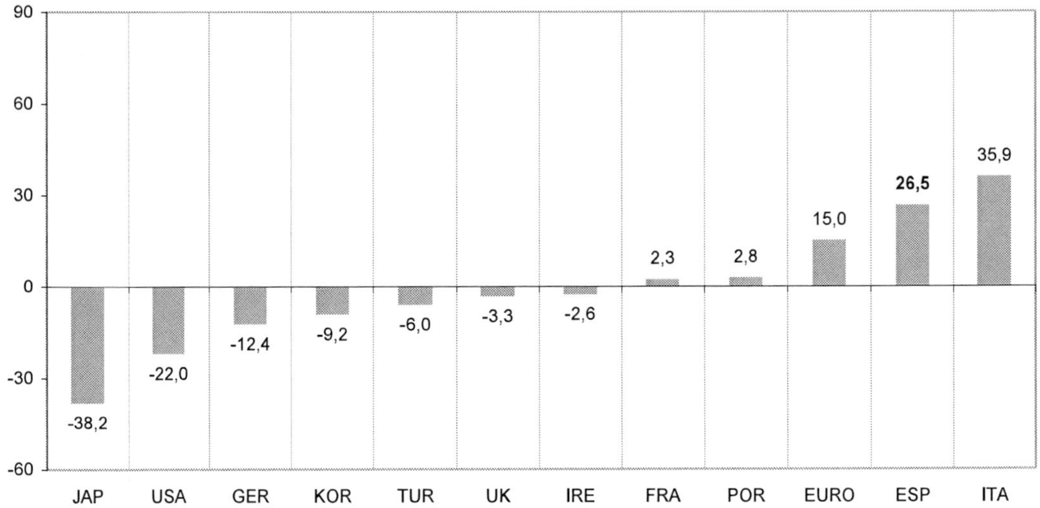

Source: OECD.

Graph 1. Competitiveness indexes calculated with relative unit labour costs in manufacturing (Cumulative changes in percent; over 1999-2008).

At the same time, the relative loss of market share was smaller in countries such as Italy or Spain, despite the significant decline in their competitiveness. Consequently, as Graph 2 shows, no strict relationship was found between price competitiveness and share of export trade.

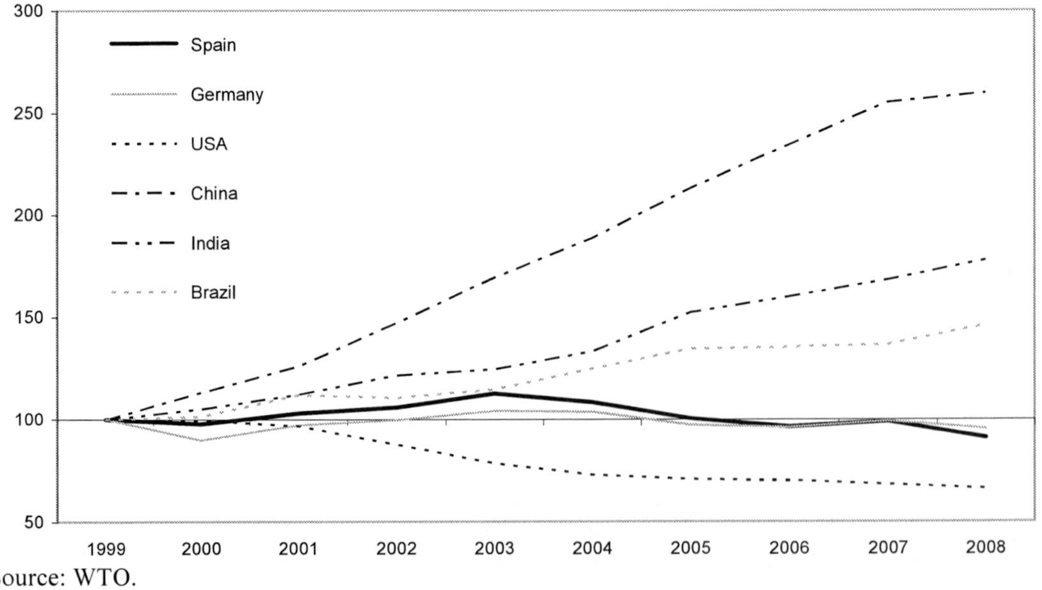

Source: WTO.

Graph 2. Export market shares in merchandise trade (Market share in 1999 = 100).

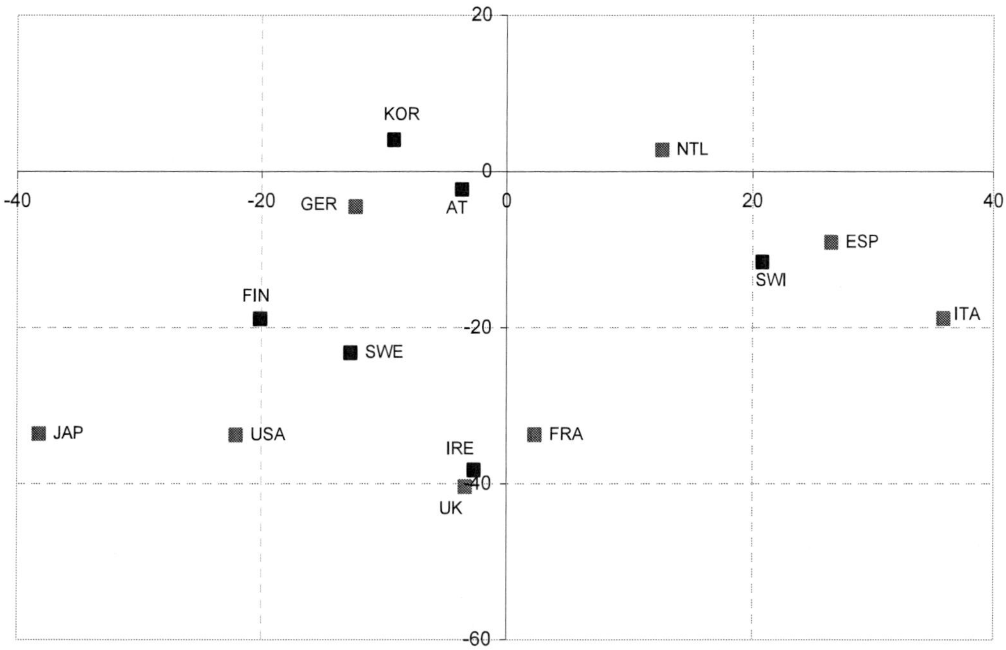

x-axis: change in competitiveness indexes calculated with relative unit labour costs in manufacturing.
y-axis: change in market shares.
Source: OECD and WTO.

Graph 3. Price competitiveness and export market shares (Cumulative changes in percent; over 1999-2008).

In fact, as noted in a recent European Central Bank report (2008), trends in major export countries' world market share appear to be an outcome of structural factors unrelated to price, such as China's growing participation in world trade since its full membership in the World Trade Organization. Graph 3 shows that the export majors' weight in world trade has undergone substantial change since 1999. China's growing influence has made it the world's second largest exporter, while non-energy export countries such as Brazil and India have also increased their share of world trade.

In addition, as the European Central Bank's report notes, other factors explain the mismatch between competitiveness and export share trends, such as globalization-related changes in export specialization or world-wide demand, or the relocation of production in host countries production factors are in abundance.

3. Competitiveness and Export Endeavour: Case Study of the Spanish Economy

The Spanish economy is analyzed below in an attempt to further explore other structural factors that explain competitiveness. While Spain's share of world-wide merchandise trade declined from 1999 to 2008, the loss was smaller than recorded for other OECD countries. This is an indication that the loss of price competitiveness has not had any intense effect on exports.

Factors associated with industry-wide and geographic patterns explain the relatively positive course of Spanish exports.

From the industrial standpoint, the OECD's 2008 report on the Spanish economy notes that the country's exports comprise a fairly large percentage of goods in high world-wide demand, such as transport equipment. Its sustained export performance may be explained by that pattern of trade.

At the same time, a focus on more dynamic export target countries instead of traditional European Union partners has led to a more diversified geographic pattern, a structural improvement in the Spanish economy's competitiveness.

This improved performance of extra-Community exports is the outcome of the increase in the extensive margin for such targets, i.e., the appearance of new companies that export to those markets.

Indeed, Spanish exports grew in the period 2000-2007 at a cumulative rate of 46 percent and a nominal year-on-year rate of 5.6 percent, i.e., two points lower than the nominal GDP.

The rise in exports in that period may be due to the entry of new exporters or the expansion of existing companies' mean export volumes. If exports in the period analyzed were determined essentially by an increase in existing companies' exports, the rise may have been due to factors associated with enhanced productivity or a decline in such companies' export margins, or to exchange rate-related factors that may have contributed to heightening competitiveness.

To analyze the importance of these two determinants, export growth in the period considered was broken down into two components, the intensive and extensive margins, and companies were divided into three groups:

- Existing companies—companies exporting at the beginning and end of the period.
- Companies that ceased to export at the end of the period.
- New companies—companies exporting at the end but not the beginning of the period.

With this classification in place, each component's contribution to total export growth was found:

- the contribution made by companies existing at the beginning of the period (2000) whose mean export value rose—known as the "extensive margin";
- the net contribution resulting from the difference between new companies' exports computed at the end of the period (2007) and the exports of companies existing at the beginning but not at the end of the period—known as the "intensive margin".

Consequently:

Export growth = intensive effect + extensive effect [3]

In the papers published to date on Spain's intensive and extensive margin[3-4], the former has been found to be conditioned by the number of companies existing at the beginning and end of the period.

This study calculated the exact number of companies existing at the beginning of the period (initial inventory of companies), the number that had withdrawn by the end of the period, and the number of new companies (net flow of companies). That calculation yielded the exact increase in the mean exports by the companies existing in a given period of time, regardless of the number of companies existing at the end of the period.

According to the data on exporters furnished by the Customs Registry for the period 2000–2007[5], 25 of the cumulative 46.6% rise in exports in the period was accounted for by increases in existing companies' export volumes, and the remaining 21% by the contribution of the net difference between new and withdrawing companies.

As Graph 4 shows, these findings varied when the same analysis was performed for whole countries.

In the graph, the red line connects the points where the intensive and extensive margins were equal, while the dashed line gives the breakdown of the two contributions to total export growth. The points for the various countries denote their contribution to the two types of growth. The differences between EU and OECD countries and emerging economies are clearly visible.

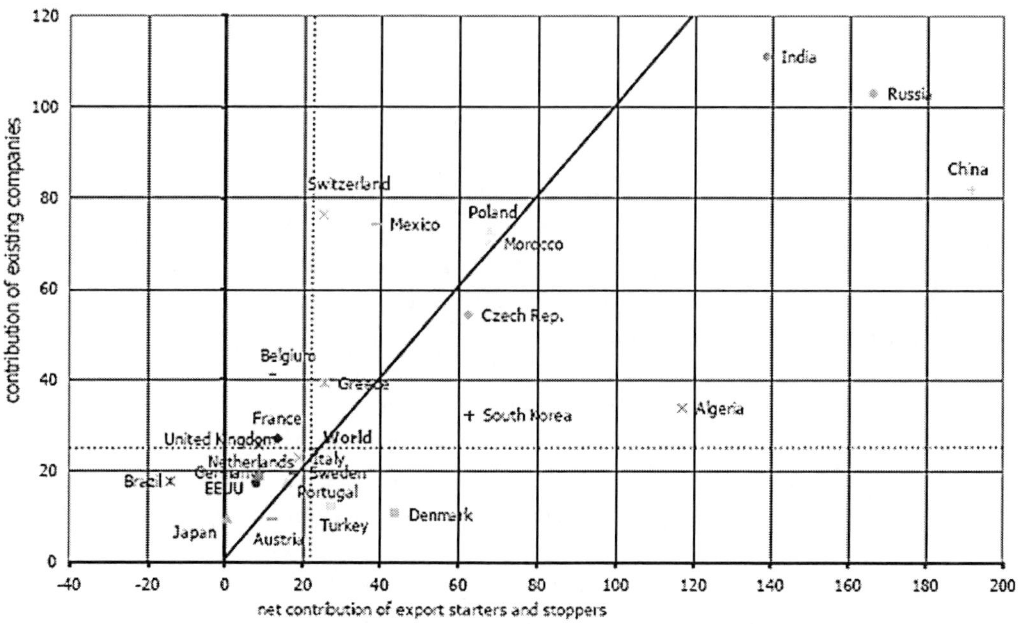

Source: Own calculations based on Custom Registry data.

Graph 4. Contribution to aggregate export growth (percentage points of aggregate export growth 2000–2007).

---

[3] De Lucio, Minguez (2008)
[4] Such an analysis can, however, be found in Wagner (2007) for the German state of Lower Saxony.
[5] Only exporters with a yearly export turnover of over €200,000 are included.

Emerging economies such as India, Russia, China, Morocco or Algeria exhibited higher export growth than the EU countries, the United States and Japan. The increase in emerging economy exports can be explained essentially by the entry of new exporters, whereas the increases recorded for OECD countries would be primarily the result of more intense export activity by existing companies.

For this reason, the increase in the number of companies exporting to new target countries would explain Spain's good performance in this regard, regardless of factors directly associated with price variables.

Nonetheless, while geographic and sectoral pattern-related factors would explain the relatively small decline in the Spanish economy's share of the world-wide merchandise market compared to other euro area countries, the adverse trend in price competitiveness did seem to affect output in national industries competing with imports. The following is a model that identifies the industries that have been most heavily impacted by international competition, namely industries with scantly differentiated, medium-low and low technology products.

4. Competitiveness of National Industries Competing with Imports in the Spanish Economy

International competitiveness has traditionally been defined as an economy's capacity to maintain or grow its presence on world markets, including the domestic market. And indeed, international trade also poses sizeable challenges to national industry. A more open economy also implies that domestic companies are increasingly exposed to international competition. For instance, many industries have been impacted by the entry of new foreign actors that heighten labor cost competition and require domestic firms to develop strategies geared to enhancing innovation. Moreover, given that the manufacturing industry generates a little over 15% of gross added value in OECD economies, competitiveness trends directly affect output and employment.

For the foregoing, an analysis of the joint behavior of output and competitiveness appeared to be an interesting exercise to determine the extent to which they necessarily go hand-in-hand over time. The approach adopted to that end was sectoral, for each industry is conditioned by different cost and demand factors. For instance, China's entry on the international marketplace would have affected labor-intensive more than technology-intensive goods. To study joint output and competitiveness trends for Spanish industry in 1996-2007, the results were compared for two sub-periods, 1996–2001 and 2001–2007. The aim of comparing two periods of similar duration was to ascertain whether decisive events for Spanish trade relations such as China's membership in the WTO in 2001 and its enhanced role in world trade, along with the advent of the euro, impacted domestic industry.

This analysis focused solely on manufactured goods. Services were excluded because the rather limited domestic and international information on this macro-sector is subject to many other shortcomings as well, such as lack of disaggregation, rigor and standardization.

The output data were based on the industry classification laid down in Spain's National Business Classification (CNAE-93), while the export and import figures were referred to the

European Union's integrated and statistical customs nomenclature item groupings[6]. Since the two classifications are not fully concurrent, the respective figures were previously matched to ensure consistency. Moreover, in light of the large number of industries involved, they were grouped under only 32 headings for readier visualization of the results.

The 32 sectors studied were then divided into four technology intensity categories: low, medium-low, medium-high and high. The classification used was the OECD's proposal[7] on technology intensity, which is based on variables such as percentage of turnover devoted to RandD.

The two variables defined for study in the aforementioned period and industries were output and competitiveness. The proxy used for output was industry turnover. Measuring competitiveness was more complex. From the technical standpoint, an industry's ability to compete on international markets is determined by the existence of a comparative advantage in terms of greater relative efficiency. Efficiency is associated with lower opportunity costs, such as the use of fewer inputs per unit of product or the lower opportunity cost of domestic resources. Nonetheless, since relative efficiency is very difficult to measure in practice, in 1965 Balassa[8] proposed to infer competitive advantage from actual trade flows, for the exchange of merchandise reflects differences both in relative costs and other questions that are not directly cost-related. To that end, the present analysis used comparative advantage indexes (CAI):

$$CAI_i = (100 \text{ x } (X_i - M_i) / (X_i - M_i)) + 100$$

where X_i is a country's exports of goods *i* and M_i its imports of goods *i*. The values of this index range from 0 to 200, in which 0 means that a country's total consumption of *i* is imported and therefore that it has no comparative advantage whatsoever, while 200 denotes a maximum comparative advantage, i.e., that its entire output of *i* is exported. The mean yearly variation in the variables, i.e., turnover as a rough estimate for output, and the comparative advantage index, were calculated for each sub-period to analyze industry vitality.

On the grounds of this methodology, maps were charted for each industry, showing the variation in CAI on the y-axis and the variation in output[9] on the x-axis. The findings are shown for the two sub-periods defined. Four maps were charted to obtain conclusions for each technology class.

---

6 TARIC (EU customs tariff database) classification

7 According to the OECD, low technology intensity industries spend less than 1% of their output on R&D, directly and indirectly. Industries with medium-low technology intensity tend to spend from 1 to 2.5% of the value of their output on R&D, including direct and indirect expenditure. Direct and indirect R&D spending accounts for from 2.5 to 7% of medium-high intensity industries' output. High technology intensity industries are characterized by high growth in international demand and the beneficial effect of their development on other industries.

8 A number of authors have used trade figures to measure comparative advantage (LIESNER 1958, BALASSA 1958, VOLLRATH 1991, SCOTT Y VOLLRATH 1992, among others); BALASSA (1965), however, was the first to call this type of analysis revealed comparative advantage For a full review of the indexes that have been historically used to measure revealed comparative advantage, along with a discussion of their theoretical validity, see VOLLRATH (1991).

9 The average annual rate of change (AARC) values were re-scaled to -10,10 to facilitate analysis. In grey, the figures for 1996-2001 and in black for 2001-2006.

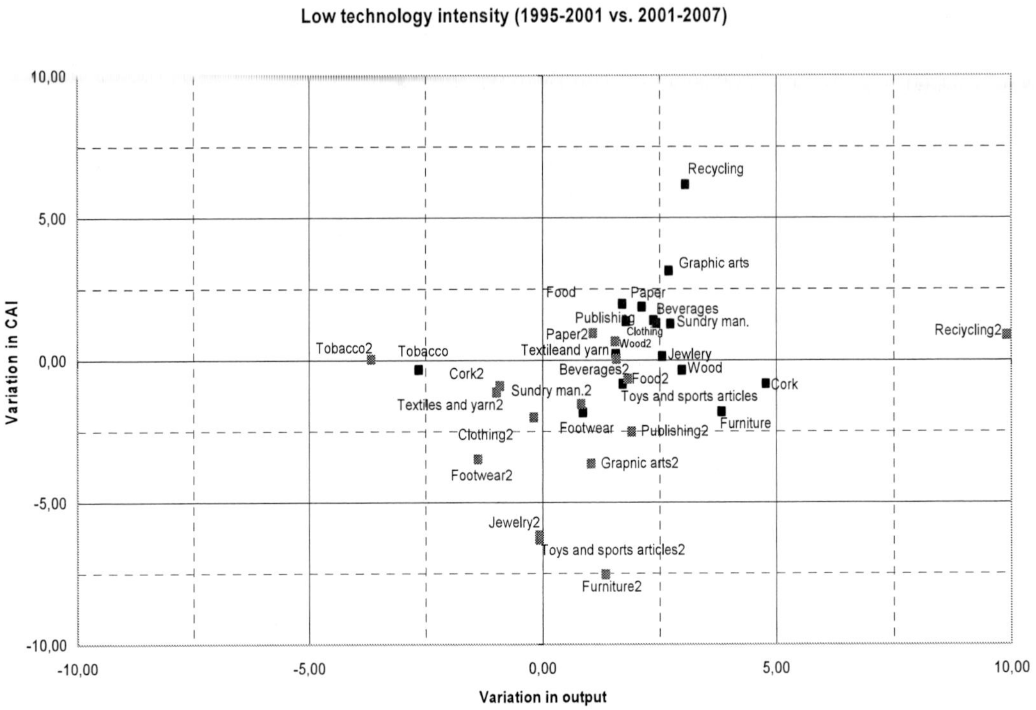

Graph 5. Low technology intensity.

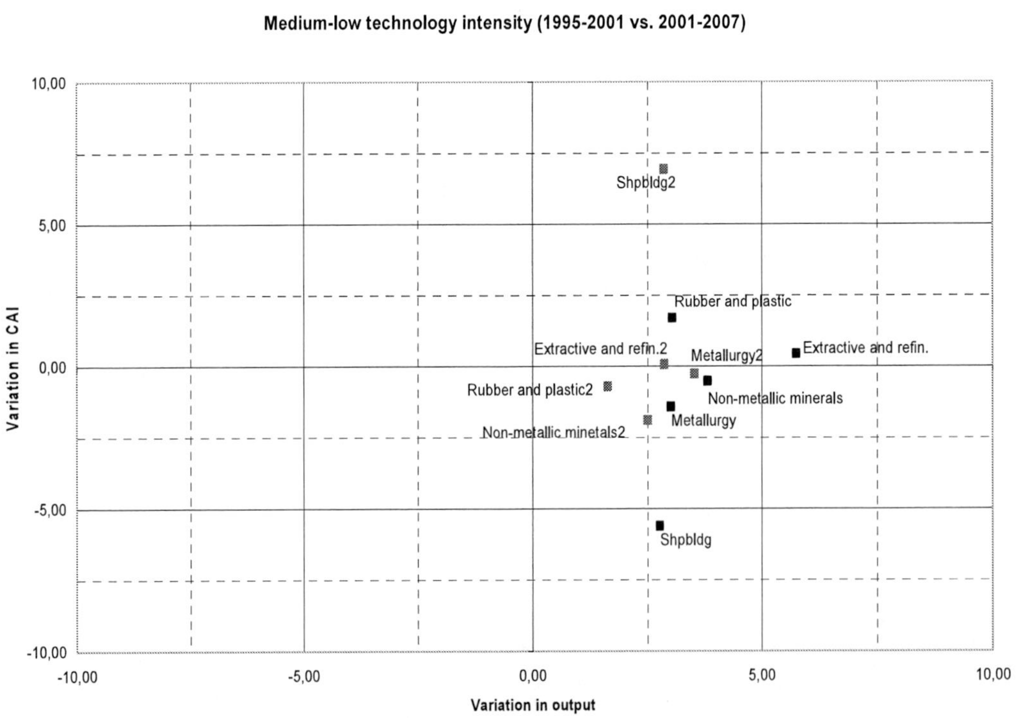

Graph 6. Medium-Low technology intensity.

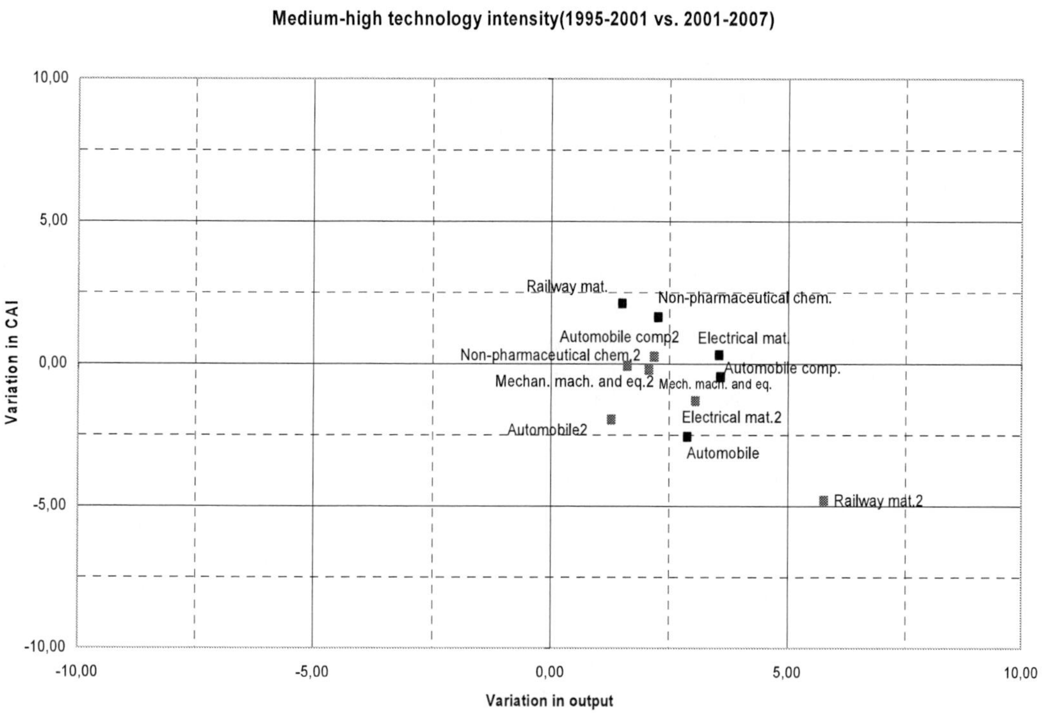

Graph 7. Medium-High technology intensity.

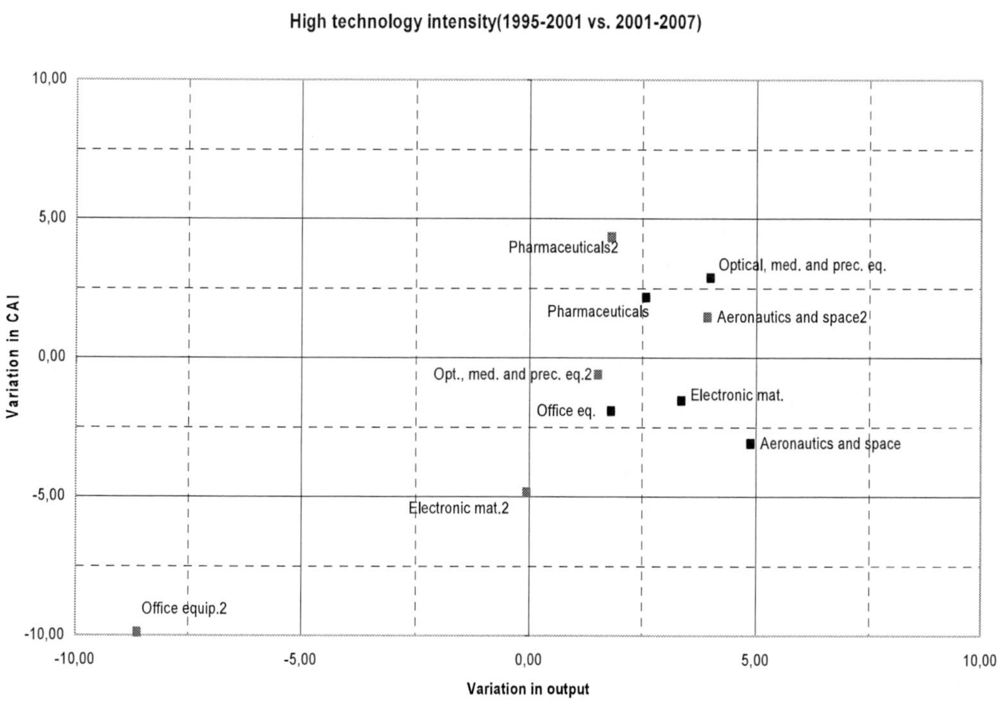

Graph 8. High technology intensity.

The first conclusion drawn was that the comparative advantage for low technology intensity industries tended downward, with poorer results in 2001–2007 than in 1996–2001. This went hand-in-hand with smaller rises or even declines in output. The downturn in output was more visible in industries such as footwear, textiles, apparel, jewelry and other sundry manufactured items that were more exposed to direct competition from emerging countries new to world trade.

Most low-medium technology intensity industries also lost comparative advantage; the exception was shipbuilding, where output apparently did not decline. In any event, growth was slower in the second sub-period in all industries.

Similar results were observed for medium-high technology industries: under pressure from heightened international competition, their growth rates, while not negative, were clearly lower in the later period.

Finally, the results were more promising for high technology industries, where both competitiveness and output grew for cutting-edge businesses such as pharmaceuticals and aeronautics. Such good results were not observed for all high technology industries, however, because some were exposed to fierce competition from countries such as China or the enlargement countries. Nonetheless, the possible relocation of some of these industries cannot be ruled out

Consequently, the loss of competitiveness, measured by the comparative advantage index, may be said to have directly affected output in industries where technology intensity was lowest and where downturns have already been recorded in domestic production. These conclusions are consistent with the fact that these same industries were the ones most heavily impacted by international competition.

CONCLUSION

Maintaining international competitiveness has become one of the chief economic policy priorities in both developed and developing countries, particularly since emerging economies have begun to participate fully in world trade. For that reason the factors determining competitiveness constitute a concern for economic policy makers, especially in countries that are parties to Economic and Monetary Unions where the margin for national monetary and fiscal policy is very narrow. The variation in the share of world trade accounted for by the main OECD exporters appears to imply that competitiveness has gradually become more closely associated with structural factors and less directly with price competitiveness indicators. In this regard, the present analysis shows that for the Spanish economy an increase in the export base, and in particular the rise in the number of exporters operating in emerging markets, constitutes a competitiveness factor, for it has contributed to trade target diversification. The results are less favorable, however, for low technology industries that compete with imports. These industries have exhibited a loss of comparative advantage and associated declines in national output, from which it may be concluded that the loss of competitiveness has had an adverse impact on industries more exposed to international competition from emerging countries, which benefit from cost advantages.

REFERENCES

Arias Segura, J. and Segura Ruiz, O. (2004). Índice de ventaja comparativa revelada: un indicador del desempeño y de la competitividad productivo-comercial de un país. Instituto Interamericano de Cooperación para la Agricultura. Noviembre 2004.

Balassa, B. (1965). Trade Liberalization and "Revealed" Comparative Advantage. *Manchester School* N° 33, May.

Bernard, Andrew B. and Jensen, J. Bradford (2004) Entry, Expansion and Intensity in the US Export Boom, 1987-1992. *Review of International Economics*, 12(4), 662-675.

Bravo, Soledad, and Gordo, Esther (2003). Los factores determinantes de la competitividad y sus indicadores para la economía española. *Boletín Económico del Banco de España*. Septiembre, 73-86.

Dbaere, P. and Mostashari, S. (2005). Do Tariffs Matter for the Extensive Margin of International Trade? An Empirical Análisis. CEPR, DP5260.

De Lucio, Juan José and Minguez, Raul (2008). ¿Cuáles son las fuentes del crecimiento del comercio exterior?. *Boletín Económico de Información Comercial Española*, n° 2946, 25-31.

DTI (2006). International Trade and Investment, The Economic Rationale for Government Support. Economics Paper No.18, July.

Durand, M. and Giorno, C. (1987). Indicators of international competitiveness: conceptual aspects and evaluation. *OCDE Economic Studies* 0, 147-182.

Fagerberg, J.and Verspagen, B. (2000). Productivity, RandD spillovers and trade, in B. van Ark, S. K. Kuipers and G. H. Kuper (eds.). *Productivity, Technology and Economic Growth* (pp.345-360). Dordrecht: Kluwer Academic Publishers.

Freenstra, R. C. (1989) (Ed.). *Trade Policies for International Competitiveness*. NBER conference volume. Chicago: University of Chicago Press.

Mandeng, O. J. (1991). International competitiveness and specialisation. *CEPAL Review*, n° 45, December, 39-52.

Mauro, Filippo and Forster, Katrin (2008). Globalisation and Competitiveness of the euro area. European Central Bank. Occasional Paper Series n° 97, September.

OECD Economic Surveys (2008). Spain, Paris.

Porter, M. (1990). The competitive advantage of nations. *Harvard Business Review*, March–April, 73-91.

Scott, I. and Vollrath, T. (1992). Global competitive advantages and overall bilateral complementary in agriculture. USDA/IRS Statistical Bulletin N° 850.

Siqgel, Eckhard (2007). International Competitiveness and Comparative Advantage. A Survey and a Proposal for Measurement. Center for Economic Studies and the IFO Institute for Economic Research, July.

Subdireccion General de Análisis, Estrategia y Evaluación. Ministerio de Industria, Turismo y Comercio (2008). Dinamismo y competitividad de los sectores industriales españoles. *Boletín de Información Comercial Española*, Julio, 3-11.

Vollrath, T. (1991). A theoretical evaluation of alternative trade intensity measures of revealed comparative advantage. *Weltwirtschaftliches Archiv*, 264-280.

Wagner, Joachim (2003). On the micro-structure of the German export boom: evidence from establishment panel data. 1995–2002, HWWA discussion paper 249.

In: International Political Economy
Editors: M.A. Galindo Martin, E. Nissan
ISBN: 978-1-60876-172-2

Chapter 8

VARIATION OF NET BENEFITS IN THE GLOBAL ECONOMY: THE CASE OF NAFTA AND EMU

***Lall Ramrattan*[1] *and Michael Szenberg*[2]**
[1]University of California, Berkeley Extension
[2]Pace University, USA

ABSTRACT

We present an assessment of net financial benefits for the U.S. and the European Monetary Union (EMU) against the rest of the world (ROW). While other assessments of regional integration in the Global economy are possible, NAFTA and EMU affects nearly 40 percent of world trade. The assessment results from Computational General Equilibrium (CGE) method using GTAP data sets. On balance, we find positive net benefits, which tend to decline in the EMU after the initial impact. A popular explanation is that the benefits for a currency union can be sourced to the saving from having a single currency. Another explanation is that profits fall as convergence takes place. Overall, globalization reflects reduction of interest rates, deficits, and unemployment rates.

INTRODUCTION

A union implies a movement away from autarky or individual rationality towards group rationality where certain authorities are relinquished. A monetary union such as the EMU, which includes Austria, Belgium, Finland, France, Germany, Greece, Ireland, Italy, Luxembourg, the Netherlands, Portugal, and Spain, making up the EU12, involves relinquishing monetary authority and exchange rate policies from member countries to the European Central Bank (ECB). Gains to the member of the union accrue not only from free trade and liberalization, but also from the use of a common currency. In a game of the EMU versus other regions, the net benefits to the union are managed mainly by centralized monetary policies, decentralized fiscal policies, the mobility of factors of production, and the stability and the reduction of transaction costs from the adoption of a single currency. The focus of this paper is on the theory and estimates of those benefits.

The word monetary union has broad and narrow definitions. A broad definition refers to a group of countries sharing a single currency. Usually, the U.S. dollar is likened to a hub, and the U.S. territories such as Guam, American Samoa, The Virgin Islands, and Puerto Rico are represented by spokes emanating from the Hub. Such a hub and spoke arrangement represents a broad definition of a monetary union that is practiced by approximately 30 percent of the 184 IMF country members (Baldwin 2006, 5). Although the U.S. dollar is used by all the states within the union, such a monetary union is different from the EMU in which all the members maintain their sovereignty. In this sense, the EURO in the EMU represents a narrower definition of a monetary union, and we do not find this experiment replicated anywhere else in the world. Economic history revealed that a number of monetary unions have failed in the past. An early example is The Latin Monetary Union that involved France, Belgium, Italy and Switzerland, Greece, and Romania that started in 1865. Also the Scandinavian Monetary Union that involved Denmark, Norway, and Sweden started in 1873. Both unions failed by the beginning of the First World War. Belgium and Luxembourg formed a union in 1921, which is now included in the EMU. The EMU has been strong for approximately eight years now, and is expected to be stronger, although we cannot predict how long it will last.

Robert Mundell (1961, 658) laid out the architecture for a monetary union with the following highlights. If a single currency were contemplated, a single central bank (CD) would be necessary. More than one single currency would require cooperation of many CBs, and their activities would affect reserves and convertibility. Adjustment mechanism for one currency versus many single currencies would therefore vary at the interregional and international levels even if the exchange rate were fixed. McKinnon (1963) research found that small countries trade more internationally and experience less price rigidities, characteristics that are more conducive to the formation of a monetary union. Kenen (1969) holds that the more diversified a country is, the less likely it will join a monetary union.

The incentive for a Monetary Union varies with the individual country's responses to its economic problems. Some of the major problems for the European Monetary Union (EMU) are summarized in a manifesto advanced by Franco Modigliani and others (1998). The manifesto claimed that demand side management with limited supply side policies have resulted in high unemployment rates in the EMU. From 1981 to 1990, the average unemployment rate in the EUR 11 and EUR 12 countries was approximately 9 percent, or 2 percent above the U.S. rate of 7.1 percent. From 1991 to 1992, the average unemployment rate increased to 10.4 percent, or approximately double the U.S. rate of 5.6 percent (Modigliani, 2005, 340). In "October 1998, the average rate of unemployment in these countries is 11% (19 million), with peaks of 15-20%, while in the 60s and early 70s it was almost universally well below 3% and nowhere over 5%. Such a huge rate of unemployment results in an immense waste of resources, through loss of output, that can be estimated at some 15% or more and even larger loss of saving-investment potential" (Modigliani et al., 1998, p. 1).

Modigliani and others sourced the problems of unemployment in the EMU to the European Union or the Maastricht Treaty that was signed on February 7, 1992. Briefly, the facts are that by February 27, 1998, the EU published some criteria regarding fiscal deficit and debts, and around June 1998, the European Central Bank (ECB) had control of monetary policies. A single currency was launched in January 1, 1999. From the start of the union to the adoption of a single currency, countries abided by an Exchange-Rate Mechanism (ERM). The

ERM II allowed countries in the EU that did not join the union by January 1, 1999 to let the values of their individual currencies fluctuate from the EURO by 15 percent.

Modigliani and others claimed that the fiscal and monetary disciplines established by the Maastricht Treaty have created the high unemployment rate in the EMU. Aggregate demand policies of the fiscal, monetary, and exchange rate types were considered restrictive. The consequence was high unemployment that in turn lowered government revenue and decreased government spending on infrastructure. As countries maintained a narrow band on exchange rates as specified by the ERM, monetary policies became tight, increasing interest rates, lowering investments, and therefore, lowering employment. Aggregate supply side policies that also contributed to the unemployment rate included widespread minimum wage rates, job security legislation that discouraged hiring, work-sharing, and early attrition through retirement policies.

The policy mixes for managing the EMU became bifurcated where the ECB controls monetary policy and each member country control its fiscal policy. The independence of these two policies can be appraised through a non-cooperative Nash game (Dixit and Lambertini, 2006, 978). In that game, fiscal policy discretion becomes expansionary, as each country tends to use that instrument that they see fit for the problem at hand in order to increase their level of output. Discretionary or committed monetary policies can be tight as when the ECB seeks to control inflation. One risk with this two-pronged approach is that discretionary fiscal policy can destroy commitment on monetary policy. As these policies are combined, sub-optimal Nash equilibrium may result. One prediction of the game is that the levels of output and inflation can be more extreme than if the member countries had control of both fiscal and monetary policies.

The role of labor unions provides yet another view of net benefits impacts in the EMU. According to Acocella et al., 2006, the substitution between tax and labor market distortions is also a strategic goal for the targeting of fiscal and monetary policies. An ECB monetary policy that lightens a tax burden can cushion labor market distortions. Fiscal policies by the member countries and monetary policies by the ECB are pitted in a Nash (sub) game where the decentralized fiscal policy can have a moderating effect on wages.

Studying the GDP gap data the EMU, Baghli et al., 2006 identified an asymmetric inflation-output Phillips curve trade-off for the individual countries and the EMU as a whole. The non-linear Phillips curve had an S-shape, which is both convex and concave. One implication is that excess demand will influence inflation more that excess supply will reduce it, resulting in output lags that will cause inflation to persist. This finding predicts that the ECB needs to be relatively more swift and significant in conducting monetary policies than in the case where the Phillips curve is normally sloping.

The EURO currency has been introduced for the benefit of the EMU areas, which at a minimum means the reduction of transaction costs. Since its introduction in 1999, the EURO has become second only to the US dollar in the international trade. One measure of its performance is its volatility, which can be defined as the percent of log changes of nominal exchange rates against the U.S. dollar. Mussa found that the volatility of the EURO had been no greater than the average volatility of the predecessor currencies of the EMU member states. In the short period of five years, the average of the predecessor currencies varied from 2.3 to 3.5 percent for the five-year period from 1974 to 1999. For its first five years from 1999 to 2003, the EURO volatility was 3.1. (Mussa, 2005, p. 447) In the long period, more volatility is discerned--$1.16 at its birth, $0.83 in November 2002, and $1.36 in December

2004, which in log form represent a 34 percent depreciation and 49 percent appreciation, respectively. Yet these long period swings are within the history of some predecessor currencies. The recent depreciation of the dollar has fundamental explanations traceable to the U. S. current account deficit, which remain large, and therefore, warranting some further depreciation. This does not necessitate further appreciation of the EURO. The overall assessment of benefits seems not to lie with exchange rate policies, which have not been out of historic trend in both short and long periods, but to lie with fiscal or monetary policy mixes.

Since the introduction of the EURO, the EMU area had experienced a boost in its foreign direct investment. Petroulas (2006) found that the EURO resulted in a 16 percent increase in FDI inflows to the EURO countries, based on data from1992 to 2001. Non-members countries also benefited to the extent of 11 percent increase in FDI inflows. FDI increased by 8 percent from non-member countries to the EURO area. From a theoretical point of view, increases in FDI follow from a stable currency. The cumulative inflow of FDI for 1990 to 2003 to the EU15 was $839.2 Billion in US dollars, largest for the United Kingdom (418.1 Billion USD), followed by France ($347.5 B), Germany ($142.6 B), Netherlands ($116.6 B), and Italy (38.2 B) (OECD Factbook, 2005, p. 69).

Andy Rose (2000) has postulated that the adoption of a common currency has a large effect on international trade. In his model, the coefficient for the share currency variable indicates that trade will increase by 235 times when a common currency is shared. Rose's results was embraced as too good to be true—model misspecification, omitted variable, and even a reverse causation to the effect that a large trade volume causes a common currency and not the reverse, were proposed as objections. Some rough corrections lowered Rose's estimate to approximately 1.9 times, which is still large (Baldwin, 2006, 14). For the EU15 countries, the gain was approximated at 6 percent higher among member countries, for a sample from 1992 to 2002 (Baldwin., 2006, p. 31). However, Baldwin eventually settled for a 9 percent internal, and a 7 percent external/outside effect (Baldwin, 2006, p. 55). In another argument, a common currency may be a result from countries wanting to stabilize their trade volume (Baldwin., 2006, p. 26). Overall, the consensus is that the benefits from the EMU were immediate, occurring around 1999, and ranging 5 to 15 percent. The consensus posits gains from trade creation, i.e., external trade, and not trade diversion among member countries (Baldwin., 2006, p. xiii).

The benefits and costs approaches we looked at in this paper are intended to capture the broader demand and supply side policies of the EMU. The net effect of these policies would be to either increase or decrease welfare benefits sourced to allocation efficiency, terms of trade effect, and policy mixes efficiency of the EMU versus other regions in the global economy. For such evaluations, we looked at Computational General Equilibrium (CGE) analysis to assess the benefits. To also analyze the financial impacts, we further isolated the financial sectors in the CGE model to ascertain the direction of a change in net benefits.

BENEFIT AND COSTS SIDES OF A UNION

We can get a feel of a country's benefits through an analysis of its preference for inflation and unemployment, and economies of a single currency. Assuming the natural rate hypothesis

(NRH) where output is at its full employment level, countries may have different rates of inflation, and therefore different unemployment rates. No policy can improve this income, and an independent monetary authority such as ECB cannot change this. In other words, the monetary union with its common currency and ECB cannot change what is known as the non-accelerate inflation rate of unemployment (NAIRU).

The long run view of the NRH protracted a no cost situation of unemployment and inflation for the union. Matters are different in short-run situations. High inflation and unemployment are costly in the short run. As countries can trade-off inflation and unemployment in the short run, the decision turns on whether the cost that they will bear individually is higher or lower than through membership in the union. The net benefits of being a member of a union should be more positive than net benefit of autarky.

A monetary union with a SC obviously has an exchange rate costs to a country. The countries lose a degree of freedom in the policy area from giving up its exchange rate policy. A SC also means a central back will conduct monetary policies, thereby losing another degree of freedom for members, namely monetary policy. The burden of adjustments for member countries therefore, falls on fiscal policies, which is also constrained by debt to GDP ratio. But taste and preference might mitigate these costs, however monumental they may appear to be.

A theoretical feeling of cost analysis is usually looked at under conditions of trade. The operation of supply and demand conditions affects a country's current account, which is modeled as domestic output less domestic spending. If a fall in the demand for one country's output is not accompanied by a decline in its spending, the current account records a deficit. This current account deficit will require adjustments that require wage flexibility and labor mobility. As a country's demand increases, wage rates will go up, which will dissuade hiring, cut back supply, increase prices, dissuade purchases, and lower current account surplus, restoring equilibrium. In the case of labor mobility, labor will move from areas where demand falls off to where demand increases, stabilizing employment. The current account will be automatically restored to equilibrium because in a country where demand falls off, the unemployed do not have to spend without producing, which would by definition of the current account cause a deficit. Rather the unemployed will now migrate.

With sticky wages and immobile labor, a country that has greater demand will have inflation. Inflation can be managed through restrictive monetary and fiscal policies. A current account surplus can only persists if higher inflation is accepted. Revaluing its currency will decrease the country's competitiveness, and the exchange rate adjustment will reduce aggregate demand for its product. However, this adjustment is not allowed to take place in a Monetary Union like the EMU with a single currency. Countries with lowered demand will have unemployment; countries with higher demand, inflation.

Fiscal policies such as an increase in taxes can dampen demand, but some transfer of these tax revenues to other countries in the union with lower demand would be necessary. The transfer of tax revenue will act a means to finance the lower demand country's current account deficit. When countries maintain their sovereignty as in the EMU, the transfer of tax revenues is not practical. Transfer works well, however within different regions of a nation, such as in the U.S. and its states, where the government collects federal taxes, and make transfer payments base on income in different regions.

SOME PRE VS. POST EMU STATE OF THE ECONOMY VARIABLES

The situation of the member countries selected state of the economy variables for 1997 and 2001 are in Table 1. Government deficit was a major criterion for entry into the EU. The stability pact held at Dublin in 1996 set a limit on government deficit of 3 percent of GDP for entry into the EMU.

Recall that government deficits are generated when revenues, defined as tax, social contributions, dividends and other property income, is less than expenditures, defined as compensation to government workers, social benefits, interest on public debt, subsidies and gross fixed capital formation. The first data entry in Table 1 indicates government budget deficit by a negative sign.

Countries sharing a single currency in the EMU that ran deficits include a mix of both large and small countries: France, Germany, Netherlands, Portugal, and Spain. Except for Portugal, the other four countries running a deficit show a small deficit between 1997 and 2001.

According to the Ricardian Equivalence theorem, a country's equilibrium interest rate, consumption, and investment should be invariant to changes in its budget deficit (Barro 1989, p. 204). The long-term rates in Table 1 are the implied prices for bonds with 10 years maturity. Data for Germany and for Greece in 1997 are not available. The rates for Greece from 1998 to 2000 were much higher than show in the table.

Except for Portugal where deficit has increased, the other three countries for which data is available indicated a tendency for the long-term rates to fall. The fall is in line with the expectation for rates to converge to some long-term level in the Union. The current deficit persisted for Austria, Greece, Portugal, and the U.K. It turned from surplus to deficit for Ireland, Italy, and Spain.

The major change in the period from 1997 to 2001 is the single currency that eliminated exchange rates among member countries.

The new challenge for the EMU countries is how to balance discrepancies between exports and imports. Ordinarily, a member country would depreciate its currency when exports exceed imports.

After the EMU member countries have discretionary fiscal policies to enhance their competitiveness. Greece and Portugal show higher than the 3 percent government deficit in managing their economy. But it is hard to conclude that the single currency is too heavy a burden.

Table 1 also shows that interest rates in the EU, U.S., U.K., and Japan decreased between 1997 and 2001. The ECB has managed to keep the EU rates consistently below the U.S. rates for that period. The U.K. is only part of the EU and therefore managed to keep its rate below that of the U.S. in 2001.

The unemployment rates came down from 10 to 7.4 percent for the EU between 1997 and 2001.

The unemployment rates for the EU, however, are still much higher than that of the U.S. and Japan. They are close to 10 percent for approximately half of the EMU countries, lending some credence to Modigliani's manifesto argument mentioned above.

Table 1. Pre vs. Post EMU State of the Economy Variables

Countries	Government Deficit (% GDP)		Unemployment Rate		Current Account (%GDP)		Long-term Interest Rates	
	1997	2001	1997	2001	1997	2001	1997	2001
Austria	-1.96	0.11	4.4	3.6	-3.1	-1.9	5.68	5.08
Belgium	-1.96	0.57	6.2	6.7	5.6	3.7	5.59	5.06
Denmark*	0.35	2.83	5.3	4.3	0.4	3.1	6.26	5.09
Finland	-1.25	5.2	12.7	9.1	5.4	7.2	5.96	5.04
France	-3.04	-1.53	11.5	8.4	2.7	1.6	5.58	4.94
Germany	-2.72	-2.82	9.7	7.8	-0.4	0.2	na	na
Greece	-4.03	-3.67	9.6	10.4	-4.4	-8.1	na	5.30
Ireland	1.46	0.97	9.9	3.9	2.4	-0.7	6.26	5.02
Italy	-2.7	2.67	11.6	9.4	2.9	-0.1	6.86	5.19
Luxembourg	3.21	6.42	2.7	2.1	11	9	5.60	4.86
Netherlands	-1.11	-0.09	4.9	2.5	6.6	2.1	5.58	4.96
Portugal	-3.57	-4.44	6.8	4	-5.7	-9.5	6.36	5.16
Spain	-3.18	-0.39	17	10.6	0.5	-2.8	5.84	4.87
Sweden*	-1.02	2.85	9.9	4.9	4.2	3.9	6.61	5.11
UK*	-2.2	0.68	6.9	5	-0.1	-2.4	7.05	4.94
US	-0.79	-0.39	4.9	4.7	-1.5	-3.9	6.63	5.58
JPN	-3.79	-6.13	3.4	5	2.3	2.1	2.37	1.32
EU	-2.64	-1.71	10	7.4			5.96	5.03
	-1.58	0.62	8.61	6.18	1.87	0.35		

Source: OECD, Factbook, 2005.

CGE ANALYSIS

In this section we assess benefits from the general equilibrium point of view. Countries in the GTAP database are grouped into regions. Equilibrium conditions are established from which trade liberalization policies can be analyzed. First, we will look at net benefits from the typical group of industries such as food manufacturing and services over the aggregated regions, which belong to the non-financial sector. Second, we will isolate the financial sector from the other sectors to ascertain any change in net benefits. Any difference in benefits from the two models will have an impact on the financial sector. Throughout the analysis our focus will be on the EMU countries versus the U.S. and the rest of the world.

TOTAL CGE MODEL

We undertake a Computational General Equilibrium model to ascertain benefits to a Monetary Union. The model we use is in the spirit of Hertel's 1997 study. In this model, we used symmetric assumptions on distortions on output subsidies, export subsidies, and import tariffs between the EMU and US. For instance, if the EU nations place an x-percent import tariff on food imports from the U.S. then the U.S. will reciprocate. The symmetry assumption standardizes the model for comparison with other periods for which we have data. The data sources used for the results in Table 2 are from the GTAP5 and GTAP6 database for the years 1997 and 2001, respectively. These years bracket the formation of the EMU, providing insights into its pre and post conditions of the countries in the union.

The symmetry assumption is further solidified by using default parameters, and a standardized technique for simulation purposes. First, the GTAP data is aggregated into three sectors—food, manufacturing, and services, and eight regions—USA, Great Britain (GBR), Germany (GER), France (FRA), Sweden (SWE), Finland (FIN), The Rest of the union (EU), and the Rest of the World (ROW). When this aggregation is made, then elasticities for substitution in trade and transformation between primary factors and other parameters for mobility are generated as default parameters.

Along with the default parameters, the GTAP framework allows a choice among three methods, for which we standardize on the Johansen technique to generate the welfare benefits indicated in Table 2.

In summary, Table 2 presents welfare benefits of the EMU versus the U.S., and the rest of the world, using standards such as reciprocal trade policies, favorable trade policies of the EMU and U.S.A towards the world, default parameters from the GTAP model, and a standard technique of computation.

The results in the Total column of Table 2 indicate that the U. S. would gain approximately $21.7 billion in welfare benefits in 1997 under the above assumptions. Most of the benefits are sourced to terms of trade effect between the U.S. and the other seven regions. Allocation efficiency due to taxes and subsidies of the Marginal Value Product of Labor (MVPL) among the three sectors—food, manufacturing and services accounted for $0.994 billion of the gains, and approximately $1.98 billion resulted from policy mixes. In 1997, the three regions had the full array of policy mixes of their fiscal, monetary, and exchange rate policies at their disposal.

In 1997, the EMU countries were dominant in their allocation efficiency, pursuing their individual taxing and subsidy tendencies on an individual rational basis. Great Britain, Germany, France and the rest of the EU had a dominant position over U.S. in their subsidization attitudes towards the MVPL among industries, resulting in a larger percent of welfare gains to allocation efficiency. The U.S. had only a 4.6 percent gain in allocation efficiency, where the EMU countries had gains from 75.9 percent and above. The EMU countries, however, were not doing well with their policy mixes relative to the U. S. in the terms of trade and policy mixes areas, where the U.S. was getting 86.3 and 9.1 percent gains, respectively.

Table 2. Benefit Analysis EURO vs. USA and ROW 1997 versus 2001 ($Million U. S.)

	Results for 1997 GTAP Data				Results for 2001 GTAP Data			
	Allocation Efficiency	Terms of Trade	Policy Mixes	Total	Allocation Efficiency	Terms of Trade	Policy Mixes	Total
USA	993.85	18768.34	1979.72	21741.91	-555.62	14245.03	3334.27	17023.69
	4.6%	86.3%	9.1%		-3.3%	83.7%	19.6%	
GBR	3622.81	372.29	-9.21	3985.9	2391.21	-172.5	-25.88	2192.82
	90.9%	9.3%	-0.2%		109.0%	-7.9%	-1.2%	
GER	3131.25	-754.73	-130.31	2246.21	1034.02	-1046.16	-284.53	-296.67
	139.4%	-33.6%	-5.8%		-348.5%	352.6%	95.9%	
FRA	1638.69	431.34	-177.88	1892.15	15.54	458.08	-256.24	217.38
	86.6%	22.8%	-9.4%		7.1%	210.7%	117.9%	
SWE	422.64	180.26	-45.76	557.14	198.13	218.52	-92.58	324.06
	75.9%	32.4%	-8.2%		61.1%	67.4%	-28.6%	
FIN	133.2	192.54	-52.81	272.93	-77.6	78.8	-56.08	-54.88
	48.8%	70.5%	-19.3%		141.4%	-143.6%	102.2%	
EU	6998.22	-1332.87	-185.55	5479.8	2808.81	-114.58	-546.17	2148.07
	127.7%	-24.3%	-3.4%		130.8%	-5.3%	-25.4%	
ROW	37726.01	-17857.2	-1378.2	18490.64	25878.22	-13667.2	-2072.8	10138.24
	204.0%	-96.6%	-7.5%		255.3%	-134.8%	-20.4%	
Total	54666.68	0	0	54666.68	31692.71	0	-0.01	31692.71

In 2001, representing a year after a single currency was introduced, the U.S. was no longer dominant in the allocation efficiency area over all the EMU countries. First we noticed that the U.S. experienced a decline in its overall welfare benefits from $21.7 billion in 1997 to $17.0 billion in 2001. One hypothesis we advanced for this decline was due to the EMU countries trading with the world on a more enhanced basis—a single currency and ECB basis of group rationality, and not individual rationality (Ramrattan, Tully, and Szenberg, 2001, p. 260). Basically, in a John Nash gaming environment, individual countries are guaranteed a status quo benefit level, but through cooperation within a group, each country has the potential to enhance their benefit level. We discuss the variation in benefits further in the financial analysis section below for the two years 1997 and 2001.

FINANCIAL CGE MODEL

In this section we take a look at the impact from the financial aspect of the regions. The three sectors we look at are financial, food, and others. The financial sector groups the insurance, finance and business sector of the GTAP model into one. The results are in Table 3, which shows show all the available EU countries against the US and the ROW. Trade is conducted for financial, insurance, business aggregated into one industry group, which is analyzed against two other industries—food and other commodities. In this aggregation, the difference in the e world total, $30,223 billion, from the $31,693 billion in Table 2 can be a result of distortion in the model. The results show significant decline in regional benefits in 2001 vs. 1997, with benefits in Germany, Sweden, and Finland turning into negative numbers.

The financial model results of Table 3 indicated that the U.S. was not dominant in terms of trade effects in 1997, but it increased its benefits in 2001 with better policy mixes.

Table 3. Benefit Analysis EURO vs. USA and ROW: Financial 1997 versus 2001 ($Million U. S.)

	Results for 1997 GTAP Data				Results for 2001 GTAP Data			
	Allocation Efficiency	Terms of Trade	Policy Mixes	Total	Allocation Efficiency	Terms of Trade	Policy Mixes	Total
USA	830.6	16,689.2	1,642.81	19,162.6	-368.39	13.374.69	2.987.2	15,993.5
	4.33%	87.09%	8.57%		-2.30%	83.63%	18.68%	
GBR	3,615.18	213.34	-12.88	3,815.64	2.394.54	-227.22	-24.7	2,142.62
	94.75%	5.59%	-0.34%		111.76%	-10.60%	-1.15%	
GER	3102.81	-704.62	-110.33	2,287.86	1.057.35	-932.02	-257.37	-132.03
	135.62%	-30.80%	-4.82%		-800.84%	705.92%	194.93%	
FRA	1,400.81	283.48	-139.27	1,545.02	165.63	171.41	-73.73	263.31
	90.67%	18.35%	-9.01%		62.90%	65.10%	-28.00%	
SWE	355.92	113.7	-32.89	436.73	-185.26	99.28	-57.78	-143.76
	81.50%	26.03%	-7.53%		128.87%	-69.06%	40.19%	
FIN	126.59	155.4	-36.83	245.16	-165.82	279.71	-217.84	-103.95
	51.64%	63.39%	-15.02%		159.52%	-269.08%	209.56%	
EU	6,855.12	-1,006.44	-150.03	5,698.65	2788.09	-231.86	-475.61	2,080.63
	120.29%	-17.66%	-2.63%		134.00%	-11.14%	-22.86%	
ROW	36,431.46	-1,5744.1	-1,160.58	19,526.82	24.537.83	-1.2534	-1.880.18	10,123.66
	186.57%	-80.63%	-5.94%		242.38%	-123.81%	-18.57%	
Total	52,718.49	0	0	52,718.49	30.223.97	0	0	30,223.97

Such mixes can partly be viewed as a counter measure to the EMU single currency, as well as to the U.S. domestic policy management. In the allocation efficiency category for 1997 vs. 2001, Sweden and Finland benefits turned negative, in the terms-of-trade category, Great Britain turned negative, and in the policy mixes area, all the EMU members remained weak partly due to the loss of individual monetary and exchange rate policies.

Table 4 below shows that the benefits between the two models have declined in the 1997 vs. 2001 period. We analyze this in terms of a difference-in-difference technique. Although GDP data is widely available, we use the GTAP estimates to be consistent with the benefit estimates in order to express the benefits in percentage form. The 1997 period is best viewed as a pre EURO period, while 2001 is post EURO period. The U.S. benefits declined slightly less in the financial model (-.08 percent) than in the total model (-0.10 percent). The benefits to the ROW follow the same pattern, declining by -.22 and -.07 percent, respectively. The EMU benefit percentages do not show such a decline. Overall, the difference-in-difference was -.02 percent for the U.S., zero for the EMU and -.15 for the ROW. The losses amount to approximately $2 million for the U.S., and $20 million for the ROW.

One implication is that EMU's single currency in 2001, two years after its introduction, did not amount to much gain for the EMU. This finding lends support to the argument that the introduction of the single currency could have generated only short-term gains, perhaps only in the year 1999 as mentioned above.

Table 4. Difference-in-Difference Análisis NonFinancial (Table 2) vs. Financial Model (Table 4) 1997 versus 2001 (Million $)

	1997 Total Benefits	2001 Total Benefits	Percent Difference
USA—Total Model	$21,742.00 (.27%)	$17,024.00 (.17%)	-0.10%
USA—Financial	$19,163.00 (.24%)	$15,994.00 (.16%)	-0.08%
GDP From GTAP Data.	$8,057,336.50	$10,176,231.00	
Difference-in-Difference =			-0.02%
EMU—Total Model	$14,434.00 (.18%)	$4,531.00 (.06%)	-0.12%
EMU—Financial	$14,029.00 (.18%)	$4,107.00 (.05%)	-0.12%
GDP From GTAP Data.	*$7,932,385.36*	*$7,899,726.54*	
Difference-in-Difference =			*0.00%*
ROW—Total Model	*$18,490.64 (14%)*	*$10,138.24 (.08 %)*	*-0.22%*
ROW-Financial	*$19,526.82 (15%)*	*$10,123.66 (.08%)*	*-0.07%*
GDP From GTAP Data.	*$13,010,263.00*	*$13,212,685.00*	
Difference-in-Difference =			*-0.15%*

CONCLUSION

A definitive way to measure net benefits is still open. Single currency, currency union, and CGE models that look at liberalization of trade are the most common methods of approach. The total and financial models we estimated suggested gains from trade for the EU.

The results indicate that welfare benefits have declined from the pre EMU period in 1997 to the post EMU period in 2001.

The findings might seem to counter that of Andy Rose whose model predicted that the impact of a single currency might have varied from 5 to 15 percent. Such a prediction may have been only short lived, accruing to the EMU in 1999, which in this light is not contrary to our findings.

Because we use similar counterfactual parameters in the 1997 and 2001 periods for our CGE model, some of the decline in benefits can be sourced to single currency usage. As the trend of the variables in Table 1 shows, the member countries in the EMU have been adjusting their critical state of the economy variables in line with other developed countries--lowering their interest rates, deficits, and unemployment rates--indicating that a process of convergence among their member economies is still occurring.

REFERENCES

Acocella, Nicoal, Giovanni Di Bartolomeo and Patrizio Tirelli. (2007). Monetary Conservatism and Fiscal Coordination in a Monetary Union, *Economic Letters*, Vol. 94, 56-63.

Baghli, Mustapha, Christophe Cahn, and Henri Fraisse. (2007). Is the Inflation-Output Nexus Asymmetric in the Euro Area? *Economic Letters*, Vol. 94, 1-6.

Baldwin, Richard. (2006). *In or Out: Does it Matter? An Evidence-Based Analysis of the Euro's Trade Effects.* London, U.K.: Center for Economic Policy Research.

Barro, Robert J. (1989). The Neoclassical Approach to Fiscal Policy. In Robert J. Barro (Eds.), *Modern Business Cycle Theory*, (178-235). Cambridge, MA: Harvard University Press.

Claassen, Emil-Maria. (1996). *Global Monetary Economics.* Oxford, United Kingdom: Oxford University Press.

De Grauwe, Paul. (1992). *The Economics of Monetary Integration.* Oxford, United Kingdom: Oxford University Press.

Dixit, Avinash and Luisa Lambertini. (2001). Market Mechanism for Policy Coordination: Tools for the EU Monetary—Fiscal Policy Interactions and Commitment versus Discretion in a Monetary Union, *European Economic Review*, Vol. 45 , 977-987.

Hertel, Thomas W. (1997). *Global Trade Analysis: Modeling and Applications.* Cambridge, England: Cambridge University Press.

Kenen, Peter, (1969).The Theory of Optimum Currency Areas: An Eclectic View. In Mundell and Swoboda (Eds.), *Monetary Problems of the International Economy* (41-60).Chicago. Ill.: University Press.

McKinnon, Ronald I., (1963). Optimum Currency Areas. *American Economic Review,* Vol.53, 717-724.

Modigliani, Franco. (2005). *The Collected Papers of Franco Modigliani: Vol. 6.*, Cambridge, Massachusetts: The MIT Press..

Modigliani, Franco, Jean-Paul Fitoussi, Beniamino Moro, Dennis Snower, Robert.

Solow, Alfred Steinherr and Paolo Sylos Labini. (1998). An Economist's Manifesto on Unemployment in the European Union. *BNL Quarterly Review*, (No., 206, 1-22).

Mundell, Robert. (1971). *Monetary Theory.* Pacific Palisades, CA.: Goodyear Publishing Company, Inc.

Mundell, Robert A. (1961). A Theory of Optimum Currency Areas. *The American Economic Review*, Vol. 51 (4), 657-665.

Mussa, Michael. (2005). The Euro and the Dollar 6 Years after Creation. *Journal of Policy Modeling*, Vol. 27, 445-454.

Petroulas, Pavlos. (2007).The effect of the euro on foreign direct investment. *European Economic Review,* Vol. 51(6), 1468-1491.

Ramrattan, Lall B., Cathyann D. Tully, and Michael Szenberg. (2001).The European Monetary Union VS. USA, Cooperation and Competition: An Examination of Welfare Benefits. In J. Jay Choi and Jefrey M. Wrase (Eds.), *European Monetary Union and Capital Markets*, (2001, 247-265).Amsterdam and New York: JAI. An Imprint of Elsevier Science.

Rose, Andrew K. (2000).One Money, One Market: Estimating the Effect of Common Currencies on Trade. *Economic Policy*, Vol. 15(30), 7-46.

In: International Political Economy
Editors: M.A. Galindo Martin, E. Nissan

ISBN: 978-1-60876-172-2

Chapter 9

COORDINATION OF FISCAL POLICIES IN EMU

Maria-Soledad Castaño Martínez
University of Castilla-La Mancha, Spain

ABSTRACT

A certain loss in efficient national economic policies has taken place, given that the globalization of the economy and steps towards economic integration mean that the economic policies of different countries has an effect that reaches beyond their own borders, not only positive ("locomotive effect"), but also negative ("beggar your neighbour").

In addition, taking into account the efficiency problems of fiscal policy and the effects caused by other countries, coupled with the fiscal policy effects on monetary policy in the Monetary Union, the basis for coordinating national fiscal policies and the conditions set out in order to form part of the EMU, were established in the Maastricht Treaty. This process of restricting room for manoeuvre in national fiscal policies culminated in the Stability and Growth Pact (SPG)

So, this chapter is devoted to the analysis of the evolution and theories that analyze the economic effects of the use of fiscal policy. The third section undertakes the analysis of the conditions imposed by the Stability and Growth Pact and how it conditions the possibilities of using fiscal policy on the part of member states. Section four contains an empirical analysis of the evolution of public finances for countries in the Euro zone. The chapter ends with some brief conclusions

1. INTRODUCTION

The development of the welfare state came about among member states in the 1950s and 60s as a result of the development of Keynesian ideas, where the use of tax policies was proposed as a means of reactivating economic growth. Within this context, public deficit is used as a tool for achieving economic policy, fundamentally in terms of real production and employment.

Conversely, the end of the 1970s and onwards saw a situation of economic crisis where Keynesian-type policies were still being applied in an attempt to mitigate the crisis; a fact that led to high levels of deficit. Consequently, for some authors, public deficit ceases to be a tool and becomes an objective. Indeed, the reduction of the public deficit has been, and still is, a high priority objective in countries in the Euro zone, as clearly shown by the Stability and Growth Pact.

The 1990s were very special from a macroeconomic and budgetary point of view. Following the Delors Committee Report (1989) and the ratification of the Maastricht Treaty, EU member countries considerably strengthened the coordination of their monetary, foreign exchange and budgetary policies, with a view to strengthening the Internal Market and, in the second half of the decade, to allowing for a quantitative leap in the process of European integration and the creation of the EMU, with a single currency policy in the hands of the European Central Bank. The essential nature of coordinating national taxation policies among member states for the smooth functioning of the EMU also became apparent. However, the year 2000 and ensuing years saw new increases in community budget deficits.

The second part of this chapter is devoted to the analysis of the evolution and theories that analyze the economic effects of the use of fiscal policy. The third section undertakes the analysis of the conditions imposed by the Stability and Growth Pact and how it conditions the possibilities of using fiscal policy on the part of member states. Section four contains an empirical analysis of the evolution of public finances for countries in the Euro zone. The chapter ends with some brief conclusions.

2. Theoretical Considerations for Fiscal Policies

Modern fiscal policies are based fundamentally on the Keynesian theory. The 1936 publication of *The General Theory of Employment, Interest and Money* is generally considered to be the moment at which tax policies came into their own and began to play an important role in stabilizing economies.

In general terms, tax policy is considered to be the collective set of variations in expenditure programs and government income, which is carried out with the aim of ensuring that different objectives in economic policy are achieved: reducing or maintaining unemployment at a low level, an acceptable rate of inflation, growth in real production, an external equilibrium, etc. (Shaw, 1972, p. 14). In trying to look for an explanation for and a solution to the problem of unemployment, Keynes broke away from classical perceptions and, in particular, the inflexibility of traditional tax administration, inspired by the financial dogma that economic stability depended on a balanced budget in the public sector. Figure I.1 sets out how the role of tax policy has developed.

In reality, classical and neoclassical tax administration methods, which were based on an economic liberalism, granted tax policies very few options by accepting as its core principles, amongst others, a limit on public spending, reducing it to national defense, justice and policing, and on activities which the private sector either could not or would not carry out. This, together with the principle of having annual budget equilibrium, as supported by A. Smith (2001), supposed that income would, therefore, also be low (Calvo and Galindo, 1990).

However, the basis for the so-called Keynesian fiscal policy can be found in works by Hansen (1973 and 1978) and Lerner (1951 and 1961). Hansen believes that any fiscal actions undertaken should centre on maintaining the level of economic activity. As for Lerner, public income, expenditure and debt should be instruments that aim to maintain a stable and high level of employment at constant prices. Combining both points of view, the classical notion of budget equilibrium should be replaced by that of an automatically stabilizing budget, which works in tandem with the following logic: if the level of economic activity drops, taxation should be reduced and public spending be increased (something which, logically, creates the corresponding deficit), whilst should the opposite happen, then fiscal policy should go in the opposite direction (giving way to surplus).

Breaking away from the budget equilibrium offers the policy decision maker the possibility of generating what is considered to be the necessary level of public spending, according to the economic situation at the time. This is carried out in order to achieve a determined economic objective which is generally focused on reaching a level of full employment despite not having the public income to finance it. In other words, it favours public deficit.

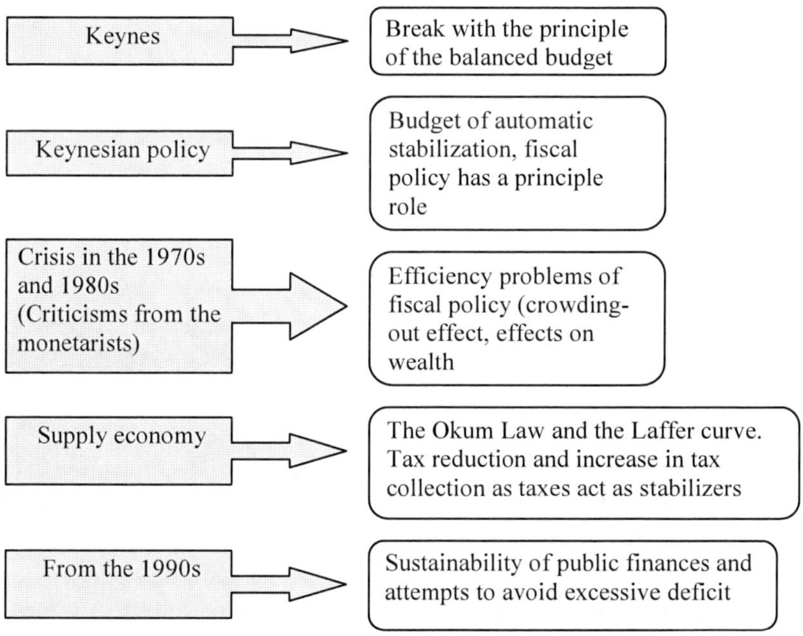

Source: compiled by author.

Figure 1. Definition of fiscal policy

However, since the crisis of the 1970s and 1980s, huge inefficiencies were seen due to the expansive policies in demand to combat the crisis. This gave way, according to monetarists, to a set of negative effects such as "crowding out" and the wealth effect, as well as changes to the economic environment, globalization and economic integration. This caused the previous approach to be revised, questioning the value of the benefits derived from said public debt (ECB, 2002).

Likewise, in the 1980s and at the beginning of the 1990s, the contributions brought about by the "Supply Sliders" started to be seriously considered in fiscal policy. For those authors belonging to this school of thought, this served to underline the importance of incentives caused by taxation in economic results. According to these authors, and in accordance with the Okun law and the Laffer curve which use taxes as an automatic stabilizer, reducing them would increase the amount of income available, causing an increase in consumption, investment and savings, something which generates employment and increases tax collection. That is why having heightened tax rates reduces tax collection, fosters tax fraud and generates unemployment, in addition to work being replaced by leisure, something which influences economic growth and has an effect on marginal work productivity (Sanchez and Sáiz Álvarez, 2006, p. 68).

On the other hand, a certain loss in efficient national economic policies has taken place, given that the globalization of the economy and steps towards economic integration mean that the economic policies of different countries has an effect that reaches beyond their own borders, not only positive ("locomotive effect"), but also negative ("beggar your neighbour").

According to Iranzo (2002, pp. 125-126), sustained economic growth produced in the world's economy over the last decade, is owed to an increasing awareness on the part of national governments as to the detrimental effects caused by using indiscriminate policies on demand in order to stabilize the economy. This resulted in economic policy having to focus on reducing inflation and public deficit, creating a more favourable environment for investment and employment growth. Therefore, what is being asked of macroeconomic policies, rather than just contributing to stability, is that they are, themselves, stable, with an increasing relevance in supply policies which are aimed at improving an economy's competitiveness and flexibility as a tool for increasing economic health.

3. The Economic and Monetary Union and the Stability and Growth Pact

Taking into account the efficiency problems of fiscal policy and the effects caused by other countries, coupled with the fiscal policy effects on monetary policy in the Monetary Union (Castaño and Carrasco, 2009, ECB, 2008, Beetsama and Debrun, 2004, Andersen 2002 and 2005, De Grauwe, 1997), the basis for coordinating national fiscal policies and the conditions set out in order to form part of the EMU, were established in the Maastricht Treaty. This process of restricting room for manoeuvre in national fiscal policies culminated in the Stability and Growth Pact (SPG).

The Werner report (1970) set out a proposal for an extensive common budget which included a fiscal harmonization process and a centralized control of national fiscal policy. Similar arguments were put forward by the MacDougall Report (1977). This stated that regional stabilization of individual countries is achieved automatically through fiscal system benefits. The Report suggested that it would be necessary to have different transfers between countries through a central community budget to counteract the effects felt in each country (Castaño and Carrasco, 2009).

Contrary to the recommendations in the Werner Report (1970) and the MacDougall Report (1977), the Maastricht treaty left economic policy explicitly in the hands of member states and stated that the EC's economic policy would "be based on the close coordination of the member states' own economic policies" (section 1, article 4, TEU). This, along with the negative repercussions of an unstable and unsustainable fiscal policy, was one of the main causes of uncertainty when the institutional fiscal framework was designed in preparation for the Economic and Monetary Union (EMU) (ECB, 2002). The Maastricht Treaty put great emphasis on establishing quantitative and qualitative regulations for budgetary discipline. Without these, granting greater independence to the European System of Central Banks seemed insufficient in guaranteeing credibility for the aim of price stability (González-Páramo, 2001).

In fact, the Treaty contains three important restrictions in this respect. These closed the door on any possible future monetization of public debt through credits or overdrafts (art. 101), access to chartered finance in the financial system (art 102) and any agreement between public administrations of all levels within the Community (art. 103). These regulations, in force since January 1994, could have, in principle, been considered sufficient as a way of ensuring that public finance was put on a sound footing (González-Páramo, 2001).

The criteria eventually incorporated into the Treaty was a less than perfect compromise between the working definition of the rules, the reflection of national specialities and the credibility of sanctions should the rules be breached. However, its justification and effectiveness has attracted diverse criticism in specialized literature (Beestma and Debrun, 2004). Although it had a supposed federal design, this policy could have been made easier if the budget had carried out automatic transfers to countries affected by asymmetric disruptions, and the reduced size and impossibility of indebtedness which characterized the EU budget prevents this stabilizing function from progressing (Bustillo and Bonete, 2000).

Furthermore, the Treaty meant a distribution of power between the different public national and supranational institutions and has established some fundamental links which oblige the member states "to consider their national economic policies as a question of common interest" at the same time as submitting their national economic policies to an extensive network of coordination and multinational supervision (ECB, 2001, pp. 54-56 and ECB, 2008).

However, one has to take into consideration that decentralization of policies bears a risk: the economic policies of member states are interdependent and their application generates externality (Cooper, 1985, Hamada, 1985, Andersen, 2002 and 2005), which is why it is necessary to coordinate policy on a European scale, as previously indicated.

This distribution of power is also a result of member states not being prepared to grant more authority to the European Union or, in this case, not being prepared to grant more fiscal control. Therefore, even though the efficiency in distributing resources persists, above all, by way of the creation of a single market, the functions of redistribution and stabilization are left, predominantly, in the hands of the member states. The EU budget consists of a limited redistribution, as we have already pointed out, mainly through structured funds which aim to finance regional and social policies geared towards increasing the level of employment and breaching the income gaps that exist between the different regions of the Union.

Under such circumstances, the European Union Treaty set out some criteria for nominal convergence which had to be fulfilled in order to form part of the EMU, but the fear remained that once countries had done so, we would see a relaxation in budgetary discipline, as previously mentioned, something which caused the Dublin City Council to approve the Stability and Growth Pact in December 1996. Under this pact, countries committed themselves to limiting public debt deficit to 3% and public debt at 60% once they were in the Monetary Union, except when under extremely difficult circumstances.

Furthermore, these limits are justified, given that if a country embarks upon a path of unsustainable increases in public debt, it would have a negative knock-on effect for the rest of the European Union. A country that allows its GDP debt ratio to advance continually will have to increase resources to the Union's capital market, subsequently raising interest rates in the union, at the same time as leaving a burdening debt for the rest of the countries. If the other countries decide to stabilize their public debt/GDP ratios, then they will be forced to adhere to more restrictive policies.

The existence of external effects is based on the supposition that the capital market does not function adequately, whereas, if capital markets were efficient, there wouldn't be any knock-on effects and other governments would not suffer the consequences of a particular country facing a heightened level of debt. Despite the fact that this argument is important, the possibility also exists that, under certain conditions, moneylenders would find it difficult to assign a risk premium to a country with heightened debt. Therefore, these moneylenders will think that, should there be a significant debt crisis, for example, if the country facing heightened debt is incapable of meet their demands, then the other countries are going to act as guarantor to the previous country so as to make sure that the crisis does not extend to the rest of the financial system. The certainty that this guarantee is in place reduces their risk premium, as the capital market will not be able to assign the correct price of debt for such a high level.

With this taxation on exact limits, in other words, limiting the deficit/GDP ratio, it conditions the spending policy, something which, indirectly, has an influence on the ability to absorb asymmetric "shocks" as well as carrying out redistribution policies.

By virtue of the SPG, each member state commits itself to achieving the medium-term goal of having a budget close to equilibrium, in such a way that when automatic stabilizers take action, the deficit always remains below 3% of the GDP. This increasing vigilance is, more precisely, the obligation of presenting an annual "program of stability" which details the medium–term budget objectives (three or four years), forecasted validation methods, predictions on microeconomic trends and an analysis of awareness. Countries which do not form part of the EMU should present "convergence programmes" of a similar content. The SPG commits the member states to maintaining a budgetary position of equilibrium or one of surplus over the medium-term. In order to do this, preventative measures must be in place, such as the Commission and Council's continual supervision (charged with assessing the consistency of budgetary policies and ensuring that excessive debt does not occur and with the Broad Guidelines for Economic Policy) and deterrents (González-Páramo, 2001).

Despite the fact that the SPG has provided the system with certain flexibility, one of the major problems that remain is that it could force a country, whose growth begins to slow down with public finance of around 3%, to undertake a restrictive economic policy just when it needs it the least. If the country in question cannot resort to the exchange or monetary policy and the SPG makes it impossible for them to apply a more expansive fiscal policy in a downturn (Gallategui, and Zubiri, 1999, pp. 347-348), it will result in an inability to absorb asymmetric "shocks" and will have to seek help from a supranational entity, due to the fact that this entity will be that which possesses the necessary instruments to face up to these problems (Galindo and Castaño, 2006).

Lastly, we are going to assess the effect the SPG has on stabilization and the sustainability of public finance, taking into account that this is considered to be a priority for the ECB (1999, 2001, 2003, 2008). The Council for the Monetary Union has declared that it is necessary to reach a situation of budgetary equilibrium so that, when there is an economic crisis, it can allow the automatic stabilizers to act appropriately without having to exceed the limit of 3% of the GDP. The problem with this position is that if a country finds itself on the verge of this limit, then there will be little room for manoeuvre in the normal functioning of the automatic stabilizers, something which could pave the way for a more precarious stabilization and product volatility higher than historical trends. This situation could be aggravated if members have a limited range of instruments (above all, taxation policy) as a result of integration into the EU. Under these circumstances, stabilization could be invoked by way of the EU's budget (ECB, 2002).

Therefore, according to the ECB (2002 and 2008), writing off public finance is centred on controlling expenditure. Fiscal strategy has to be broken down into income and expenditure. Once again, it is worthwhile distinguishing between writing off and stabilizing. As previously mentioned, discretional measures are needed to reach the main objective. There is ample empirical evidence that shows that, by doing this, controlling spending is more appropriate than increasing taxation. The credibility factor and the outlook for tax reductions in the future, induced by controlling spending, usually have a more positive effect on investment and private consumption. Reorganization, based on controlling spending can, additionally, help authorities to put structural spending reforms into practice.

As you will see in the following section, as from 2000, public accounts for the Euro zone began to worsen, something which caused the SPG to reform in 2004. That is to say, faced with the impossibility of adhering to the SPG in periods of economic recession and once the single currency was in place, the SPG has become more flexible so that the minimum regulations in force with regards to fiscal policy can be met and do not jeopardize the adequate functioning of the EMU (Galindo and Castaño, 2006).

We must add the economic crisis, which began in 2007, to the section above, as it was a situation in which the most intense of discretional measures were undertaken in member states' fiscal policies. Theses centred mainly on spending, along with a sharp decline in tax collection. This brought about increases in public deficit ratios which were finally translated into an increase in public debt ratios.

Furthermore, the use of fiscal policy is becoming excessive and, at times, even inefficient. This is due to the fact that it is the only relevant tool at the disposal of policy makers in member states as they do not have the possibility of using either the monetary or the exchange policy.

4. Evolution of Public Finances in Euro-Area

In this section, it is realised an empirical analyze of evolution of public finances of some euro-area countries. For it, it is realised a comparative study of evolution of deficit rate (general government balance), public debt rate and GDP growth for Belgium, Germany, Greece, Spain, Ireland, France, Italy, Luxembourg, The Netherlands, Austria, Portugal and Finland.

However, it is necessary to indicate because the euro-area countries have used fiscal policy of intensive way. In table, it is summarized evolution of unemployment rate. In this table, it is possible to observe that in 2009 the unemployment rates are increase in all countries, and this situation could deteriorate in 2010. Besides, actual economic crisis, it is characterized for a high decrease of private consumption and private investment, for it, policy makers in member states are using expansive fiscal policy, increase public expenditure, next to decrease of tax collection, then, deficit rate are increase and it is not possible to archive balance budget target al shot-term in euro-area countries.

Table. 1. Evolution of Unemployment rate

Unemployment rate	2005	2006	2007	2008	2009	2010
BELGIUM	8,5	8,3	7,5	7	8,5	10,3
GERMANY	10,7	9,8	8,4	7,3	8,6	10,4
GREECE	9,9	8,9	8,3	7,7	9,1	9,7
SPAIN	9,2	8,5	8,3	11,3	17,3	20,5
IRELAND	4,4	4,5	4,6	6,3	13,3	16
FRANCE	9,2	9,2	8,3	7,8	9,6	10,7
ITALY	7,7	6,8	6,1	6,8	8,8	9,4
LUXEMBOURG	4,6	4,6	4,2	4,9	5,9	7
THE NETHERLANDS	4,7	3,9	3,2	2,8	3,9	6,2
AUSTRIA	5,2	4,8	4,4	3,8	6	7,1
PORTUGAL	7,7	7,8	8,1	7,7	9,1	9,8
FINLAND	8,4	7,7	6,9	6,4	8,9	9,3

Source: European Commission (2009)

Later, in follow figures it could observe the evolution of deficit rate, debt rate and GDP growth, in each countries of euro-area. In general terms, euro-area countries present a improvement of deficit rate in period 1995-1999, since this criteria was fundamental to achieve to unique coin. This criterion is possible to achieve not only for measures to take by the state member, but also, for an economic growth greater that not predicted, that reduced the cost of fiscal consolidation.

However, since 2000, deficit rate became to deteriorate, fundamentally, France, Germany, Italy and Portugal. In addition, in 2003, Germany, France and Netherlands exceed the limit of 3 % of the public deficit rate. This fact provoked the reform of SPG.

In addition, actual economic recession provoked that the prevision for 2009 and 2010 countries euro-area will not carry out the conditions of SPG. The worse situation is presented by following countries Spain, Ireland, and Portugal, theses countries are also that they will present greater estimated unemployment rate and are the countries with more problems competitiveness. However, theses countries are not higher debt rate, the countries could present problems of rate debt are Belgium, Italy and France.

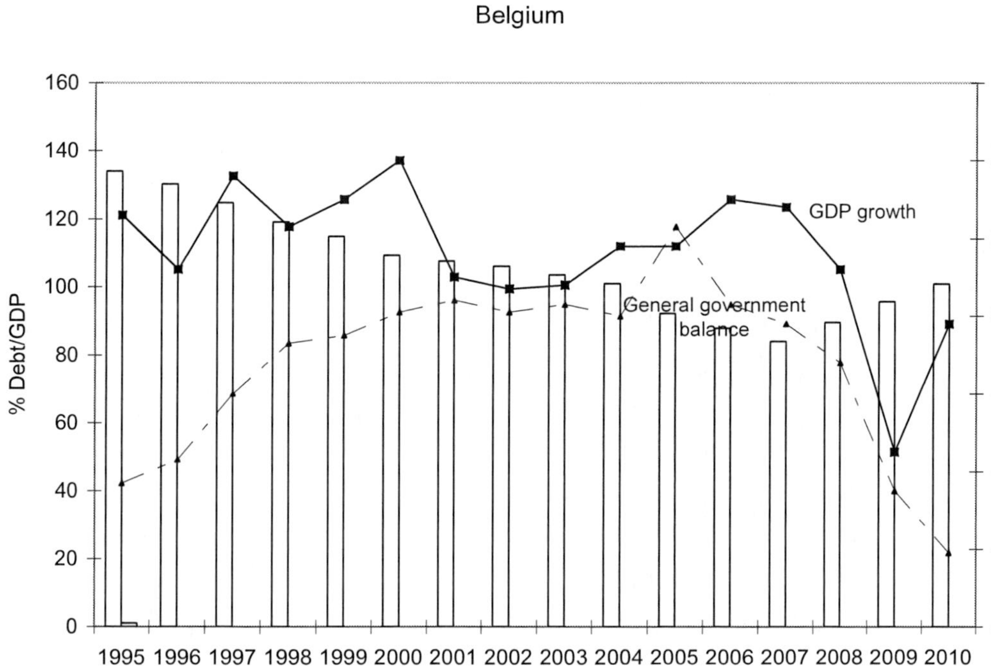

Source: European Commission (2002, 2004, 2009)

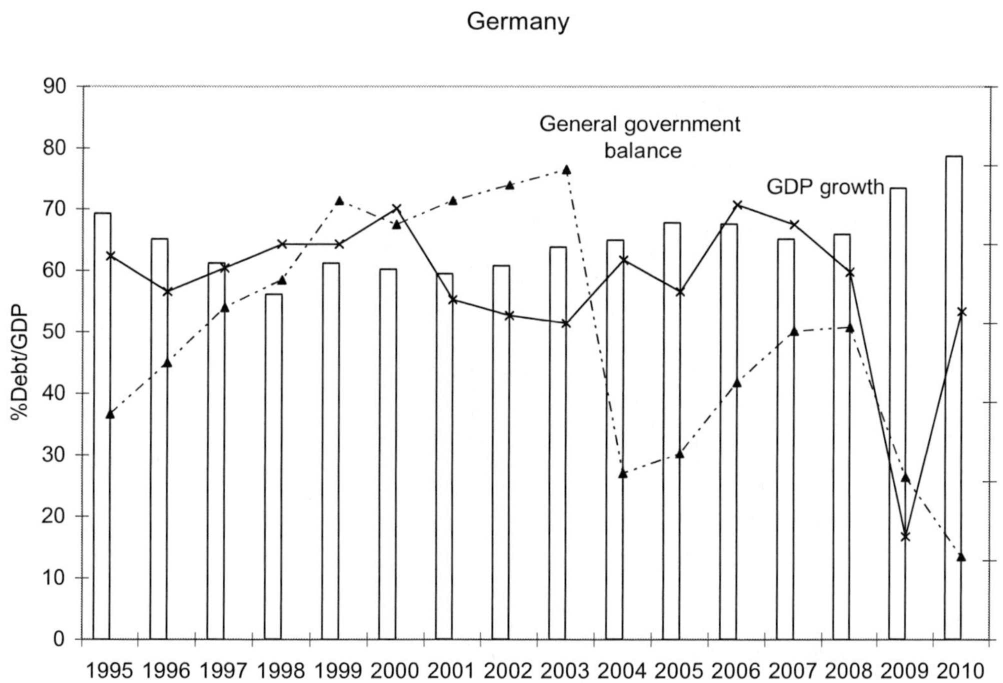

Source: European Commission (2002, 2004, 2009)

Figure 2. (continued)

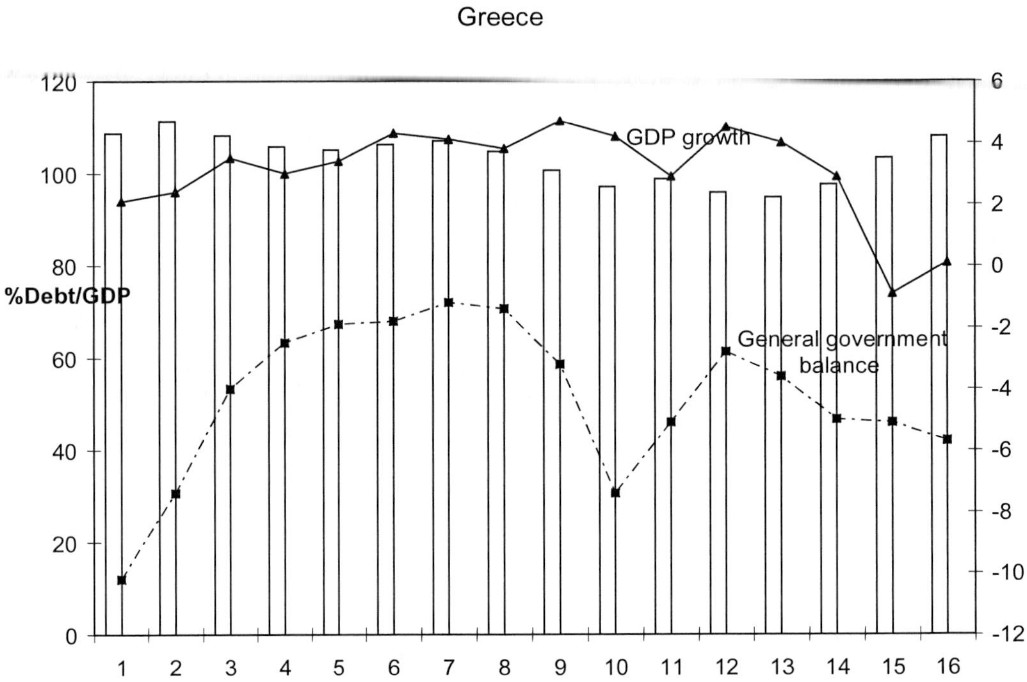

Source: European Commission (2002, 2004, 2009)

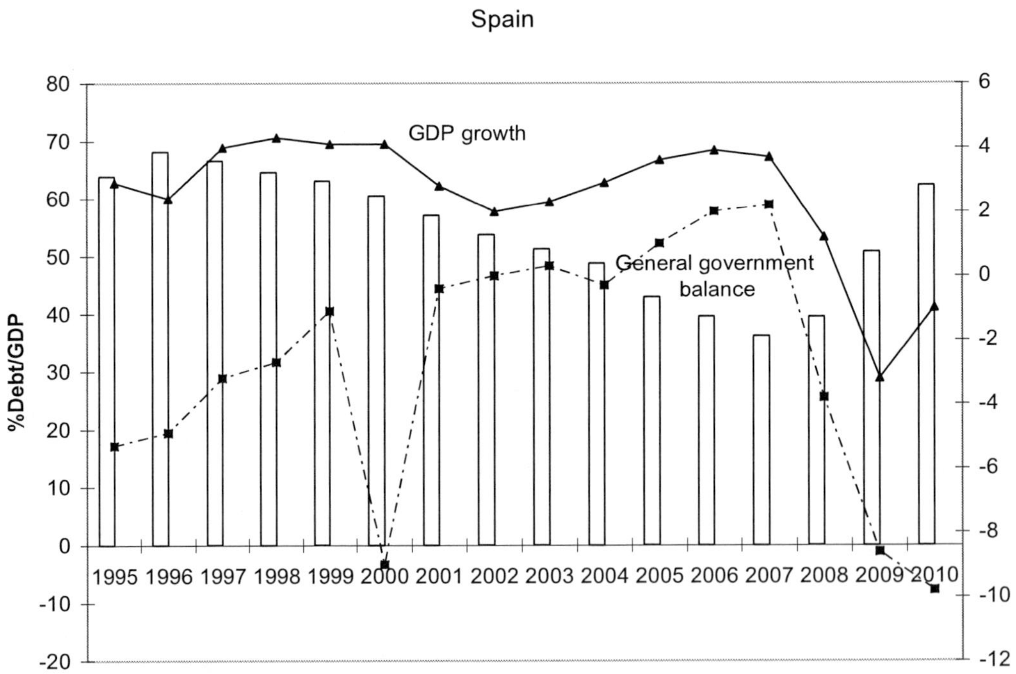

Source: European Commission (2002, 2004, 2009)

Figure 2. (continued)

Ireland

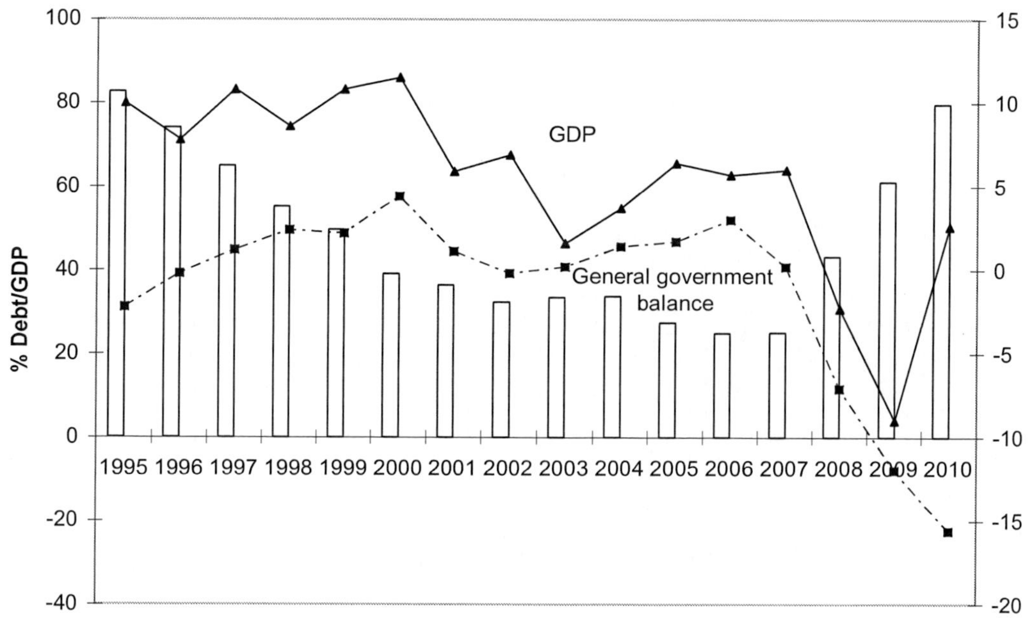

Source: European Commission (2002, 2004, 2009)

France

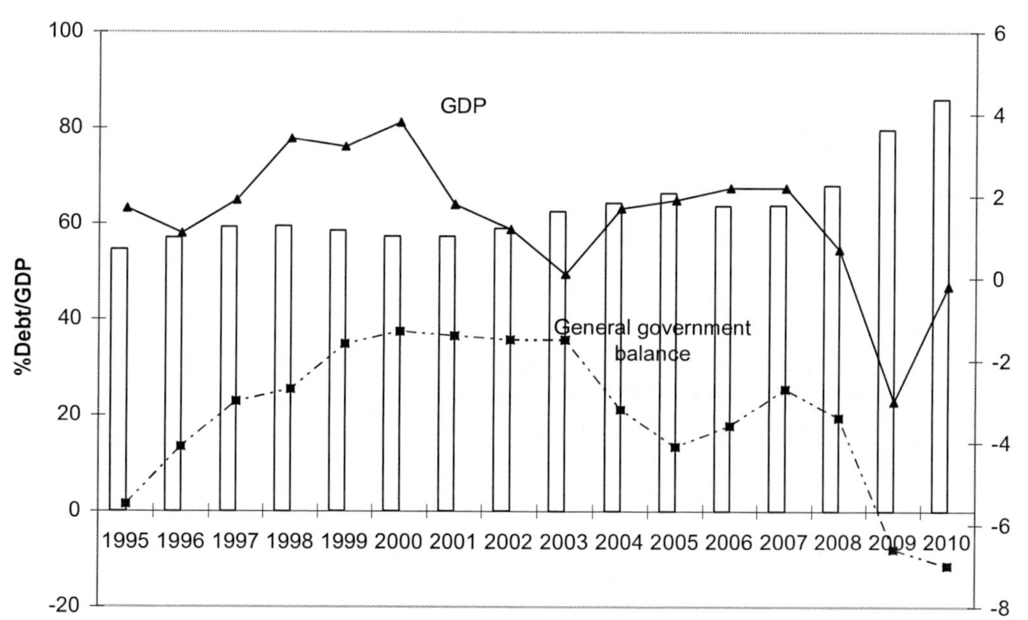

Source: European Commission (2002, 2004, 2009)

Figure 2. (continued)

Italy

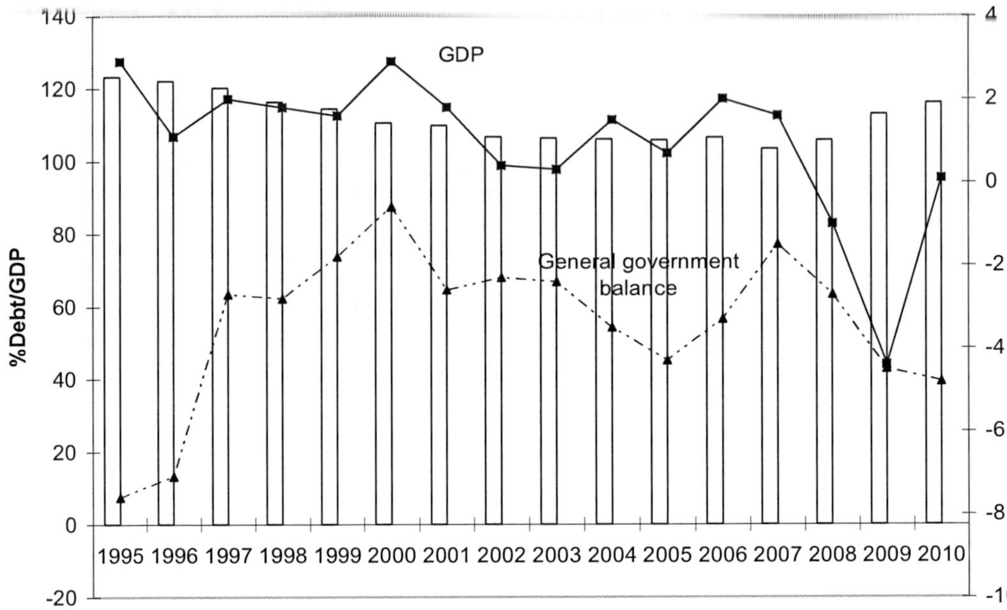

Source: European Commission (2002, 2004, 2009)

Luxembourg

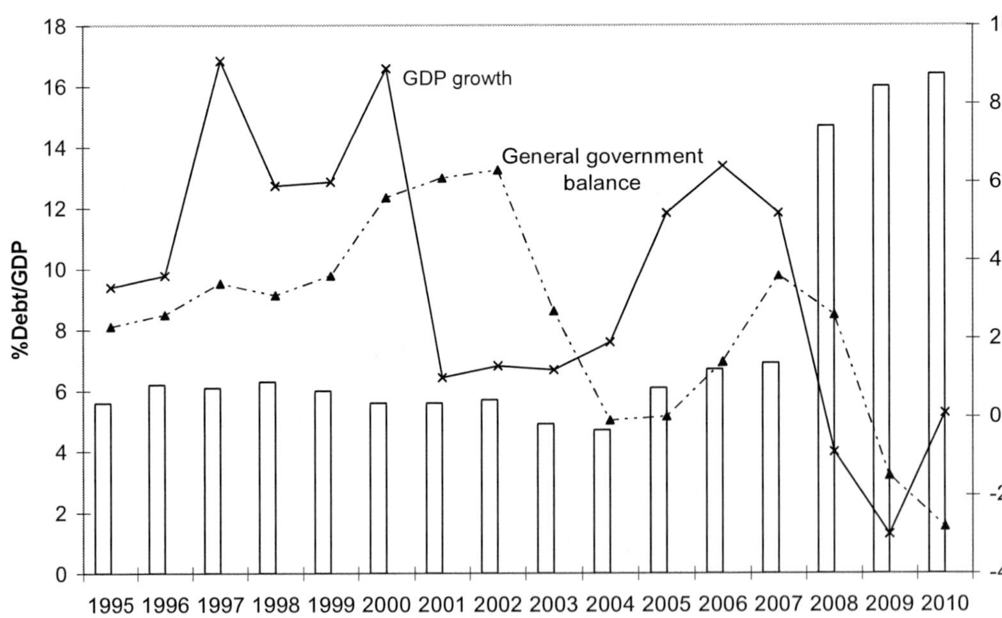

Source: European Commission (2002, 2004, 2009)

Figure 2. (continued)

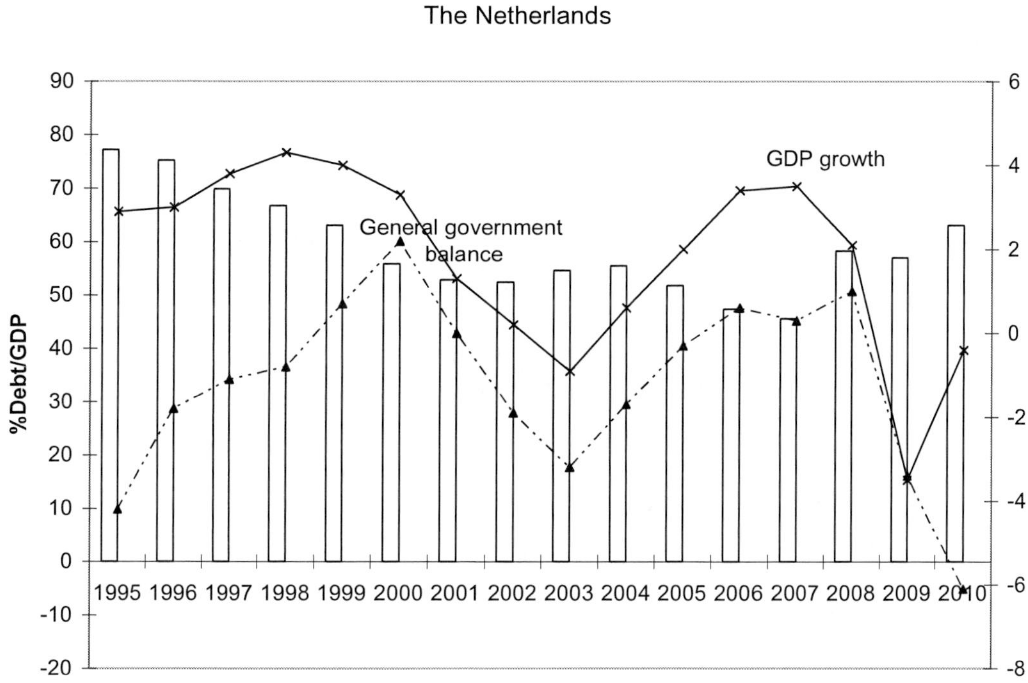

Source: European Commission (2002, 2004, 2009)

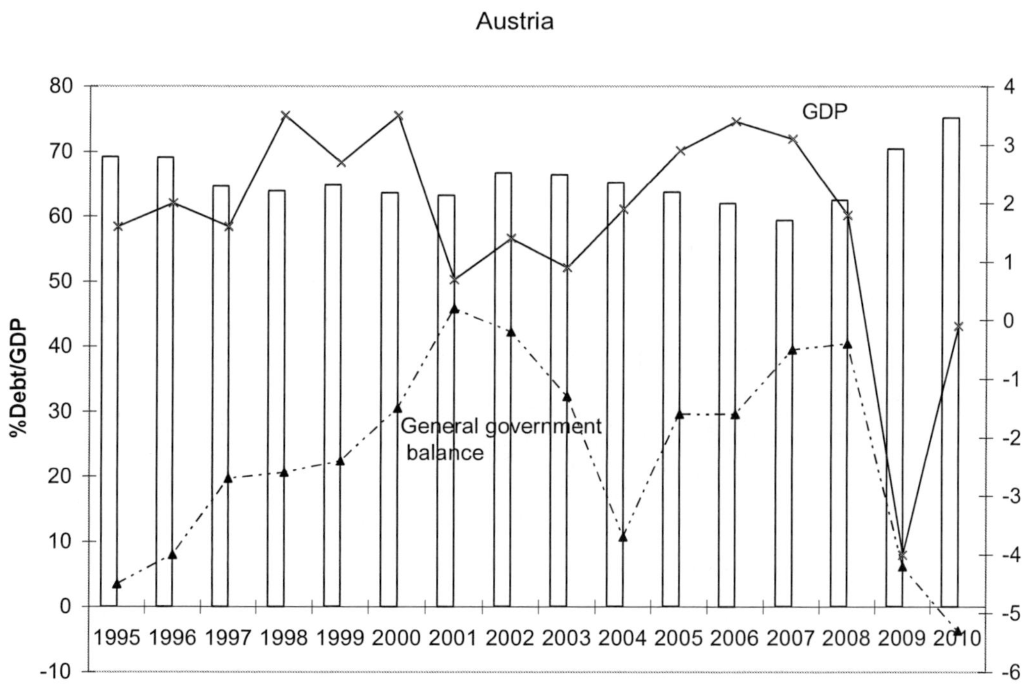

Source: European Commission (2002, 2004, 2009)

Figure 2. (continued)

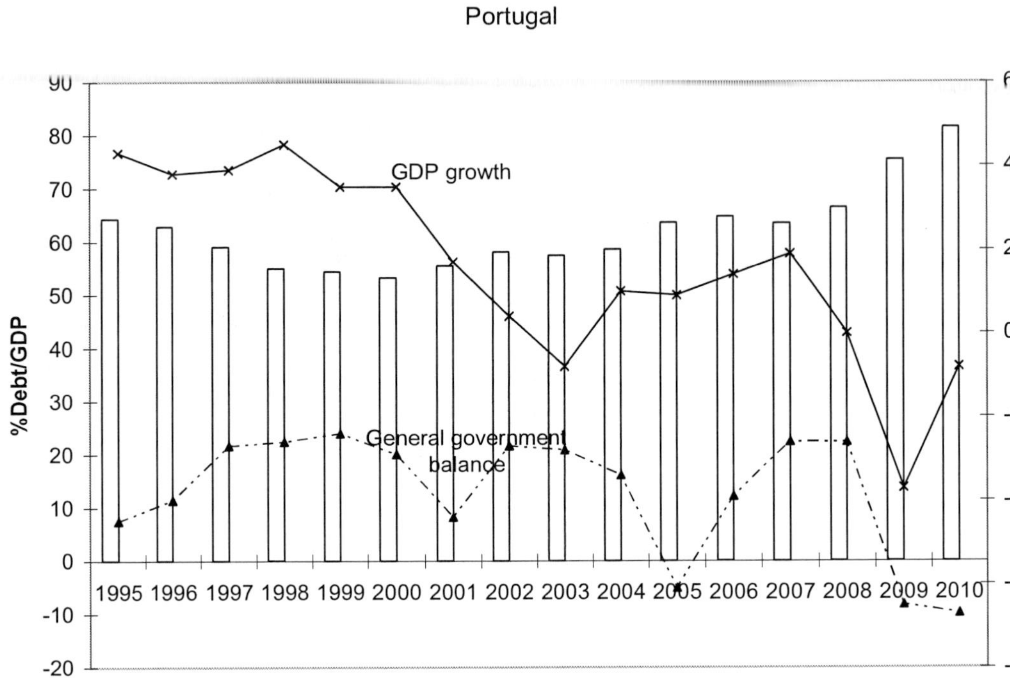

Source: European Commission (2002, 2004, 2009)

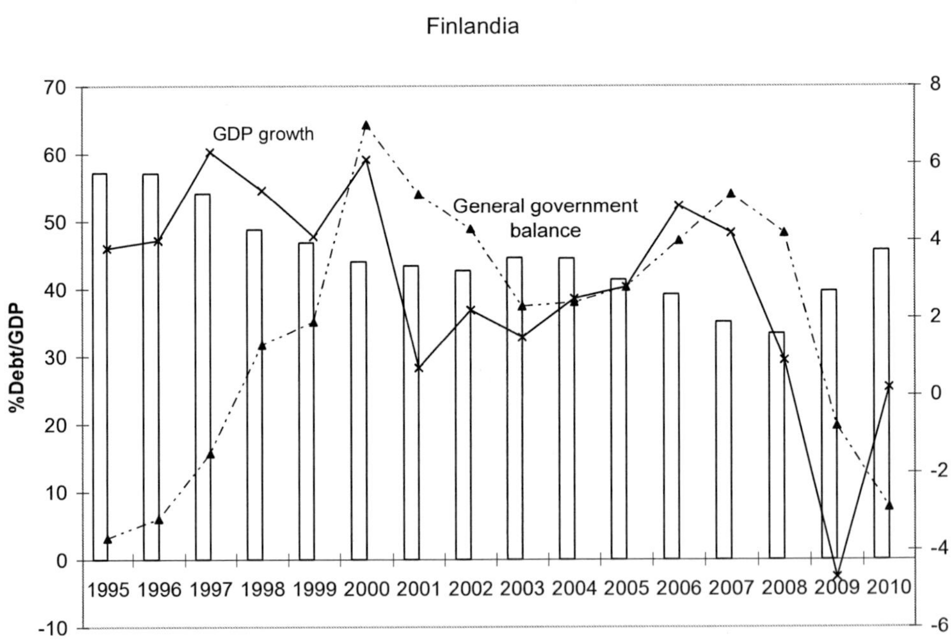

Source: European Commission (2002, 2004, 2009)

Figures. 2. Evolution of public finances in euro-area

Definitively, with actual economic recession it is impossible to achieve of target of SGP, in this situations it is necessary the coordination of fiscal policies of euro-area countries to avoid negative effects before indicate, essentially, penalty of capital markets via increase interest rate and outward financial flows.

CONCLUSION

In this chapter a study of necessity of coordination of fiscal policies in EMU, where fiscal policy is the only relevant tool at the disposal of policy decision markers in member states to try to resolve the economic recession, but, if decision markers of member states do not coordinate theses decisions, it could generate negative effects in the rest of countries of euro-area or also, it is possible that capital markets punished the countries with high public debt rates. Also, in case of euro-area, where monetary policy is centralized it is possible that des-coordination of fiscal policies of member states it translate at long-term in increase of inflation rate and increase of interest rate.

If the situation of economic recession has provoked that it is not possible to achieve of target of SGP, it is necessary it is necessary the coordination of fiscal policies of euro-area countries and European monetary policy to try archive the target of economic policy, economic growth and increase of employment with less cost possible.

REFERENCES

Andersen, T. M. (2005). Fiscal stabilization policy in a monetary union with inflation targeting. *Journal of Macroeconomics* 27, 1–29

Andersen, TM, (2002). *Fiscal Policy Coordination.* *www.regeringe.se/propositioner/sou/pde/remiss.pdf.*

Beetsma, R, & Debrun, X (2004). "The interactions between monetary and fiscal policies in monetary union: a review of recent literature", in R. Beetsma, C. Favero, A. Missele, A. Muscatelli, P. Natale, & P. Tirelli (Eds.), *Monetary Policy, Fiscal Policies and Labour Markets,* (edition, pp. 91-133). Cambridge UK: Cambridge University Press.

Bustillo, R & Bonete, R. (2000). *Introducción a la Unión Europea: Análisis desde la economía.* Madrid: Alianza Editorial.

Calvo, A. & Galindo, M. A. (1990): *La teoría de la política fiscal.* Madrid: Dykinson.

Cangiano, M. & Mottu, E. (1999). Will Fiscal Policy be effective under EMU?. Working Paper.IFM. 98/176. http://papers.ssrn.com/sol3/papers.cfm.

Castaño, M.S. & Carrasco, I. (2009).Interactions Between Monetary and Fiscal Policies: The Case Of The European Monetary Union. In W. N. Squires and C. P. Burdock (Eds.), *Monetary Growth: Trends, Impacts and Policies*, New York: Novapress.

Cooper, R. (1985). Economic interdependence and coordination of economic policies. In R.W. Jones and P.B. Kenen (Eds.), *Handbook of International Economics,* vol. II. North-Holland, Amsterdam: Elsevier.

Gallategui, M. C & Zubiri, I. (1999). El diseño del sector público en la UME: algunas sugerencias de reforma. In Fundación BBV. *El euro y sus repercusiones sobre la economía española.* (edition, pp. 333-402). Madrid: Fundación BBV.

De Grauwe, P. (1997). *The Economics of Monetary Integration*, New York: Oxford University Press.

European Central Bank (1999). Estrategia de política monetaria del Eurosistema orientada hacia la estabilidad. *Boletín Mensual del BCE*, January, 45-57.

European Central Bank (2001). La política fiscal y el crecimiento económico, *Boletín Mensual del BCE*, August, 41-58.

European Central Bank (2002). Funcionamiento de los estabilizadores fiscales automáticos en la zona euro, *Clm.economía,* vol. 1, 147-172.

European Central Bank (2008). One monetary policy and many fiscal policies: ensuring a smooth functioning of EMU, *Monthly Bulletin*, July, 65-78.

European Commission (2002). *Eurostat. Yearbook. 2002*. Eurostat

European Commission (2004). *Eurostat. Yearbook. 2004*. Eurostat

European Commission (2009). *The Commission's economic forecast programme. http://ec.europa.eu/economy_finance*

Galindo, M.A. & Castaño, M.S (2006). La política fiscal y el Pacto de Estabilidad y Crecimiento (PEC). In J.M. Sáiz Alvarez: *¿Hacia dónde vas Europa?.* Madrid: Ediciones FIEC.

González-Páramo, J.M. (2001). *Costes y Beneficios de la Disciplina Fiscal: la Ley de Estabilidad Presupuestaria en Perspectiva*. Madrid: Instituto de Estudios Fiscales.

Hamada, K. (1985). *The Political Economy of International Monetary Interdependence.* Cambridge: MIT Press.

Hansen, A. H. (1973). *Política fiscal y ciclo económico*. México: Fondo de Cultura Económica.

Hansen, A. H. (1978). *Guía de Keynes*. México: Fondo de Cultura Económica.

Iranzo, J. (2002). El cambio de rumbo de la política económica: de la estabilización a la estabilidad. *clmeconomía*, vol. 2, 123-146.

Lerner, A. P. (1951). *Economics of Employment.* New York: McGraw-Hill

Lerner, A. P. (1961). The Burden of Debt. *Review of Economic and Statistics*, 43: 750–755

Sánchez, L. & Sáiz Álvarez, J.M. (2006). La Política Fiscal, In M.A Galindo, & Y. Fernández (Eds.), *Política Socioeconómica en la Unión Europea,* (edition, pp. 65-78). Madrid: Delta publicaciones,

Shaw, C. K. (1972). *Fiscal Policy*. London: Macmillan Studies in Economics.

In: International Political Economy
Editors: M.A. Galindo Martin, E. Nissan
ISBN: 978-1-60876-172-2

Chapter 10

SCIENCE AND INNOVATION POLICY: EVOLUTION AND CHALLENGES

Mikel Gomez Uranga and Jon Barrutia Güenaga
UPV/EHU

ABSTRACT

From both the macroeconomic and microeconomic or business perspectives, innovation is a path that can lead to sustainable success on today's current scene. In other words, the way innovation policy is posed is of great relevance. The existence of a market failure is often used as a justification for innovation policies. The scope of application for innovation policy is also a key point. Here we can find the idea of Regional Innovation Systems (RIS) and their evolution. The relationship between science policy and innovation policy is therefore important and often not sufficiently examined. It is important to analyse, in turn, the role of clusters and the policies relating to them.

1. INTRODUCTION

From both the macroeconomic and microeconomic or business perspectives, innovation is a path that can lead to sustainable success on today´s current scene. The decisions made to draw up the map for innovation in a certain socioeconomic sphere are extremely important to strategy. In other words, the way innovation policy is posed is of great relevance.

The existence of a market failure is often used as a justification for innovation policies. The classic debate on public vs. private concerning how much margin should be left to private initiative or the market is largely empirical rather than theoretical. As Richard Nelson says: "There is no satisfactory normative theory regarding the appropriate roles of government in a mixed economy" (Nelson,1987, p. 556).

The scope of application for innovation policy is also a key point. According to successful experiences and results, it seems that the generation of networks between innovative agents and firms where knowledge is shared does better in local settings and specific territories. Here we can find the idea of Regional Innovation Systems (RIS) and their evolution which is influenced by the new scientific-technological paradigm and its link with innovation. The relationship between science policy and innovation policy is therefore important and often not sufficiently examined.

The way innovating agents, scientists-technologists and firms form groups is a key factor in this approach. For this reason, it is important to analyse, in turn, the role of clusters and the policies relating to them.

Consideration of these points offers us a complete view of innovation policy in the framework of social and economic competitiveness.

2. Innovation Policies

Justification for Innovation Policies

For decades, neoclassical economists have ignored technology. There was no place for explanation of technical change in their economic models. The first outstanding neoclassical economist to contemplate technical change as generated by variation of the relative price of factors was Hicks. The Nobel Prize winner, the economist Arrow, admitted that the market was not capable of efficient allocation of resources from inventions due to the following: uncertainty, spill overs, economies of scale, information asymmetry and the indivisibility of inventions. Thus, public intervention should be allocated to cover these "market failures". Post-Keynesian economists, paying greater attention to the system's instability and structural unemployment caused by the crisis, claimed government intervention was the main drive of demand. The belief that state intervention allows us to stabilize the economy and develop techno-scientific potential based on public intervention and state regulation contrasts with the Public Choice position that calls for the least possible government intervention since, in symmetry with Arrow's thesis, "policy failures" exist in that case (Vence, 2007).

The authors that focus their analysis on innovation are the ones that recovered Schumpter's tradition. They understand it as the strategic variable that explains economic growth and cycles of the capitalist economy.

Post-Schumpeterian theses provide a number of interesting concepts and ideas to describe macroeconomic growth as an ever changing disequilibrium process (Castellaci et al., 2005).

Going beyond a methodological vision that sets the center of innovation almost exclusively in the firm itself, requires understanding that firms can also be innovative with other agents (other firms, others in the firm's chain of values and others in the system). The Innovation System concept shows a more general formulation of inter-agent collaboration (also including governments and institutions). It admits that innovative centrality should not lie only with firms. In this systemic vision, the knowledge (or learning) based economy proposed by Lundvall and Edquist is understood, considering knowledge as the key resource in today's economies and learning as the process which allows for the best inter-agent collaboration or relationships. From this perspective, policy intervention from government is justified through "system failures". One risk must be recognized: from this perspective, both public and private relationships may be contemplated in a functional manner as maximum efficiency is exclusively pursued. The system tends to be considered self-regulated, ignoring any conflict derived from socio-economic relationships.

From our point of view, system failures are not on the same plane as market failures because institutions and governments are included in the innovation system. In this latter case, we should perhaps refer to changes in the logic of system agents' actions rather than failures.

The following table shows an initial outline which introduces rationality, objectives and levels as well as roles of public intervention in the field of innovation from the different methodological approaches relevant to economics.

The outline shown above gives us initial information on the methodological bases that underlie the different science, technology and innovation policies we will examine in the rest of the chapter.

Table 1. Theoretical Rationales for Science, Technology and Innovation Policy

	NEOCLASSICAL	SCHUMPETERIAN	NEO-MARSHALLIAN	SYSTEMIC	EVOLUTIONARY
Rationale for public intervention	Information-transmission failures Appropriability failure	Support to accumulation of endogenous RandD	Flexible "external economies of agglomeration"	System failure, Institutional failures System dysfuntions	Learning failures, Cognitive gaps, Block-in dysfunctions Lack of diversity
Objective of intervention	Substitute for less than optimal use of resources	Create conditions of increasing returns to RandD	Reduction of costs in information, Transports, Promote locally based networks of cooperation and competition	Overall coherence of the system, roles and function of actors, Adequate institutional settings	Avoid lock-in
Level of intervention	Centralised-national level No differentiation of levels of intervention	Centralised – national level, but with focus in more advenced regions	Regional level but also National level with regional focus (decentralised)	National and Regional levels	Increase cognitive capacity Improve diversity and selectivity Multi-level Balances centralised with decentralised intervention
Role of policy maker	Compensate for less than optimal private investmenT	Incentivate accumulation of "monopolistic" gains	Creation of a collaborative industrial community	Coordinating the system, help in networking	Identification of technology specific failures, Design of segmented targeted intervention

Source: Laranja et al. (2008, pp 823–835).

The first generation of public innovation policies was directed to subsidizing and promoting RandD, while also making use of fiscal initiatives. As we see in the outline, these policies responded to the logic of market failures. Methodological orientations of systems inspired in neo-Schumpeterian evolutionist currents were gradually imposed in innovation policy, converging with orientations similar to neo-Marshallian approaches, which in turn, are the ones that gave rise to cluster policies.

However, what changes in the evolution of economic systems can explain such major policy changes? Some cases in point are the following:

a) High development of information networks as the fundaments of a knowledge- based economy, which has been linked to increased technology transversality. This has exponentially increased costs and the need for collaboration between different groups on the international scene.
b) The increasing need to mobilize all available material, human, financial and technological resources with relatively significant, coordinated and coherent orientations.
c) Greater participation of science in economic activities.
d) The increasing importance of intellectual property.
e) Greater awareness that man is facing new global problems, some of which are related to the very survival of economic systems and even civilization itself.

The contribution of evolutionist type methodology from innovation systems provides or emphasizes the logic of collaboration and relationships between agents, which calls for more holistic intervention looking to offer more global solutions. This keeps competence from being parceled in government and political centers as it is assumed that the problems are systemic and that all the agents are part of the problem as well as part of the solution.

Geographic proximity is a key factor in innovation processes. There are various proximity instruments: infrastructures such as technology parks, specialized equipment, regional SME networks, clusters around universities, multinational RandD corporative centers, etc.

The concept of RIS (Regional Innovation System) is widely used in innovation policy all over the world. It can be understood as "a set of private and public interests which interact, as well as institutions and other organizations that function through institutional and organizational agreements and relationships that lead to generating and spreading knowledge" (Bruijn, 2005, p. 1155).

Inventory of the Content of Public Innovation Policies

Without aiming to offer a complete list, studying authors like (Cimoli et al. 2006), we propose carrying out a first inventory of policies and public bodies that subsidize research for innovation classified from different perspectives.

Thus, the following points are considered:

a) Public policy in the field of innovation, which may have a direct effect on innovation agents' incentives structures. They consist of regulations, aid, subsidies and direct action to create resources. Policies that regulate and foster RandD, both in the field of business and organizations involved in certain research that may benefit firms.

b) Measures that affect business property structures, mainly privatization of state firms, dealings with multinationals and local firms as well as state banks and those public or semi-public organizations that offer venture capital funding.
c) Policies and legislation on international trade as well as laws on intellectual property. Those policies and practices which affect competition and everything related to anti-trust laws, etc.
d) Policies orientated to improving innovation systems and which stress, above all, the search for greater coordination between the different agents. These would include flow and distribution of information between the different stakeholders in economic-financial networks such as: clients, suppliers, financial institutions, shareholders, workers, etc. that are subject to different market legislation (labour, products, etc.) and the ways in which governance is organized.
e) Policies whose main objective is to create the conditions for the creation or development of innovative firms and their contribution to commercialising the results of certain segments of scientific research.
f) Policies, laws and possible public institutions that are involved with learning and management of technical knowledge in the business sphere. There are political instruments and institutions in many countries such as: Policies and laws on science for training researchers, doctoral candidates and universities as well as public and private research centers for all fields of knowledge, technical training policies that affect training centers and polytechnic schools.

The Real Context Calls for Complex Political and Regulatory Action

The big sectors that formed the backbone of industrial economies were monopolies and often public monopolies until the 90s. In almost every country, telephony and telecommunications services were public monopolies. This sector underwent one of the largest deregulation processes known in the history of the economy. Big business groups were gradually segmented into different lines of activity, and public property was later privatized. Other different networks began to grow almost at the same time as this deregulation took place. We are referring to the spread of Internet. The complementary nature of these technologies made it necessary for networks to use large routes from telephony services which belonged to private sector firms and were somewhat smaller than conventional firms. The spread of new Internet services firms led to the coexistence of network servers, carriers and owners, private sector, reconverted public sector, quasi-public firms, rules to regulate connections and regulatory gaps in Internet itself. All of these factors caused the evolution of the world's most important technological, economic and social paradigm to be very complex in technological and regulatory terms, and very different from the traditional definitions of market, state or private or public sectors. An increasing amount of advances and inventions are being achieved in this hybrid industry of electronics and telecommunications, but especially in hardware and also software industries.

Anti-monopoly regulations may have a positive effect on competition and improvement in the field of RandD as well as fostering patents in certain industries. If a large firm purchases another that owns a patent relevant to the evolution of a technology sector, a regulatory agency could determine that the patent owner firm should make the previously patented technology available to competitors as a condition for purchase.

Larger numbers of inventions and researchers are coming from the world of universities as well as firms, both private and state owned. University graduates create firms and new paradigms and clusters are emerging from universities and developing during the 2000s. In other words, a large part of research tasks and the capacity to renew existing paradigms and propose new ones is taking place in universities despite business and private evolution and their large contribution to RandD. Mobilising knowledge resources is one of the most complex tasks that world governments must respond to. Among them is the job of preparing education systems to form technicians and qualifications that contribute to adapting the economy to new techno-scientific paradigms with broad possibilities of revolutionizing the economy and society. An example of this is biotechnology.

Innovation sources are not exclusively found in firms themselves but are often at the intersection between firms, universities, research laboratories, suppliers and consumers (Powel et al., 1996). There is increasing empirical evidence of large public participation in RandD, and its greater influence on growth and business improvement. While subject to rules, initiatives and policies, either public or combined in a certain governance framework, knowledge based economies have considerable levels of public intervention.

Flow of knowledge from scientific research centers toward business innovation is often possible through government intermediation. Intellectual property, especially patents, is still necessary to maintain creation and knowledge. It also continues to be vital to the competitive strategies of big firms and countries. However, it is also increasingly the material base of many mercantile and innovation agreements between university and industry.

Research is seldom the result of totally free decisions. It is conditioned by social, political and commercial needs. Big lines of research are set down in world governments' major decisions and treaties. The economic and financial conditions needed for research (all types of infrastructures and means) affect these choices. Laws, policies and regulations allow or prevent knowledge from being maintained, spread or exploited. Major orientations and objectives also condition the spheres we have mentioned. Some examples are depletion of conventional energy sources, climate change, moral and ethical problems and the destruction of traditional wealth and biodiversity.

In this context of change and makeup of a new scientific, technological and innovation paradigm, it seems reasonable to make some conjectures about the relationship between competitive business innovation channels and science. Above all, since this issue is increasingly understood in a systemic and cluster-like manner, both from the theoretical perspective as well as in public-private decision making. In order to make our conjectures more effective, the subjects of analysis will be science policy, business innovation and the university as reference for the scientific agent.[1]

---

[1] On the other hand, the university may assume the role of nexus between scientific knowledge and firms within the so called "university's third mission" (Shiles, 2002, Sheen, 1992, Clark, 1998), which also makes it a reference as a subject for study.

3. Science Policy and the University: Design and Management for Innovation

Previous Considerations

We consider the relationship between policy on science and innovation to be real and positive. This starting point is based on the present parameters of knowledge generation and acquisition, technological development and competitiveness, reasons for which business innovation looks to science as a source of quality and distinction.

While innovation is a complex social global phenomenon, reflection of this issue centers on business innovation as the clearest expression of competitiveness and the value generating factor.

Without aiming to offer a totally comprehensive view, the Science-University relationship is justified to the extent to which the latter is a key agent in generating, collecting and spreading scientific knowledge.

Thus, UII (University-Industry Interaction) can be established, understanding it as one of the routes to bring business closer to science, and therefore to competitive innovation.

From this perspective, we will examine the transfer routes found in the sphere of patenting, the creation of spin offs and consulting while excluding previous and continuous Human Resource (HR) training that is not related to research personnel.

The objective of the reflection is to understand the functional dynamics between science policy and UII and their possible effects on business innovation.

Science Policy Implemented by Public Administration (PA)

Some aspects of science policy are general and therefore common to Public Administration's policy and management decisions in any other field. In synthesis, these aspects can be limited to two: the new conception of the relationship between PA and citizens and new public management.

The new conception of the relationship between PA and citizens is based on the concept of Relational Public Administration which envisages a more continuous participative role of citizens in public problems and decisions as well as higher levels of mutual commitment.

New Public Management (NPM) (Barzelay, 2001, Pollit and Bouckaert, 1999) introduces competitiveness, efficiency and effectiveness parameters in the traditional bureaucratic system. Proof of this is quality management, programme contracts, rendering accounts, institutional assessment or outsourcing formulas. One general principle, shared and vital to NPM, is considering the citizen as a customer. All of these aspects, a continuous relationship, based on participation and mutual commitment and understanding the citizen to be a customer, can be synthesized as Public Governance[2]. We can therefore say that science policy is directly affected by Governance as it is part of PA.

[2] Relational Administration and Governance have been amply developed with the inclusion of ICTs in public action. In fact, study of these fields is now focusing on e-Administration and e-Governance. See Criado and Ramilo (2003) for a global systematic examination of this point. Also see Ahrens(2000), Jesoop(2001), Swyngedow (2005).

One of the unique features of science policy is that, in the short term, it is directed to a very specific group of agents and operators (scientists, universities, research centers, technology based RandD departments in firms, etc.) although this policy should benefit the society as a whole in the long term. In other words, it is focused on a minority whose essential feature is their professional and organizational profile determined by their relation to science.

This "target population" is further reduced if we center on the university, which is one objective of this chapter. Therefore, we can affirm that a sub-group of the "science population" with a tradition of research is concentrated in the university, within an organization called to serve and take part in the community it belongs to.

The risk of the stock of knowledge becoming obsolete quickly is very high since science is an activity characterized by permanent rapid progress. This progress should also generate high levels of competition between the different science "producers" on the international scene given the universal nature of scientific knowledge.

The Functional Relationship of Science Policy and the University in View of UII for Business Innovation

Firms receive strong stimuli to increase their levels of knowledge and technology in today's globalised competitive environment. This decision to undertake internal generation and/or external acquisition[3] in order to achieve this objective is relevant (Borg, 2001). Internal generation (Beneito, 2003) presents many advantages, as does external acquisition (Caloghirou, et al., 2004). There are also positions in favour of combining both options (Helfat, 1997), (Cassiman and Veuglers, 2004).

Furthermore, firms observe that RandD + i is becoming more complex and raises costs. Therefore, a logical consequence is the search for collaboration with "specialized organizations" such as the university. In this sense, the new scientific-technological paradigm, synthesized under the term analytical innovation (Asheim et al., 2007), (Jensen et al., 2007) becomes a key factor from the perspective of competitive leadership. In order words, it is a vital factor when business looks to successfully tackle innovation so firms must pose methods to approach the field of science[4]. Seen from the perspective of UII, (Okubo and Sjoberg, 2000), it is in this context that universities, given their intensity and expectations, can carry out new activities.

On the other hand, the university as a whole is undergoing institutional and socio-political changes that range from fewer available public funds to European processes like the Bolognia Declaration of 1999. This will prompt the university to take on structural and relational changes (Michavila and Calvo, 2000), (Van der Wende, 2000) (Barrutia, 2001), (Mook and Lo, 2002), (Flavian and Lozano, 2004), (London Communique, 2007). In this manner, the university will open up to the market and firms out of sheer "necessity". This opening up is quite successful in certain economies, according to empirical evidence (Shane, 2002 and Mowery, 2005).

---

[3] We understand "external acquisition" as that coming from cooperation with other agents..

[4] Including those related to generating, adapting or setting up internal knowledge in order to assimilate and integrate acquired knowledge. (Zhara and George, 2002).

All of these forces and factors converging to support UII can be synthesized as follow (Marzo et al., 2008):

A new scientific-technological paradigm, an uncertain environment and fewer public funds, changes in the administrative-political makeup and high RandD costs.

On the whole, this presents a favourable context for UII, both from the point of view of firms and universities. In this context, the university emerges as a specific body in the new scientific-technological paradigm where science is a priority. We can therefore establish a link between science, university and firms with innovation as the central nexus.

The key role played by the community of professors in university management gives the institution a specific character. In this sense, we understand the university to be an Professional Bureaucracy (Mintzberg, 1984; Mintzberg and Rose, 2003).[5] One reason for this may be the nature of scientific knowledge. The high entry barriers that must be overcome to acquire, generate, collect and distribute this knowledge are important indeed. This makes science professionals holders of "know how" which sets up functional and productive hierarchies as opposed to formal or structural ones. In comparison, the latter type is devaluated, making it very difficult to administer these organizations as a whole with habitual parameters.

The main consequence is that any action or decision related to directional vocation is moderated or altered by the "professionals bureaucracy" effect and this also applies to science policy.

As holders of the competence on science policy, Public Administrations show two basic problems that must be considered.

On the one hand, sometimes there is not a sole Public Administration intervening in the field of science policy. On the other, in the specific scope our study focuses on, Public Administrations are situated beside/opposite universities which are autonomous bodies with competence for management and internal organisation based on the principle of the freedom of professorial chairs.[6]

In relation to the first point, it is not uncommon to find different Public Administrations intervening in science policy for the same research or university sphere. This is because of the federal or decentralized structures of certain countries or geo-political areas (see the EU, for example).

These structures hinder effectiveness and achievement of targets while also generating coordination, negotiation and control costs.

[5] From the sphere of analysis of university organisation, it would be more precise to mention Clark's coordination triangle (Clark, 1983) and its evolution (Jongbloed and Koelman, 2000). This makes it possible to visualize the different possibilities of organization for higher education. The reality of the university in the scope of analysis (above all, public universities) and the moment of reference would come closer to what we could call predominance of the "academic oligarchy". Therefore, in spite of the risk of simplifying, we prefer to emphasise this point by fully adopting the features of an organization of professionals. This organization is based on standardization of knowledge and skills rather than processes. It has a highly decentralized autonomous structure in which professionals work with a great deal of independence and are key players in the organization. This is due to the fact that they take part at all levels, from the operative to the strategic and also control selection and training, which gives them a great deal of power.

[6] While university autonomy and freedom of professorial chairs are the subject of many studies and research as well as reason for constitutional legislation, this issue exceeds the limits of our study. We shall, therefore, identify freedom of professorial chair with freedom of thought and understand that meddling in this field in democratic nations is severely penalized, not only by law but by society itself in terms of values

Concerning the second point, the Public Administration-university relationship can be placed, in general and in the case of science policy, within the logic of the agency problem (Jensen and Meckling, 1976).

All the costs associated with agency relationships should be considered from this perspective, with special mention of those stemming from moral hazard (Holmströn, 1982) and adverse selection (Akerlof , 1970) problems.

In this section, we cannot overlook the effects of Public Governance or the fact that we consider universities as organizations of professionals.

Furthermore, if we aim to set up a nexus with UII, we cannot leave out the business sector.

These latter factors, Public Governance, organizations of professionals and the business sector, lead us to consider the influence of university scientists and business representatives in the Public Administration itself, with capacity to take part in and affect science policy. Given the features of this influence, we also think that they could be assimilated to those attributed to stakeholders.

These include power based influence, legitimacy, urgency, vocation of permanence and stable long term results (Daake and William, 2000) (Mitchell et al., 1997) (Mitchell and Agle, 1997) (Clemens and Gallagher, 2003).

When exercising science policy, Public Administrations cannot overlook certain problems that come from institutional organization as well as the practice of Public Governance. Consideration of the two groups of stakeholders which finally modulate initial science policy is also necessary.

This can be shown as follows:

SP(PA) = F(ID*A*PG*SI) for UII effective in the field of innovation (1)

Key: SP = Science policy
PA = Public Administration
A = Agency
ID = Institutional design
PG = Public Governance
SI = Stakeholders' influence
F = Function
A = F(C*MH*AS) (2)

Key: C = costs
MH = moral hazard
SA = adverse selection

PG = F(P*MC*PE) (3)

Key: P = Participation
MC = Mutual commitment
PE = Public evaluation

SI = (PB*IBS) (4)

Key: PB = Professional Bureaucracies' influence
IBS = Influence from the business sector

Resulting in:

$$SP(PA) = F(C*MH*AS*P*MC*PE*OPI*IBS) \quad (5)$$

Design and Management of Science Policy

Having put forth the functional relationship between SP and the fundamental variables it depends on, we can analyse the possible factors that are relevant to design and management when approaching innovation.

The following normative considerations[7] can be set forth, in a synthesized form, from the central problem examined in this chapter:

- Science policy should be approached in a manner which is entirely autonomous and independent of UII, taking the sole objective of promoting knowledge as a value within itself. Automatic regulation mechanisms (markets, quasi-markets, chance...) will cause this knowledge to transcend to society as a whole or not. The criteria of the scientific community are the ones which generate rationality in decision making.
- While science policy must be related to innovation, specifically through UII, it should not be mixed with innovation policy as these issues are considered to be independent for purposes of long term coordination. In practice, the latter coincides with the former in many aspects.
- Science policy must intervene in innovation to a greater extent than mere long term coordination with innovation policy. Therefore, its design and management should put forth effective action for adequate UII. In this case, the criteria are more blurred and cannot simply respond to one environment or be inflexible or closed. In contrast, they would be part of a whole which would include Public Administration, university and industry (triple helix model)[8].

These normative positions take shape through a set of design and management factors for science policy. A linear relationship can be set up between each normative position and a subset of design and management factors.

These factors include the variables specified in the expression (5), above all and very explicitly in the case of the third normative position.

Thus, we can express this relationship between SP and design and management factors in the following manner, as it is shown in table-2.

[7] We shall not explicitly consider the normative choices on science policy orientating research or understanding it freely to give this chapter a wider focus. This is also the case for basic and applied percentages looking to foster (although with the new scientific-technological paradigm, this division has been overcome) how much effort to devote to science and big science. However, it is clear that they are all implicitly included.

[8] See Etzkowitz and Leydesdorff (1996).

Table 2. Relationship Between Science Policy and Design and Management Factors

Normative considerations	Factors
Science policy should not be considered completely independent of UII	Moral hazard and adverse selection with the university, participation of the university group obliged through a number of design and management mechanisms (Science Boards, Science and Technology Committees, Evaluation Commissions...) Dominant input indicator. Solely endogenous output (publications in prestigious journals, nº. of PhDs, nº. of projects) Dominance of the Professionals Bureaucracies. Short term execution.
While science policy should be related to innovation, specifically from UII, it should not be mixed with innovation policy.	The same factors as in the previous situation, jointly with more coordination mechanisms with innovation policy (basically of an institutional nature, interdepartmental commissions for government….) Short term execution.
Science policy should be connected to UII in order to foster business innovation.	Moral hazard and adverse selection with the university although attenuated by the influence of business and participation of the university group. This is also the case for the business sector, in this instance attenuated by the influence of the university group. Emphasis on incentivating university students to achieve proper UII, interest from PA and business in the organisative structure and means of the university for innovative UII. (Quality of the ILOs,…).Broad participation of all the sectors involved, coordination necessary from the administration, based on the involvement of many different departments. Decision making and long term management. Output indicators (patents and licences, spin-offs…) Triple helix. Positive consideration of the innovation system and grouping in clusters. Longer term execution.

In agreement with the purpose for analysis of the latter, science policy in connection with the UII in order to foster business innovation, which is the most interesting one. From this perspective we can look into some of the conditions needed for a science policy-UII connection:

- Science policy linked to UII for innovation. This can be considered necessary in today's competitive context and with the new scientific-technological paradigm.
- This science policy centered on universities should also consider participation of the university science group to be necessary, starting from the double direction Public Administration-university (governance) and university-Public Administration (stakeholders).

- The business sector must also be considered in this same double direction.
- The triple helix relationship is developed, in which it is necessary to clearly and concisely set down the incentives that guide scientific work towards innovative UII.
- The university must be incentivated to set up UII means for effective innovation, which will be a positive indicator for firms.

An approach which should certainly consider the complexity of the issue and therefore cannot overlook the systemic and grouping vision of the different agents taking part in the process.

For this reason, it is important to also consider what cluster policy is like.

4. Science-Based Cluster Policies Become More Systemic

Is it innovation that fosters the creation and development of clusters? Or, in contrast, is it the makeup of clusters that fosters innovation? The key to clusters lies in the coordination of industries that are located on a common economic mesolevel. These firms must collaborate with agents outside the cluster nucleus.Furthermore, those firms are rooted in a specific institutional framework. Thus, creating innovation outside the natural environment where the cluster is located cannot be considered. Nowadays, there is broad consensus on the influence of clusters on economic growth and that the learning dynamics which go with innovation are related to the evolution of clusters.

The most advanced clusters (like bios) have a wide variety of external connections. These relationships are necessary to renovate base knowledge so they must be well connected, above all, to research organizations (Rosiello and Orsenigo, 2008) Agents sometimes integrate into local networks as a means to later internationalization. Collaboration and the capacity to cooperate with different researchers and agents is often more important than the ability to produce knowledge (Frenken and Van Oort, 2004).

At present, knowledge as a source of wealth, as well as innovation and learning, are viewed from a more regional and cluster perspective than from the national level (Cooke et al. 1997). From the perspective of traditional industrial economics, economies of scale associated with large firms are said to determine the generation of innovation due to their capacity to combine technologies, maintain large organizational structures and make big investments (Lazonick, 1991, Florida and Kenney, 1990). Vertical integration and flexible organizations are also qualities of clusters and are related to innovation.

We can define clusters by reference to (Parto, 2008) as "A cluster is a sectoral and geographical concentration of enterprises. The starting point of the debate on clusters and clustering is that firms not innovate and grow in isolation. They rely extensively on external knowledge sources. Geographic proximity tend to en certain advantages. Geographic agglomeration promotes innovative activities above and beyond locally specific collaborative arrangements focused for research and development. In clusters, the diffusion of innovation is assisted by geographic proximity and a host of locally specific, formal and informal arrangements" (Parto, 2008, p. 1012).

There are two different types of logic for strategies involving clusters; one is top-down which is based above all on government initiatives and the other is bottom-up, based mainly on initiatives from private firms. At present, a combination of both strategies is used for most biosciences clusters everywhere (Fromhold and Elsebith, 2005). In different studies on the evolution of two science based sectors: biotechnologies and nanotechnologies (Gomez Uranga et al., 2007), some of the most representative variables that necessarily go with evolution of these two sectors are chosen. A set of policies to overcome the weaknesses observed in the variables studied should be proposed.

The table -3 shows different reinforcers that can be used to evaluate to what extent any bios or nanos clusters need to be fostered.

Table 3. Reinforcers as responses to weaknesses on bios and nanos

First level reinforcers. Response for quantitative variation	Second level reinforcers, systemic in nature (qualitative changes)
Need to increase innovation (products and processes) Increase the number of bios and nanos firms (start-ups, spin-offs, etc.) Increase the number of patents Allot more resources to research (RandD) Increase financing and attract investors (VC and others) Increase qualifications focused on bios and nanos	Improve culture of collaboration between the different agents Foster multidisciplinary approach in research and education Boost changes in government policy and regulations Carry out legal and regulatory changes Foster learning dynamics and processes (between different agents, following evolutionist models like the Triple Helix) Encourage changes in university and corporate cultures

Source:Gomez Uranga et al.(2007)[9].

Most science-based clusters are distinctive for the high number and rapid growth of start-ups. These organisations are the best prepared to respond to very specific market demands and needs. Management of small firms is potentially more flexible than large ones. The origin of start-ups in the field of biosciences and nanotechnologies has to be linked to research in laboratories and universities. These companies' main function is to commercially exploit research results. In other words, these firms work in the field of exploiting intellectual property rights. Entering the "spin-outs" route is a big challenge for researchers. Many of the SMEs in the sectors mentioned have appeared recently, sometimes registering short life expectancy, but undergoing constant transformation.

In a financially diverse context, funding figures which are better suited to needs appear according to the stage of the business life cycle. Funds for start-ups may mainly come from Business Angels during the first stage. The consolidation stage of start-ups is carried out by the entry of venture capital. These funds will sustain firms until they reach a level in which their survival and feasibility are guaranteed. It is not usually common to reap profits in the non consolidated stage. For this reason, the only way many start-ups can survive is through venture capital investment.

[9] The following section develops some of the features shown in the chart which are more fully explained in the article by Gomez Uranga et al. (2007)

On the European scene (except for the UK), the absence of a culture of venture capital has caused the public sector to carry most of the weight for these types of funding. The uncertainty of these activities is due to the fact that research projects become business projects. In this case, aid comes from local and regional governments. For instance, in Japan, biotechnology start-ups are financed by governments; legal and regulatory changes go with grants, loans and equity financing to start-ups from various government agencies (Lehrer and Asakawa, 2004).

The evolution of universities calls for learning processes in order to function in the world of hiring and litigation concerning licensing, as is shown in the study of the Triple Helix model. In this sense, ILOs (Industry Liaison Offices) devote a great deal of time to developing learning focused on management of licenses and patenting. This is what the author (Owen-Smith, 2003) calls 'experimental learning'. The academics are given the right to that intellectual property. But, on the other hand, utilisation of those scientific products is permitted through licences of commercial application to industry.

The Bayh Dole Act law (1980) was presented in the USA by the federal government. The purpose of this law is to strengthen relations between the university and industry. Its aim is to establish a policy of innovation in the USA, to allow universities to retain the ownership titles of the inventions developed, to provide incentive to universities to collaborate with industry. Although as Mowery, Nelson, Sampat and Ziedonis highlight, firms benefit from academic research through publications, conferences, informal channels of information and consulting, more than through patents (Mowery et al., 2001).

The Nanoforum report (Malsch and Oud, 2004) highlights two main difficulties involved in developing and creating dynamics for start-ups and small firms in the field of nanotechnology: Firstly, lack of highly qualified staff and, secondly, lack of collaboration and cooperation between universities and this type of firms or between research organisations and firms. These difficulties are even considered more important than the financial needs of firms of this type; biotechnology firms must resort to alliances and consortia to make up for or acquire the knowledge they lack internally if they wish to manufacture new products and/or services.

Universities are usually financed through public budgets. The predominant cooperation networks in the EU are mainly between university researchers. However, private sponsors are playing an increasingly greater role in this financing. For instance, participation of industry in basic research is increasing although recently there has been a greater relationship between the different organisations (university, industry, governments) in the field of research.

Collaborations between universities and non-academic organisations is more localised geographically than collaboration between universities (Frenken and Van Oort, 2004). In spite of the relative internationalisation of academic contents, universities are deeply rooted and depend on general and budgetary frameworks which may in some cases be national and in others state (in the U.S.), regional or local. These may sometimes be completely public or have more diversified sources. These general and budgetary financing frameworks also determine their possibilities and, in part, their possible relationships.

Regional and central governments can support universities to strengthen ILOs and thus their capacity to create spin offs. A first example of this is the UK Finance Ministry's participation in promotion of spin offs and spin outs (Benneworth and Charles, 2005; Lokett and Wright, 2005). In Belgium, ISLs also receive public aid from regional government (Debackere and Veugelers, 2005).

The EU supports cluster policy, which comes from three sources:

- From policy, industry and firms. Policy which improves innovation is vital to the development of SMEs. These policies are coherent with the objectives set down in the Lisbon agenda for the European Union, looking to improve competitiveness and develop a knowledge based economy in Europe.
- From policy in the field of RandD, focused on activating regional research driven clusters, fostering the Triple helix type dynamics in different local areas, through use of the one of the main Community tools, the VII Framework Programme.
- From European Union regional policy to support disadvantaged regions through structural funds (OECD, 2007).

Innovation is one of the key points in the OECD study on clusters for a large group of nations which carry out cluster policy, both at the industrial and regional level. Science and technology policies are used by a larger number of regions worldwide when industrial and regional policies pursuing innovation are implemented jointly.

One of the reasons that cluster policy is mainly directed to SMEs is to counteract their costs of searching for information, which are usually high. These policies are also focused on fostering networking. The United States has some very consolidated programmes: Small business innovation research (SBIR) and Small business technology transfer (STTR), centering on innovation.

Clusters programmes show strong connections between science and technology with links between university and business research playing a key role. Spin-offs often arise, mainly in the field of biotechnology. The economic resources devoted to science and technology are increasingly focused on the need to increase innovation. Science sometimes sets down its own priorities which are accepted in decision making on innovation policy. This is mainly centered on a few clusters. Clusters policy also fosters inter-agent collaboration as well as between firms and the relationship between technological and scientific research (OECD, 2007).

As a cluster policy, the European seventh framework programme has been adopted for the period 2007-2013. Among the objectives of this initiative, the following are important: Transnational cooperation; The dynamism, creativity and excellence of European Research at the frontier of knowledge; strengthen human potential in research and technology in Europe; the dialogue between science and society in Europe.

In order to achieve these objectives it is necessary to foster four types of activities: transnational cooperation on policy defined themes (the cooperation programme); investigator driven research based on the initiative of the research community (the ideas programme); support for individual researchers (the people programme); and support for research capacities (the capacities programme).

Under the ideas programme, activities should be implemented by a European Research Council (ERC) to develop high level frontier research at the European level. Under the capacities programme, the use and development of research infrastructures should be optimised, and capacities of SMEs and their ability to benefit from research should be strengthened.

The programme shall support the research activities in the following areas: health, food, agriculture and biotechnologies, ICTs, nano sciences, nano technologies, materials and new production technologies; energy; environment, including climate change; transport and aeronautics, socio economic sciences and humanities; security.

The Commission introduced the concept of Joint Technology Initiatives as a new way of realising public- private partnerships at the European level. The amount shall be distributed among the activities as follows: In EUR million; Cooperation 32413; Ideas 7500; People 4750 Capacities 4097; Non nuclear actions of the joint research 1751.

European Technology Platforms (ETPs) : "Are an effective means of defining research and development priorities, timeframes and action plans on a number of strategically important issues where achievement of Europe's future growth, competitiveness an sustainability objectives is dependent on major research and technological advances in the medium to long term". (CEC, 2005, p.5)

ETPs have been an important input to the identification of the thematic priorities for the Seventh Framework Programme, are in line with the timescale for the FP for 2007-2013. They cover the whole economic value chain, ensuring that knowledge generated through research is transformed into technologies and processes, and ultimately into marketable products and services.

ETPs address technological challenges that can contribute to the key objectives which are essential for Europe's competitiveness, including:

- Timely development and deployment of new technologies that offer the potential of radical change in one or more industrial sectors, for instance, nanomedicine and hydrogen and fuel cells.
- Technology development to meet different policy objectives with a view to sustainable development (i.e., water supply, sanitation and photovoltaics).
- New technology-based public goods services with high entry barriers and uncertain profitability but which offer significant economic potential, i.e., mobile and wireless communications.
- Achieving the necessary technological breakthroughs to remain at the leading edge in high technology sectors that have significant strategic and economic importance, i.e., aeronautics and nanoelectronics.
- Renewal, revival or restructuring of traditional industrial sectors such as steel, textiles and clothing.

CONCLUSION

Innovation policy has evolved over time, jointly with the requirements imposed by international competitiveness. The role played by the different public institutions as well as private agents in this policy is vital as long as all of them are considered a system. They are integrated in mutual interdependence and linked to specific territories. Empirical evidence shows increasing participation from a public initiative, and its important impact in terms of competitive innovation. This participation takes on broad forms of application since it can range from design of a normative framework to direct intervention through investments.

The new scientific-technological paradigm in relation to competitive innovation brings forth the need to link innovation to science and, at the same time, conditions it to the dynamics of social, political and commercial influence.

In this sense, the relationship between innovation policy and science policy increasingly determines competitive innovation. Thus, this science policy must connect with UII and should set up a wide multiple sector network for participation (Public Administration, industry and university).

How networks and policy are made up is also relevant in the scope of competitive innovation. Clusters are determining factors as inter agent "modes of organisation" to achieve this.

Due to its complexity, management of this systemic innovative "whole" is carried out through participative governance formulas and mutual commitment between parties, without overlooking the dynamics of stakeholders and their influence on how the entire system works. Big public institutions are aware of this and a case in point is the EU´s support for clusters policy.

REFERENCES

Ahrens, J. (2000). Governance and Economic Development. A comparative institutional approach. Cheltenham. Edward Elgar.

Akerlof, G.A. (1970). The market of lemons: Qualitative, uncertainly and the market mechanism. *Quaterly Journal of Economics* 89, 488-500.

Asheim, B. (2007). Sistemas regionales de innovación y bases de conocimiento diferenciadas: un marco analítico, in Buesa, M. and Heijs, J. (coord.). Sistemas regionales de innovación: nuevas formas de análisis y medición. Madrid: Fundación de las Cajas de Ahorros.

Barrutia, J. (2001). Algunas condiciones necesarias para la gestión y organización en la universidad. *Cuadernos de Gestión*.1 (2ª época), 13-30.

Barzelay, M. (2001). The New Public Management. California: California Sage Publications.

Beneito, P. (2003). Choosing among Alternative Technological Strategies.An Empirical Analysis of Formalsources of Innovation. *Research P*olicy, vol. 32, 4, 693-713.

Benneworth, P., and Charles, D. (2005). University spin off policies and economic development in less successful regions: Learning from two decades of policy practice. *European Planning Studies*, 13(4), 535-557.

Borg, E. (2001). Knowledege, information and Intellectual Property. Implications for Marketing Relationships. *Technovation,* vol.21, 515-524.

Bruijin (DE) P,and Lergendijk, A. (2005). Regional innovation systems in the Lisbon strategy. *European Planning Studies* Vol 13, 1153-1172.

Caloghirou, Y., Kastelli, I. and,Tsakanikas, A.(2004). Internal Capabilities and External Knowledege Sources. Complements or Substitutes for Innovative Performance. *Technovation*, vol 24, 29-39.

Cassiman, B. and Veugelers, R. (2004). RandD Cooperation and Spillovers : Some Empirical Evidence from Belgium. *The American Economic Review*,vol. 92, 4, 1169-1118.

Castellaci, F., Grodal. S., Mendoca. S, and Wibe, M. (2005). Advances and challenges in innovation studies. *Journal of Economics Issues*. 1, 91-121.

Cimoli, M., Dosi, G., Nelson, R. and Stiglitz, J.(2006). Isntitutions and Policies Sahping Industrial Development : An Introductory Note. LEM Working Paper Series.Sant´Anna School of Advanced Studies, Italy, 2006/02.

Comission of European Communities (2005). Report on European Technology Platforms and point technology Initiatives?. Working Document,Brussels.

Clark, B.R. (1983). The Higher Education System: Academic Organisation in Cross national Perspective. Berkeley: University of California Press.

Clark, B. (1998). Creating Entrepreneurial Universities.Organisational Pathways of transformation. NewYork International Association of Universities and Elsevier Science.

Clemens, B.and Gallagher S, (2003). Stakeholders for Environemental Strategies: The Case of the Emerging Industry in Radioactive Scrap Metal Treament, in J. Andriof, S Waddock, B. Husted. and, S. Rahman (ed): Unfolding Stakeholder Thinking 2, Greenleaf; Sheffield, UK, 128-144.

Criado, J. I. and Ramilo, M.C. (2003). De la Administración Pública electrónica a la Administración Pública Relacional, en Joan Costa i Quim Gil.(Coor.). Comunicaciones grupo 8 Democracia y Participación Ciudadana en la Sociedad interconectada. 1er Congreso On Line del Observatorio para la Ciber sociedad. Available at cibersociedad.rediris.es/congreso.

Cooke, P., Uranga, M. andEtxebarria, G. (1997). Regional innovation systems: Institutional and organisational dimensions. *Research Policy*, 26, 475-491.

Daake, D. and William, P. (2000). Understanding Stakeholder Power and Influence Gaps in a Health Care Organization: An Empirical Study. *Health Care Management Rev*, vol. 25, 3, 94-107.

Debackere, K. and Veugelers, R. (2005). The Role of Academic technology transfer organizations improving industry science links. *Research policy*, 34, 321-342.

Etzkowitz, H. and Leydesdorff, L. (1996). Emergence of a Triple Helix of University-Industry-Government Relations. *Science and Public Policy*, vol. 23, 279-286.

Flavián, C. and Lozano, F. J. (2004). La orientación al mercado de la universidad pública: un reto para el sistema universitario español. *Revista Internacional de Marketing Público y No Lucrativo*, vol.1, 2, 9-28.

Florida, R. and Kenney, M.(1990) The breakthrough illusion. New York: New York Basic. Books.

Fromhold-Eisebeth, M. and Eisebeth, G. (2005). How to institutionalize innovate clusters? Comparing explicit top-down and implicit bottom-up approaches, *Research Policy*, vol 34, 8, 1250-1268.

Frenken, K. and, Van Oort, F. G. (2004). The geography of research collaboration: Theoretical considerations and stylized facts in biotechnology in Europe and the United States, in P. Cooke and A. Piccaluga (Eds) Regional Economics as Knowledge Laboratories, (pp. 38-57),Cheltenham: Edward Elgar.

Gomez Uranga M., Etxebarria G. and Campás, J. (2007). The Dynamics of Commercialization of Scientific Knowledge in Biotechnology and Nanotechnology. *European Planning Studies*, 15.9, 1199-1214.

Helfat, C.E. (1997). Know-How and Asset Complementary and Dynamic Capability Accumulation: The case of RandD. Strategic Management Review, vol.18,.5 , 339-360.

Holmström, B. (1982). Moral Hazard in teams. *Bell Journal of Economics*, 13, 324-340.

Jensen, M.C. and, Meckling, W.H.(1976). Theory of Firm: management Behavior, Agency Cost and Ownerships structure. *Journal of Financial Economics*, vol 3, 4, 305-360.

Jensen, M.B., Johnson, B., Lorenz E., and Lundvall B.A. (2007). Forms of knowledge and modes of innovation. *Research Policy*, vol.36, n5, 680-693.

Jessop, B. (2001). Institutional re(turns) and the strategic-relational approach. Environment and Planning, nº33, 1213-1235.

Jongbloed, B.W and Koelman, J.J (2000). Vouchers for higher education? A survey of the literature. Study commissioned by the Hong Kong University Grants Committee. Ensechede: Cheps.

Laranja, M.,Uyarra, E. and Flanagan, K (2008). Policies for Science, technology and innovation: translating rationales into regional policies in a multi-level setting. *Research policy*, vol.37, 5, .823-835.

Lazonick, W. (1991). Business organisation and the myth of the market economy. Cambridge. Cambridge University Press.

Lehrer, M. and Asakawa, K. (2004). Rethinking the public sector: Idiosyncrasies of bioltechnology commercialisation as motor of national RandD reform in Germany and Japan. *Research Policy* 33, 921-938.

Lokett, A. and Wright, M. (2005). Resources capabilities,risk capital and the creation of university spin out companies. *Research Policy*, 34, 1043-1057.

London Communiqué (2007). Towards the European Higher education Area: responding to challenges in a global world. London, 18.

Malsch, I. and Oud, M. (2004). Outcome of the open consultation on the European satrategy for nanotechnology,December.Nanoforum.org European Nanotechnology Gateway. Available at http://www.nanoforum.or Accessed March.

Marzo, M., Pedraja, M. and Rivera, P. (2008). Un modelo de relaciones empresa-universidad. *Revista Europea de Dirección y Economía de la Empresa*, vol 17, 1, 39-56.

Michavila, F. and Calvo, B. (2000). La Universidad española hacia Europa. Madrid: Fundación Alfonso Martin Escudero.

Mintzberg, H. (1984). The structuring of organizations. Englewood Cliffs, NJ: Prentice-Hall.

Mintzberg, H and Rose, J. (2003). Strategic Management Upside Down: Tracking Strategies at McGill University from 1829 to 1980. *Canadian Journal of Administrative Sciences*, 20/4, 270-290.

Mitchell, R., Agle, B.and Wood, D. (1997). Toward a Theory Stakeholder Identification and Salience: Defining the Principle of who and what Really Counts. *Academy of Management Review*, vol.22, 4, 856-886.

Mitchell, R. and, Agle, B. (1997). Stakeholder Identification and Salience: Dialogue and Operationalization. *Proceedings at International Association for Business and Society*, 365-370.

Mook, J. and Lo, E. (2002). Marketisation and the changing Governance in Higher Education: a comparative study. *Higher Education Management Policy*, 14, 1, 51-82.

Mowery, D., Nelson, E., Sampat, B.and Ziedonis, A (2001) The growth of patenting and licensing by U.S. universities. *Research Policy*, 30 (1), 99-119.

Mowery, D. C. (2005). The Bayh-Dole Act and High-Technology Entrepreneurship in USA Universities: Chicken, Egg, Or something Else? In: Gary Liebcap (ed.). University Entrepreneurship and Technology Transfers (pp. 38-68). Amsterdam: Elsevier.

OECD (2007): Competitive of Regional Clusters. National Policy Approaches. OECD Reviews of regional Innovation.

Nelson., R.(1987). Roles of Government in a Mixed Economy. *Journal of Policy Analysis Management* 6, 540-557.

Okubo, Y. and Sjoberg, C. (2000). The Changing Pattern of Industrial Scientific Research Collaboration in Sweden, *Research Policy*, vol.29, num 1, 81-98.

Owen –Smith, J. (2003). From separate systems to a hybrid order: Accumulative advantage across public and private science at Research One universities. *Research Policy*, 32, 1081-1104.

Parto, S. (2008). Innovation and economic activity: An institutional analysis of the role of clusters in industrializing economies. *Journal of Economics Issues*.r 4, 1005-1030.

Pollit, CH. and Bouckaert, G. (1999). Public Management reform: a comparative analysis. New York: Oxford University Press.

Powel, W.W, Koput, K.W. and Doers, L.S. (1996). Interorganisational collaboration and the locus of innovation networks of learning in biotech. *Administrative Science Quaterly* 41, 116-145.

Rosello, A. and Orsenigo, l. (2008). A critical assessment of regional innovation policy in pharmaceutical biotechnology. *European Planning Studies*, vol 16,3, 337-357.

Shane, S. (2002). Selling University Technology:Patterns from MIT. *Management Science*, 48, 122-137.

Sheen, D.(1992). Barriers to scientific and technical knowledge acquisition in industrial RandD. *RandD Management*, 22, 135-143.

Shiles, D. (2002). Higher Education Funding Council HEFC9 Methods in the 1990s: National and Regional Developments and Policy implications. *Public Administration*, 8014, 711-731.

Swyngedow, E. (2005). Governance innovation and the citizen: the Janus face of governance-beyond-the-state. *Urban Studies*, vol.42, 11, 1991-2007.

Van der Wende, M.C. (2000). The Bologna Declaration: enhancing the transparency and competitiveness of European higher education. *Higher Education in Europe*, 25, 3, 305-310.

Vence Deza, X. (Ed) (2007). Crecimiento y Políticas de Innovación, nuevas tendencias, experiencias comparadas. Madrid: Pirámide.

Zahra, S. and George, G.(2002). Absorptive Capacity:A Review, Reconceptualization,and Extension. *Academy of Management Review*, vol. 27, 2,185-203.

In: International Political Economy
Editors: M.A. Galindo Martin, E. Nissan

ISBN: 978-1-60876-172-2

Chapter 11

CAN REGULATIONS INDUCE ENVIRONMENTAL INNOVATIONS?

Oscar Alfranca
Department of Agrifood and Biotechnology
ESAB
Av. Canal Olímpic, s/n
08860 Castelldefels
Spain
Email: oscar.alfranca@upc.edu

ABSTRACT

Sometimes environmental problems can become a business opportunity for certain companies, and more specifically, for those we can refer to as the ecoindustry. In this paper, a discussion is introduced on firms which, in their search for better environmental performance, are led to develop research activities in the area of pollution-control technologies, in order to optimize their waste management processes. This can lead to technological breakthroughs that eventually can be attractive for others. Companies adopting such a strategy could also enjoy an advantage, and even lobby governments for harder regulations.

Empirical analysis in the paper indicates that, at the mean, an increase in CO_2 emissions will present a positive effect on high technology exports. The hypothesis that improvements in water quality induce positive effects on high technology exports is rejected. Instead, a negative, although fairly small, elasticity at the mean has been estimated. The negative sign of the interaction term in the econometric model indicates that improvements in water quality and CO_2 emissions can be considered to be substitutes, rather than complements, in the high technology exports process.

1. Introduction

In this work we will discuss whether regulations can induce environmental innovations, which incentives drive process innovations, and how regulations can be designed to provide or strengthen those incentives. In this paper, processes and mechanisms through which regulations may affect incentives and the potential to induce innovations are discussed.

The hypothesis that environmental protection costs are associated with additional costs imposed by the government relies on the basic assumption that markets work well to reach an optimal use of scarce resources. Therefore, government intervention is only useful to redistribute revenues, whenever markets are not fulfilling their role properly. This is what might happen with the environment.

One of the prerequisites for the adequate functioning of markets is the existence of well-defined property rights. In the case of some environmental goods such as air or water, these rights are very difficult to assign, because frequently they can be used by agents at very low cost, whereas the social cost is certainly greater. This could cause polluters to receive the wrong signal and, given that it is possible to use these resources without paying the real price, they would be encouraged to do so in excess. The main consequence is that the market generates too much pollution if we compare it with the optimal social level.

Nevertheless, sometimes solving environmental problems becomes a business opportunity for some companies, and more specifically, for those we can refer to as the ecoindustry. In this paper, a discussion is introduced on firms which, in their search for better environmental performance, are led to develop research activities in the area of pollution-control technologies, in order to optimize their waste management processes. This can lead to technological breakthroughs that eventually can be attractive for others. Companies adopting such a strategy could also enjoy an advantage, and even lobby governments for harder regulations.

Given the growing importance of environmental issues in public policy, the challenging and controversial nature of the Porter Hypothesis (PH), and the mitigated nature of the empirical results obtained thus far, assessment of the hypotheses remains an open research question.

Porter argues that pollution is often associated with a waste of resources (material or energy, among others), and that more stringent environmental policies can stimulate innovations that may compensate for the costs of complying with these policies. In fact, there are many ways through which improving the environmental performance of a company can lead to a better economic or financial performance, and not necessarily to an increase in cost.

Porter has suggested that pollution is generally associated with resources misuse, with raw efficiency, or with energy losses. Therefore, pollution involves economic waste and unnecessary or incomplete exploitation of resources. Reducing pollution is often coincident with productivity improvements (Porter and van der Linde, 1995). From this, more stringent and flexible environmental policies (for instance taxes and tradable permits) would be fruitful for the economy, stimulating innovations that compensate for the costs which are associated with these policies. This implies that reducing pollution could generate a reduction of expenditures in resources, energy or services.

In fact, there are many ways through which improving the environmental performance of a company can lead to a better economic or financial performance, without cost increases. For instance, improvements in environmental performance can lead to an increase in revenues through the following channels: Improvements in the possibility to participate in certain markets; Opportunities to differentiate products; and the Possibility to sell pollution-control technology. On the other side, improvements in environmental performance could also guide the next cost reduction policies: Regulatory cost, Cost of material, Energy and services, Cost of capital, and Cost of labour.

Some examples exist about firms which try to improve the environmental aspects of their supply chain. Presumably, all plants with the ISO 14001 certification pay attention to the environmental performance of their suppliers since this is one of the criteria to be fulfilled in order to obtain the certification (Barla, 2005; Hess et al., 1999). Furthermore, a recent survey of the OECD, with a sample of more than 4000 facilities in seven countries, indicates that 43% of them assess the environmental performance of their suppliers (Johnstone et al., 2007).

In the economic literature, a better environmental performance is considered to be a high quality characteristic of a product (Cremer and Thisse, 1999; Bansal and Gangopadhyay, 2003). This relies on the assumption that environmentally aware consumers are willing to pay more for cleaner products. As a result, a market powered firm might find it profitable to provide a green category of this product at a higher price, or to specialize in green products.

However, environmental performance might be hard to be perceived by consumers. When a firm keeps this performance private, it can be signalled through a higher price, whenever greener products are also more costly to be produced (Mahenc, 2007). Asymmetric information on the greenest products might lead to a lemon-type market failure, which can be reduced through eco-labelling. The "lemon problem" arises when the buyers do not know the quality of the good, and then the purchase price is independent of the actual quality (Tirole, 1989).

In the economic literature, the PH has been criticized for its lack of theoretical foundation (Palmer et al., 1995). Profit maximizing firms should not ignore profitable investments in innovation, being regulated or not, in an economy with perfect markets. Recent papers have provided foundations to the PH by introducing a market failure (in addition to the one due to pollution). The environmental regulation, which is devoted to solve the pollution market failure, turns out to mitigate the other market failure to the benefit of regulated firms. Examples of such market failures include spillovers in knowledge, learning-by-doing, asymmetric information within firms, market power or specific investments with contractual incompleteness.

In this scenario, two main research lines can be distinguished to analyse the relevance of regulation to explain competitiveness:

a. The impact of environmental regulations on a firm's innovation policy and technological choice is measured by investment in R&D, capital and new technologies, and in successful patent applications.

The main objective of these studies is the test of the first premise of the Porter Hypothesis that more stringent environmental regulations could enhance innovation. Hence, more innovation is a necessary but not sufficient condition for the PH. Jaffe and Palmer (1997) estimate the relationship between total R&D expenditures (or the number of successful patent applications) and pollution abatement costs (a proxy for the stringency of environmental regulation). They found a positive link with R&D expenditures (an increase of 0.15% in R&D

expenditures for a pollution abatement cost increase of 1%), but no statistically significant link with the number of patents. Restricting themselves to environmentally-related successful patents, Brunnermeier and Cohen (2003) found a positive but small relationship with environmental regulation.

Both studies suggest a weak but positive link between a better environmental performance (through better compliance with regulation) and the firm's innovation policy. Most papers reviewed in Jaffe et al. (1995) highlight a negative impact of environmental regulation on productivity. For instance, Gollop and Robert (1983) estimated that SO_2 regulations slowed down productivity growth in the U.S by 43%, during the seventies. More recent papers find more positive results, such as Berman and Bui (2001), which report that refineries located in the Los Angeles area enjoyed a significantly higher productivity than other U.S. refineries, despite a more stringent air pollution regulation in this area. Similarly, Alpay et al. (2002) estimated the productivity of the Mexican food processing industry to be increasing with the pressure of environmental regulation. They therefore suggest that a more stringent regulation is not always detrimental to productivity. Although the mentioned studies tend to reject the Porter Hypothesis, one cannot conclude that being green harms the firm.

b. The impact of environmental regulation is estimated with variables such as productivity and costs.

The main aim of these studies is to test whether more stringent environmental policies can be beneficial to the firm. Nevertheless, these papers are silent on the process that leads to higher productivity. Porter argues that more stringent environmental policies will lead to innovations to reduce inefficiencies and this, in turn, will eventually reduce costs. This process may take some time. Some examples can be found of companies which have reduced their pollution and costs at the same time, such as British Petroleum which reduced its CO_2 emissions to 10% below their level prevailing in 1990 at no cost through an optimization of the production process, elimination of leakages or reuse of wastes (Reinhardt, 2001).

2. Environmental Organization Innovations and the Porter Hypothesis

Environmental modernization of the firm involves the implementation of management activities with the objective of reducing environmental impacts. These environmental organizational innovations enhance the firms' technological opportunities and can contribute to technical environmental innovations. Environmental organizational measures may come from environmental regulatory compliance or voluntary environmental organizational measures such as the adoption of Environmental Management Systems and other non-mandatory approaches.

A number of studies have analyzed the determinants of environmental expenditures on innovation activities (see, for example, Jaffe and Palmer, 1997, and Pickman, 1998), although the effect of voluntary environmental managerial measures on a firm's innovation activities has not been studied until recently. In general, evidence accumulated in these studies supports the idea that voluntary organizational measures carried out at firm-level present a positive impact both on product and process innovations (Rennings et al., 2006; Rehfeld et al., 2007).

Regarding firm innovations, the Porter Hypothesis is controversial. Empirical evidence relies on a small number of company case studies, in which firms are able to reduce both their pollution emissions and their production costs. As such, it can hardly be generalized to the entire population of firms.

Ambec and Barla (2005) argue that, analytically speaking, for the Porter Hypothesis to be valid, at least one market imperfection is required in addition to the environmental externality. Examples of such market failures include spillovers in knowledge (Jaffe et al., 2004) or in learning-by-doing (Mohr, 2002), or market power (Simpson and Bradford, 1996, Greaker, 2003). Alternatively, they may arise out of systemic organisational failures within the firm, such as contractual incompleteness (Ambec and Barla, 2005), asymmetric information (Ambec and Barla, 2002), and agency control problems (Gabel and Sinclair-Desgagnc 2002).

Jaffe and Palmer (1997) present three different specifications for the PH. Under this framework, the "weak" version of the hypothesis is that environmental regulation will stimulate certain kinds of environmental innovations, although there is no claim that the direction or rate of this increased innovation is socially beneficial. The "narrow" version of the hypothesis asserts that flexible environmental policy instruments such as pollution charges or tradable permits give firms greater incentive to innovate than prescriptive regulations, such as technology-based standards. Finally, the main hypothesis of the "strong" version is that properly designed regulations may induce innovation that could more than compensate for the cost of compliance. While many researchers have tested different versions of the Porter Hypothesis empirically, the studies are often partial and the results ambiguous.

Through a systematic examination of all the possibilities, we also want to identify the circumstances most likely to lead to a "win-win" situation, i.e., better environmental and financial performance to control pollution and reduce it to a tolerable threshold. To this effect, the government has at its disposal a panoply of instruments such as regulation, taxation or pollution permits', which may result in the polluters receiving the right signal, once confronted with the true cost of their actions. In short, from this perspective, consideration of the environment is necessarily associated with a cost increase for companies that have used environmental resources with impunity.

3. Technology and Regulation

Regulations can create a barrier to incorporate particular technologies in either products or production processes. An example could be the use of antifungal chemical crystal violet in farmed salmon, by the Chilean salmon industry (Perlman, 2007). The EU has banned the import of Chilean Salmon because of fear that this chemical substance is dangerous and may cause health problems to those who ingest them. This regulation however is controversial, because in Chile, there is no public official information about either the total volume and the kind of chemicals used by the salmon industry.

Regulations can also create barriers for expansion and growth within particular regions or for specific product lines. In some cases, the regulation creates technology-specific barriers to expansion. For instance emission limits. Regulations can also demand the development of entirely new products or processes, in order to substitute existing products and processes. Differences in institutionalizing regulatory regimes that affect the mechanisms are also likely to affect the kind and degree of incentives that arise.

Regulations can clearly induce positive innovation effects when they have created entirely new markets for pollution control. For instance, a combination of regulations that specify particular product qualities restricting the use of certain production factors, and regulations that could create barriers for expansion and growth within particular regions or for particular product lines.

Understanding the possibilities of promoting innovations through regulations is interesting for the interplay between corporate strategy formation, through opportunity recognition and selection on the one hand and, on the other, public environmental regulations. The basic, strategic, innovation-related reactions of firms to regulations include the following (Foster, Hilden and Adler, 2006):

a) Compliance through acquiring new technologies for pollution control. For instance, the installation of end of pipe technology. According to the US Environmental Protection Agency, end of pipe technologies are those that reduce emissions of pollutants after they have been formed. When these technologies are developed, then a certain demand for innovations among suppliers might be induced in this field. The compliance enhances diffusion, but could also provide incentives for innovations and R&D spending.
b) Technological and management research activities in order to redesign production processes to reduce such needs. For instance, reuse of waste products in the production process. This strategic reaction creates demands for innovations or in providers of production technology.
c) Closure or outsourcing of regulated products or production phases. As far as technology is concerned, outsourcing can be defined as a process in which a company delegates some of its in-house operations/process to a third party. An example is the withdrawal from particular markets. Outsourcing can, in some cases, be seen as a form of organizational innovation. In this case, technological innovations may arise in outsourced units.
d) Specific organizational innovation. By setting up joint ventures, (a joint venture is an entity formed between two or more parties to undertake economic activity together), and other similar organization structures a firm could be able to change its regulatory environment in such a way that liabilities are reduced, or that differences in regulatory regimes can be used. For instance, rules that apply to power plants may be partially different from those related to energy generation within a producing industry.
e) Active promotion of particular regulatory interventions in order to gain competitive advantage from the firm's own innovations. An example is the promotion of product standards for which the firm has already developed technology.
f) Active scanning of likely future regulatory interventions to gain competitive advantage, or innovative exploration of possibilities offered by existing regulations. For instance, these actions could induce the developing of technological solutions that clearly outperform existing regulatory demands.

4. REGULATORY REGIMES AND INSTITUTIONS

Differences in institutionalizing regulatory regimes that have an effect on the mechanisms are also likely to concern the kind and degree of incentives that could arise. Regulations can clearly present positive innovation effects when they create entirely new markets for pollution control. An example would be combinations of regulations that specify product qualities and barriers for particular product lines.

There are links between regulations and process innovations in industry, but they are not usually straightforward. The key incentives are those that clearly relate to business strategies and products.

This also means that the evaluation of regulations aiming at fostering process innovations must take into account the societal context and business environment, including the existence of pressure groups that exert their influence through the products and markets rather than through direct demands at the level of permit conditions for individual plants. The combined effects of the differences in the markets, business strategies and the regulatory policies are capable of explaining the slower progress in the environmental performance of industry plants in countries with weaker regulations than others.

5. EMPIRICAL EVIDENCE

5.1. Data sources and Variables

The econometric model of high-tech exports incorporates variables representing the effect of forest area, water quality, CO_2 emissions, life expectancy and technological exports. These are the main variables' definitions and sources:

Dependent variable:

- techexp: Commercial transactions related to international technology and know-how transfers. It consists of money paid or received for the use of patents, licences, know-how, trademarks, patterns, designs, technical services (including technical assistance) and for industrial research and development (R&D) carried out abroad, etc. The coverage may vary from country to country and the TBP data should be considered as only partial measures of international technology flows. Source: Basic Science and Technology Statistics, OECD, Paris.

Explaining variables:

- life: Life expectancy at birth and ages 40, 60, 65 and 80 is the average number of years that a person at that age can be expected to live, assuming that age-specific mortality levels remain constant.

Source: OECD Health Data. Statistics and Indicators for 30 Countries, OECD, Paris.

- water: Water quality index. It is a weighted average of selected ambient concentrations of pollutants usually linked to water quality classes.

Source: Glossary of Environment Statistics, United Nations, New York.

- forest: Land with tree crown cover (or equivalent stocking level) of more than 10 per cent and an area of more than 0.5 hectares. The trees should be able to reach a minimum height of 5 metres at maturity in situ.

Source: United Nations, European Commission, International Monetary Fund, Organisation for Economic Co-operation and Development, World Bank. Handbook of National Accounting: Integrated Environmental and Economic Accounting. Glossary, United Nations, New York.

- CO_2: It is a colourless, odourless and non-poisonous gas formed by combustion of carbon and in the respiration of living organisms and is considered a greenhouse gas. Emissions means the release of greenhouse gases and/or their precursors into the atmosphere over a specified area and period of time.

Source: United Nations. United Nations Framework Convention on Climate Change (A/AC.237/18 (Part II)/Add.1 and Corr.1). Opened for signature at Rio de Janeiro on 4 June 1992. (Section C). United Nations, New York.

- trend: Time trend.

In order to back up an intuition about the relevance of the variables used in the econometric model, the values for some descriptive statistics, such as mean, standard deviation, bias coefficient, Kurtosis coefficient, and the Jarque Bera statistic, among others, have been calculated and are included in Table 1.

Table 1. Descriptive statistics

	techexp	Forest	Life	water	CO_2
Mean	13.84615	84111.40	99.76374	67.97802	9.434066
Median	13.00000	37760.00	100.0000	76.00000	9.000000
Maximum	35.00000	275280.0	100.0000	778.0000	30.00000
Minimum	3.000000	860.0000	96.00000	7.000000	1.000000
Std. Dev.	6.994170	86915.50	0.890231	44.77541	4.703734
Skewness	0.775804	0.893426	-3.743073	10.64030	2.047879
Kurtosis	2.963285	2.586459	15.41941	175.1609	7.813670
Jarque-Bera	36.53404	51.01848	3189.308	456398.9	605.8577
Probability	0.000000	0.000000	0.000000	0.000000	0.000000
Sum	5040.000	30616550	36314.00	24744.00	3434.000
Sum Sq. Dev.	17757.38	2.74E+12	287.6813	727755.8	8031.418
Observations	364	364	364	364	364
Cross sections	13	13	13	13	13

Regarding the skewness of variables, the asymmetry of the probability distribution mainly affects the water quality index sources. As for the Kurtosis value, a high kurtosis value means that the variance is mainly determined by infrequent extreme deviations, as opposed to frequent modestly-sized deviations. Water quality shows the highest value for the Kurtosis coefficient. The Jarque-Bera test is a goodness of fit measurement of departure from normality and it is based on the sample kurtosis and skewness values. This coefficient was calculated for each of the different variables, and, in all the cases, the normally distributed error hypothesis was clearly rejected.

5.2. The Econometric Model. Results and Discussion

We have specified an econometric model of annual high-tech exports and fitted to panel data consisting of thirteen European Union countries, (Austria, Belgium, Denmark, Finland, France, Germany, Holland, Luxembourg, Italy, Portugal, Spain, Sweden and the United Kingdom), over the 1980-2007 period.

The econometric high tech exports equation is:

$$techexp = Constant + \beta_1 life_{it-5} + \beta_2 water_{it-3} + \beta_3 forest_{it-7} + \beta_4 co2_{it-10} +$$
$$\beta_5(water_{it-3} * co2_{it-10}) + \beta_6 trend_{it} + \mu_{it}, (1)$$
$$and:$$
$$E(\mu_{it}) = 0, E(\mu^2{}_{it}) = \sigma_i^2, E(\mu_{it} * \mu_{qt}) = \sigma_{iq}^2$$

where *techexp* is for high technology exports, *life* is for life expectancy, with a lag of five periods, *water* is for a water quality index with a lag of three periods, *forest* is for forest area (in square km), with a lag of seven periods, *co2* is for emissions, with a lag of ten periods, and μ is a random disturbance term representing the effects of omitted variables that are peculiar both to a country (*i*) and time period (t). It has zero mean, constant variance over time and non-zero contemporaneous correlation across countries.

Now we turn to a formal statement of hypotheses about the annual high technology exports relationship. We expect $\beta_1 > 0$, or progresses in life expectancy present a positive influence on technology exports. We expect $\beta_2 > 0$, or an improvement in water quality increases technology exports. An increase in the forest area (β_3) and reductions in CO_2 emissions (β_4) are expected to increase technological exports as well. Effects deriving from interaction between water quality and CO_2 emissions (β_5) are expected to be negative. The existence of a positive tendency (β_6) towards the increase of innovations has also been tested. The constant terms represent time invariant but unspecified factors that affect economic growth rates (e.g.: climatic conditions).

Estimation results can be found in table 2. Equations are fitted by Zellner Seemingly Related Regression, and are estimated by pooling the observations between the 1990-2007 period for the thirteen European countries in the sample.

Overall, the fitted model performs well. All coefficients are different from zero at the 5 percent significance level. The value of the t-tests indicates the hypothesis that environmental and social variables in high technology exports have no explanatory power (i.e., all coefficients are zero) can be rejected.

The hypothesis that effects of CO_2 emissions and water quality do not interact cannot be accepted, (Table 2), and a negative interaction is expected between the two variables. General effects from an increase in CO_2 emissions on high technology exports are more clearly seen from the value of the elasticity at the mean, which is 0.176%. This value indicates that, at the mean, an increase in CO_2 emissions will have a positive although moderate effect on high technology exports. The hypothesis that improvements in water quality induce positive effects on high technology exports is rejected. Instead, a negative, although fairly small elasticity at the mean (-0.0262%) has been estimated. The negative sign of the interaction term indicates that improvements in water quality and CO_2 emissions can be considered to be substitutes, rather than complements in the high technology exports process.

General effects from an increase in CO_2 emissions on high technology exports are more clearly seen from the value of the elasticity at the mean, which is 0.176. and in forest area induces positive effects on high technology exports is clearly accepted in all cases. From this, increases in CO_2 emissions induces positive effects on technology, but improvements in the environmental condition of water seem to induce a small, but negative effect on high technology exports.

It is important to point out that improvements in environmental variables such as water quality and forest area present in all cases, negative effects on high technology exports. Which could indicate that technology production for some environmental issues, can be more intensely induced with negative changes in environmental conditions, rather than by environmental improvements.

Improvements in life expectancy present a clear positive effect on high technology exports. This result could be accepted to be a proxy for a common interest on health improvements, which could be very similar to a luxury good (increasing high income increases). The sample values of the F statistic and the Chi-square tests soundly reject the null hypothesis that there are no interaction effects on growth between CO_2 emissions and water quality improvements. The Wald tests calculated in order to test the significance of the interaction term between CO_2 emissions and water quality improvements clearly reject the hypothesis of no significance. Positive Fixed effects coefficient in the model are for countries such as France, Finland, Greece, the Netherlands, Sweden and the United Kingdom. The range of values goes from Greece (1.37) to Sweden (17.032).

Negative fixed effects have been estimated for the rest of countries in the sample: Austria, Belgium, Denmark, Italy, Luxembourg, Portugal, and Spain. The minimum value is for Belgium (-14.793) and the highest is for Spain (-3.242).

Table 2. Econometric results. Determinants for High Technology Exports.

Dependent Variable: techexp

Variable	Coefficient	Std. Error	t-Statistic	Prob.
Constant	-29.32	9.601	-3.053	0.0025
Forest (-7)	-7.96	2.67E-05	-2.982	0.0032
Life (-5)	0.409	0.092	4.404	0.0000
Water (-3)	0.0396	0.00514	7.701	0.0000
CO2(-10)	0.658	0.0671	9.808	0.0000
TREND	0.322	0.00908	35.556	0.0000
Water(-3)*CO2(-10)	-0.00703	0.000839	-8.383	0.0000
Fixed Effects				
Austria	-6.681		-3.874	
Belgium	-1.479		-4.832	
Denmark	-4.070		-3.669	
Finland	1.434		-1.229	
France	1.021		-1.843	
Germany	1.372		-2.836	
Italy	-7.138		-3.768	
Luxembourg	-9.067		-4.272	
Netherlands	5.303		-2.626	
Portugal	-1.126		-4.527	
Spain	-3.242		-3.174	
Sweden	1.703		-0.989	
United Kingdom	7.979		-2.317	
R-squared	0.976	Mean dependent variable		7.974
Adjusted R-squared	0.975	S.D. dependent variable		1.856
S.E. of regression	1.013	Sum squared residuals		2.207
F-statistic	5.067	Durbin-Watson stat		1.798

CONCLUSION

The main conclusion in this paper is that some links can be established between regulations and the innovation process in industry, but that this relationship is not at all straightforward. Rather, the key incentives for companies affected by public environmental regulations are those that clearly relate to business strategies and products. This also means that the evaluation of regulations aiming at fostering process innovations must take into account the societal context and business environment, including the existence of pressure groups that exert their influence through the products and markets rather than through direct demands at the level of permit conditions for individual plants. The combined effects of differences in markets, business strategies and regulatory policies could be considered to be another tool that could help to explain the slow progress in environmental performance of industry plants in countries with weaker regulations.

REFERENCES

Alpay, E., Buccola, S. and Kerkvliet, J. (2002). Productivity growth and environmental regulation in Mexican and U. S. food manufacturing. *American Journal of Agricultural Economics*, 84, 4, 887-901.

Ambec, S. and Barla, P. (2002). A theoretical foundation of the Porter Hypothesis. *Economics Letters,* 75, 355-360.

Ambec, S. and Barla, P. (2005). Quand la réglementation environmentale profite aux pollueurs: survol des fondements théoriques de l'hpothèse de Porter. Département d'économique, Université Laval. Cahiers de Recherche, num. 0504.

Bansal, S. and Gangopadhyay, S. (2003). Tax/Subsidy Policies in the Presence of Environmentally Aware Consumers, *Journal of Environmental Economics and Mangement*, 45, 333-355.

Barla, P. (2005). "ISO 14001 Certification and Environmental Performance in Quebec's Pulp and Paper industry", Département d'économique, Cahiers de recherche, num 0503. Laval University

Berman, E. and Bui, L. (2001). Environmental regulation and productivity: evidence from oil refineries, *Review of Economics and Statistics, 83*, 3, 498-510.

Brunnermeier, S. B. and Cohen, M. A. (2003). Determinants of environmental innovation in US manufacturing industries, *Journal of Environmental Economics and Management, 45*, 278-293.

Cremer, J. and Thisse, J. F. (1999). On the taxation of polluting products in a differentiated industry, *European Economic Review, 34*, 575-594.

Foster, J., Hilden, M. and Adler, N. (2006). Can Regulations induce environmental innovations? An analysis of the role of regulations in the Pulp and Paper industry in Selected Industrialized Countries. In Hage, J. and Meeus, M. editor. *Innovation, Science and Institutional Change*. Oxford University Press, Oxford.

Gabel, H. L. and Sinclair-Desgagné, B. (2002). The firm, its procedures, and win-win environmental regulations. In Henk Folmer et al editors. *Frontiers of environmental economics*. Edward Elgar Publishing Ltd., Cheltenham.

Gollop, F. M. and M. J. Roberts, M. J. (1983). Environmental Regulations and Productivity Growth: The Case of Fossil-fuelled Electric Power Generation. *Journal of Political Economy, 91, 4*, 654-674.

Greaker, M. (2003). Strategic environmental policy. Eco-dumping or a green strategy, *Journal of Environmental Economics and Management, 45*, 692-707.

Hess, J., Kaouris, M. and Williams, J. (1999). What ISO 14000 brings to environmental management and Compliance. In: *Environmental Management Strategies. The 21st century perspective*, Upper Saddle River, Prentice Hall. 317-352.

Jaffe, A. B., Peterson, S. R., Portney, P. and Stavins, R. (1995). Environmental regulation and international competitiveness: what does the evidence tell us? *Journal of Economic Literature, 93, 12*, 12658-12663.

Jaffe, A. B. and Palmer, K. (1997). Environmental Regulation and Innovation: A Panel Data Study. *Review of Economics and Statistics, 79*. 610-619.

Jaffe, A. B., Newell, R., and Stavins, R. N. (2004). A Tale of two market failures: Technology and Environmental Policy. *Resource for the Future discussion paper RFF DP 04-38*. 1-25.

Johnstone, N., Serravalle, C., Scapecchi, P. and Labonne, J. (2007). Public environmental policy and corporate behaviour: project background, overview of the data and summary results. In: Johnstone, N. (ed.). *Corporate behaviour and environmental policy*, Cheltenham, UK. Edward Elgar in association with OECD.

Mahenc, P. (2007). Are green products over-priced? *Environmental and Resource Economics 38:4*, 461-473

Mohr, R. D. (2002). Technical change, external economics and the Porter hypothesis. *Journal of Environmental Economics and Management, 43, 1*. 158-168.

Palmer, K. W., Oates, W. and Portney, P. (1995). Tightening Environmental Standards: The Benefit-Cost or the No-Cost Paradigm? *Journal of Economic Perspectives, 9*, 119-132.

Perlman, H. (2007). *Industrial agglomeration: the salmon industry in Chile*. Ph. D. Thesis, Universitat de Lleida, Lleida.

Pickman, H (1998). The effect of environmental regulation on environmental innovation. *Business Strategy and the Environment, 7, 4*. 223-233.

Porter, M. and Van der Linde, C. (1995). Towards a new conception of environment-competitiveness relationship, *Journal of Economic Perspectives, 9*, 97-118.

Rehfeld, K; Rennings, K. and Ziegler, A. (2007). Integrated product policy and environmental product innovations: An empirical analysis. *Ecological Economics, 61, 1*, 91-100.

Reinhardt, F. L. (2001). Global Climate Change and BP Amoco, Harvard Business School, Case study 9-700-106.

Rennings, K., Schroeder, M., and Ziegler, A. (2006). The European Performance of European Stock Corporations. Does Sustainability Matters? In: Schaltegger, S. and Wagner, M. *Managing the Business Case for Sustainability*, pp. 196-210. Greenleaf Publishing, Washington.

Simpson, D. and Bradford, R. (1996). Taxing variable cost: environmental regulation as industrial policy, *Journal of Environmental Economics and Management, 30, 3*, 282-300.

Tirole, J. (1989). *Industrial Organization*, MIT Press, Cambridge, Massachussetts.

In: International Political Economy
Editors: M.A. Galindo Martin, E. Nissan
ISBN: 978-1-60876-172-2

Chapter 12

EDUCATION AND ICT: KEY FACTORS TO IMPROVE THE DEVELOPMENT IN THE WORLD

Víctor M. González Sánchez[1]
UNED – National University of Distance Education, Spain

ABSTRACT

The concept of economic development has different meanings; it's essentially, though, an aim for all countries in order to boost wealth and the welfare of their citizens. Nowadays, the Information and Communication Technologies (ICT) are becoming a key factor in allowing economic development to improve in the world. On the other hand, education itself contributes to development, while being the complement necessary to make good use of the ICT potential.

The main aim of this chapter is to analyze, from different points of view, the role that such important factors, like ICT and education, may play in the world's development. Throughout the chapter, the different aspects of each one of them will be assessed, as well as their relation to economic development, to conclude with a review of the situation in the European Union which, resulting from the implementation of the Lisbon strategy in 2000, started to devote attention to technological and educational factors, and regarded them as an improvement for the economy.

1. INTRODUCTION

Classical economics deemed that production is governed by three key factors: labor, land and capital stock. However, such a general classification leaves out other factors, such as educational training and leading-edge technology, which have, to a great extent, an influence on economic development. Occasionally, these factors are often regarded to be outside development analysis.

[1] The author appreciates the support received from UNED's Research Vice-Rectorship through 'UNED's Research Promotion Plan'.

Development encompasses many aspects such as the improvement in the quality of life of the inhabitants of a country, assessed through a greater availability of economic resources and means to get them. In this sense, technological capital and the human factor considerably govern the chances of a certain country to reach and keep a higher development level. Thus, indicators used in this chapter, like per capita income, illiteracy index and ICT availability per inhabitant, will make it possible to analyze a country's development.

The main aim of this chapter is to analyze the role that two such important factors as Information and Communication Technologies (ICT) and education, play in the world's development. Throughout the chapter, the different aspects of each one of them will be assessed, as well as their relation to economic development, to conclude with a review of the situation in the European Union which, resulting from the implementation of the Lisbon strategy in 2000, started to devote attention to technological and educational factors, and regarded them as an improvement for the economy.

2. ICT and Economic Development

ICT have become a key resource for economic activity, at least as important as other factors regarded as traditional in an economy. The importance of knowledge has been on the increase with these technologies as a result of higher speed, by means of which information and knowledge are conveyed, regardless of distance and volume, at a considerably reduced cost. Accordingly, thanks to ICT, the vicious circle of poverty and social isolation may change through learning and attainment.

By themselves, ICT don't ensure the implementation of an economic growth process or an improvement in the population's welfare. Nevertheless, as indicated in the World Bank (1998), if it is agreed that the access (although poor) to world markets is an important factor to promote long-term progress in developing countries, it can also be stated that the access to the world's knowledge provided by ICT is a key factor (although also deficient) so as to stimulate the long-term knowledge-based economic development.

There are not simple solutions for development's challenges. Consequently, ICT don't solve all the problems in a country, but they can improve the conditions to face development's challenges; since with the help of information and knowledge, human capital can become a driving force for development in any aspect. In that respect, the differences in ICT endowment are not by themselves the cause of a slower rate in development growth, but they could come to restrict the economic growth of a country. So, it can be said that the investment in these technologies has an impact comparable to any other investment made in an economy.

The impact of new ICT[2] on macroeconomics and economic development has become an outstanding fact since the last decade of the last century, beyond other considerations

[2] The availability of appropriate technology is an important factor to try to assess a country's accessibility to the information and knowledge society. Thus, among other technological devices and services, which are appropriate to study the access to this society, the International Telecommunication Union (ITU, 2003) has established a simple classification between the latest and oldest ICT, according to their more or less recent appearance, and whether or not they have been brought into general use. Some examples of both types of ICT are shown below: Old ICT: radio receiver, television set and fixed-line telephone. New ICT: mobile phones, personal computers and Internet.

regarding ICT's contribution to directly reduce the main existing development problems in the world[3]. The significant peak reached by ICT has had a considerable bearing on developed and developing countries' economy over the last few years; yet the impact on each case has depended on the proportion representing the productive sectors of goods and services relating to ICT in the economy of each country (ITU, 2006).

One of the ways to assess the relative weight of ICT on the overall economy of a country is to estimate the part representing these technologies on its GDP—either by measuring it according to the added value, or through the investment made. In the first case, as indicated in Table 1, the OECD's data on the added value provided to the economy by ICT's manufacturing sector point out that, in the case of Korea and Finland, this accounts for over a fifth of the added value of the whole manufacturing sector. As a result, while the manufacturing sector of Japan, Hungary, Ireland, Sweden and the United States is above the average set by OECD, the rest of the countries have a relatively moderate role in ICT, as far as the manufacturing sector is concerned. On the one hand, this fact reflects a greater dependence upon the ICT sector for those countries whose relative weight is larger; and, on the other hand, this implies, to a certain extent, a relative specialization in some countries, as well as an international share of the ICT sector.

Table 1. Share of ICT in value added – 2006

	Share of ICT manufacturing in total manufacturing value added	Share of ICT services in total business services value added	
		Telecomminucation services	Other ICT services
Australia	2.8	4.1	3.9
Austria	5.6	2.9	4.4
Belgium	3.5	4.0	5.0
Canada	4.6	4.1	4.6
Czech Republic	5.0	5.3	3.8
Denmark	4.8	2.9	6.0
Finland	20.1	5.0	6.8
France	5.2	2.8	5.8
Germany	5.6	3.0	4.5
Greece	3.0	6.0	0.6
Hungary	12.6	5.8	4.3
Ireland	11.5	2.6	9.9
Italy	4.2	3.5	5.2
Japan	12.8	3.3	2.4
Korea	21.1	5.6	2.7
Mexico	5.6	3.6	1.2
Netherlands	3.8	3.7	7.0
Norway	4.6	3.5	6.0
Portugal	2.8	5.5	3.0
Spain	2.3	4.3	4.0
Sweden	9.3	2.7	8.8
United Kingdom	6.0	3.9	7.9
United States	7.7	4.7	4.2
OECD average	7.2	4.0	4.9

Source: Proper making from information of OECD (2009).

[3] See United Nations (2008).

As for the service sector, from Table 1 it may also be inferred that the added value provided by ICT services as a whole accounts for an average percentage higher in OECD than in the manufacturing sector. Moreover, regarding this, the existing distances between countries placed in a better or worse position are more reduced, and the number of countries with values above OECD's average is also higher. If a distinction is made between the corresponding part of telecommunication services and all the services provided by ICT, Greece takes the lead in this instance, followed by Hungary and Korea. Nonetheless, the situation is clearly different if the data of other ICT services are analyzed. With respect to ICT services, countries with a higher added value, excluding telecommunication services, on the total added value in services are as follows: Ireland, Sweden, the United Kingdom and the Netherlands. With the exception of Finland, it can be concluded that, regarding telecommunication services, none of the countries which are above the OECD's average are above the relative average of other ICT services. As a matter of fact, Finland is the only country of the ones illustrated in Table 1 that is clearly above all the average references set by OECD, regarding the added value provided by these technologies compared to all the sectors. It's, therefore, the more balanced country with regard to the ICT sector.

From an investment point of view, the part of Gross Fixed Capital Formation (GFCF) corresponding to ICT on the total GFCF, as an integral part of each country's GDP is exemplified in Figure 1. In each case, the investment part relating to IT and communication equipment, and software investment are indicated. The United States is undoubtedly the country where GFCF is considered to be of paramount importance, especially regarding software; since, together with the United Kingdom and Sweden, it exceeds 15% of the total new investment made in the country. Actually, except for five of the countries shown in Figure 1, GFCF in software is the more significant of those carried out within the ICT sector. So, this is subject, to a great extend, to the weight of GFCF in those technologies with regard to the total investment. Generally speaking, the higher the percentage of ICT investment is in relation to the total of countries' economy, the less the relative weight of the investment in communication equipment will be.

In other words, according to OECD's data, in those countries whose levels of investment in these technologies are considerably more reduced with respect to the total, there is a greater tendency to invest in communication equipment. Largely speaking, this fact accounts for the need to make basic technological investments in communication, which, to a great extend, were already made in ancient times by those countries now allocating a greater proportion of their GFCF to information technology equipment, and software. In a way, this makes them become ICT-producing countries; so it is expected that job creation and higher incomes will be directly resulting from this greater technological investment

Studies conducted on the analysis of ICT's impact on economy disclose the considerable and growing importance attached to the market of these technologies. The aim of this chapter, among other things, is to show the relation between ICT and economic development. In this sense, in order to make an analysis by using indicators which can be reproduced in an international scale, GDP will be used in terms per capita (GDPpc), as a generally accepted reference, not perfect though, to measure the economic development of a country. Furthermore, the ICT variables used in this case are fixed-line telephone lines, regarded as old ICT and a rough reference of the basic ability of each country to take advantage of other technologies; and Internet users and broadband subscribers, as a reference of new ICT and a rough variable of the real degree of use of these technologies.

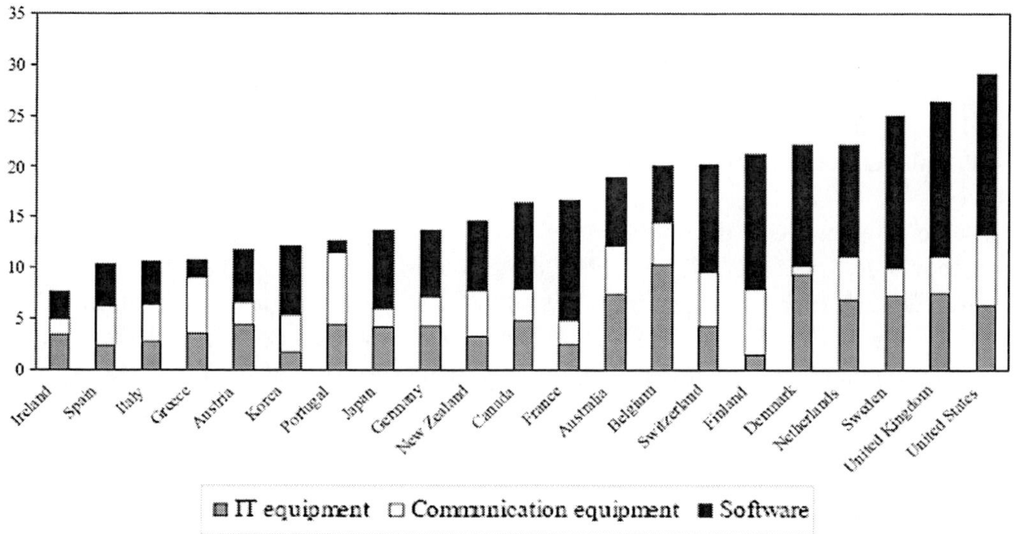

Source : Proper making from information of OECD (2009).

Figure 1. Shares of ICT investment in non-residential gross fixed capital formation (As a percentage of total non-residential gross fixed capital formation, total economy, 2007 or latest available year).

From Figure 2, it can be inferred that the existing relation between economic development and the number of telephone lines per one hundred inhabitants in the countries of the world. Although the data provided are updated, the general behaviour is virtually the same as, at least, that of two decades ago. Consequently, the relation between both variables is clearly direct and, therefore, a higher degree of economic development results in an easier average availability of telephone lines for the inhabitants of a country.

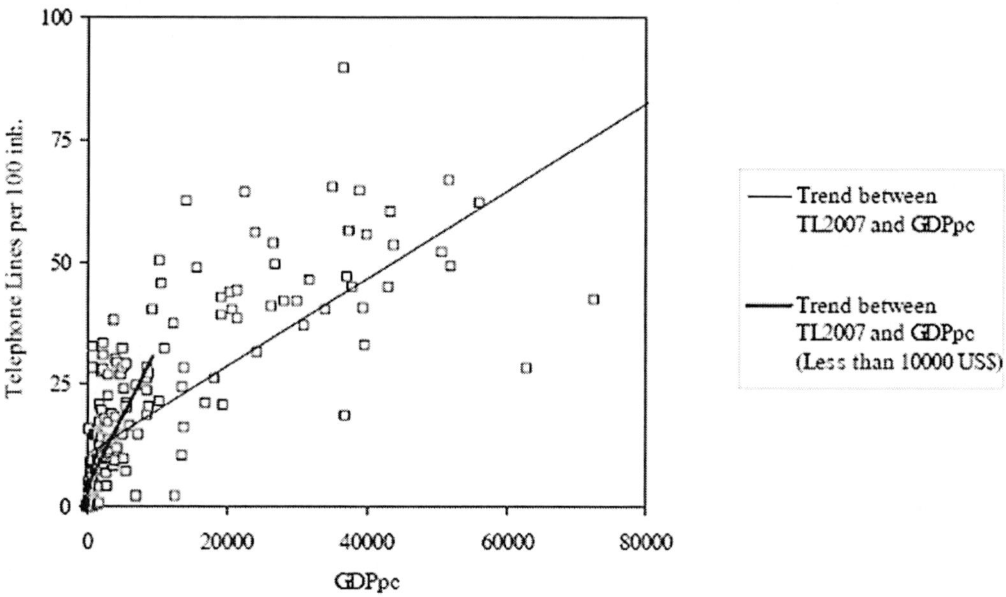

Source : Proper making from information of ITU (2008).

Figure 2.

However, as basic ICT, the use of them can be considered, to a large extend, universalized; and, therefore, there is a clear trend towards reduction. Beyond the logical replacement of fixed-line telephones for cellular phones made over the last decade[4], if the data of the countries with a GDPpc below US$10,000 are considered alone, the relation between this reference and the number of telephone lines per inhabitant differs, but it is still positive.

The relation between the reference of fixed-line telephone lines and countries with a poorer economic development implies that these countries need to increase the investment in basic ICT, so that they can take better advantage of the technological potential provided by new ICT; thus, boosting their economic development. In this way, the basic technological limitations, which are a burden for less developed countries can be checked with the fact that no country with a per capita income below US$10,000 has, at least, one fixed-line telephone per two inhabitants.

On the other hand, the use of ICT, and accordingly, the ability to have a positive impact on a country's economic development can also be measured by means of other variables like the number of Internet users and broadband subscribers. In both cases, ICT are regarded as new, so they are expected to have a greater influence on economic development.

As for the former, the relation between the number of Internet users and GDPpc is shown in Figure 3.

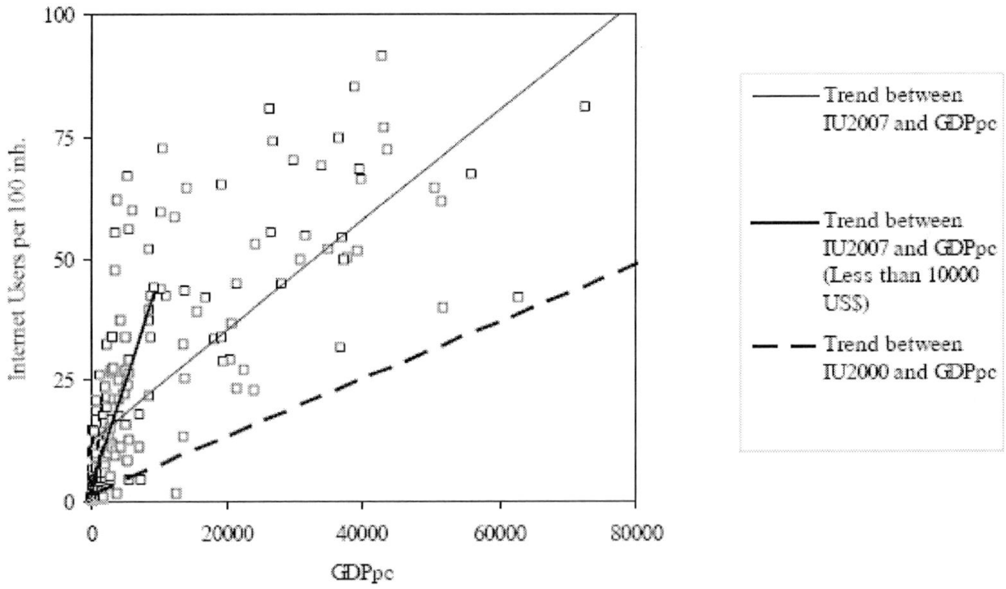

Source: Proper making from information of ITU (2008).

Figure 3.

Obviously, the relation is clearly direct; the more developed countries are those whose number of Internet users is higher. However, as it happened in the case of fixed-line telephones, if the data of those countries with a GDPpc below US$10,000 alone are taken into

[4] Nowadays, in most of the countries of the world, the number of lines for cellular phones per inhabitant is higher than the number of fixed-line telephone lines per capita.

account, the relation between both variables is modified towards the Internet users' axis. As a consequence, those countries with a poorer development will generally need more incentives to increase their proportion of Internet users and to move forward the reference improvement of economic development; bearing in mind that there are very few countries with a lower income where, at least, half of the population are Internet users.

As for the progress made by the number of Internet users in relation to GDPpc, between 2000 and 2007, there is a trend towards the increase of users in those countries with a lower income. Hence, in 2000 there were only three countries with a per capita income below US$10,000 (Malaysia, Chile and Uruguay), where over 10% of the population were Internet users; so this technological reference was regarded as a real barrier compared to the wealthiest countries. Lately, concerning Internet users, the trend has been on the increase in all the countries; the differences, as it has been mentioned before, are noticeable in favour of those with greater economic development.

In Figure 4, the relation between the number of broadband subscribers and the level of economic development of countries is represented. On this occasion, the direct relation between both references show a less generalized expansion of this technology; only eight countries, almost all of them European, exceed the barrier of 30% of subscribers per one hundred inhabitants: Bermuda, Denmark, Finland, Iceland, the Netherlands, Norway, Sweden and Switzerland.

Besides, bearing in mind that a technology whose infrastructure cost is higher, and, in any case, greater than the mere availability of a telephone line, its expansion and use in countries with a lower income is virtually token; since only Lithuania goes beyond the barrier of 10% of subscribers among those countries whose GDPpc didn't exceed US$10,000 in 2007.

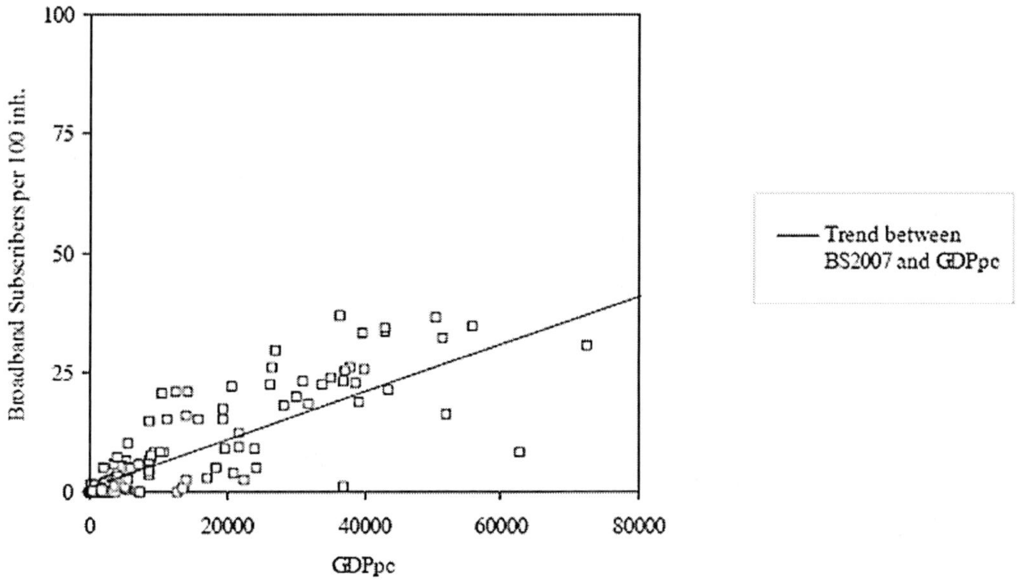

Source: Proper making from information of ITU (2008).

Figure 4.

Hence, the best access to ICT and the rise in the number of broadband subscribers is subject to a country's economic development level. Moreover, this technological handicap also conditions the development of those countries which suffer from it. The split of this vicious circle should be, to a great extend, the aim of technological and development policies for many countries in the world.

Before tackling other of the purposes of this chapter regarding the role of education in the development of countries, other topic will be dealt with in this section: the assessment of the existing relation between population's literacy rate and the percentage of people able to take advantage of Information and Communication Technologies as a tool for daily and economic use. To a certain extent, it comes down to comparing people able to read and write with those, being literate, who know how to make use of ICT.

So, Figure 5 illustrates the existing relation between the number of Internet users per one hundred inhabitants and the total adult literacy rate. As it can be concluded, for the whole of the population, the relation is positive, and very similar, should the youth literacy rate alone have been considered.

The link between the literacy rate of the population in a country and the percentage of Internet users is very high, to such an extent that only two countries, Morocco and Tunisia, whose population's total literacy rate is below 80%, exceed the number of 15 Internet users per one hundred inhabitants. It's precisely in the stretch from 80% and 100% of literacy rate where countries have better references with regard to their population's training in order to take advantage of ICT via Internet.

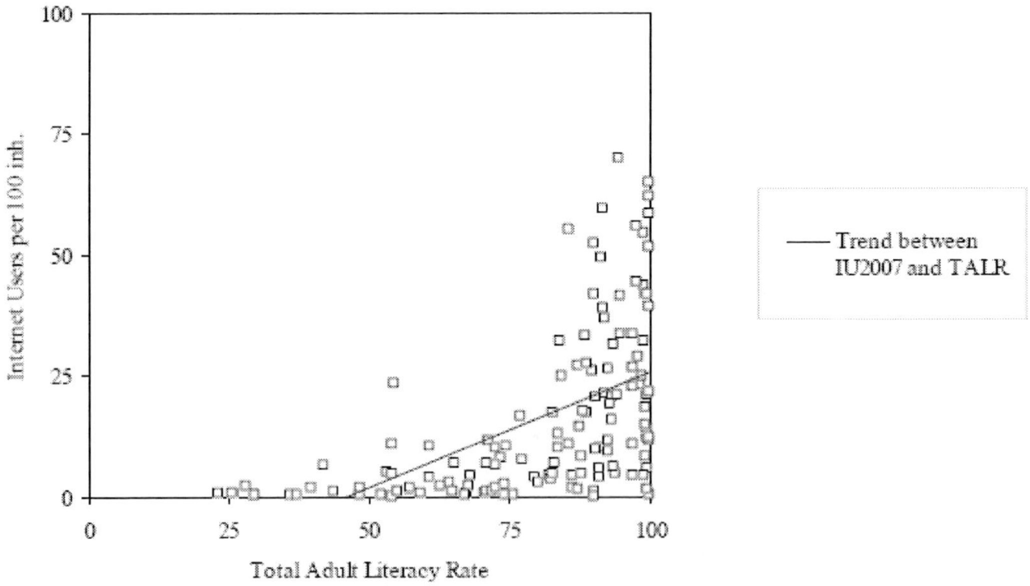

Source: Proper making from information of UNESCO (2008a) and ITU (2008).

Figure 5.

Therefore, it can be stated that, although it is not enough, it's necessary to reach a certain literacy rate in the population, so that countries can have greater chances to make use of these technologies, not only as an element of technological literacy, but also as a potential of growth and development for the present and future time[5].

3. Education and Economic Development

The relation between education and economic development is tight; both variables are very close and interdependent. As a result, a growing education attainment level within the population lays the foundations for the economic development, and this, in turn, generate resources for education. According to UNESCO (2006b), education is a fundamental human right, while being a condition essential for an equitable and sustainable economic and social development.

Countries with more developed economies began to implement literacy programs during the 1980s. They expected to get rid of illiteracy by the end of the 20th century, as well as to reduce education differences between men and women. As for less developed countries, it was expected to get education attainment levels similar to those of developed countries in a shorter term. However, although the situation has improved, women's education opportunities are still worse than men's. The educational systems of each country and the international organizations supporting them should be firmly committed to overcome these difficulties and to be successful in making education an equal right for all citizens.

In general, even today, the odds of a person being literate or illiterate in the world depend, to a large extent, on his or her residence, among other things. As a result, considering the data provided by UNESCO and ranked according to the different regions in the world depicted in Table 2, the variables geographic area, sex and age offer a first approach to the possibility of a person being literate or not.

Bearing in mind the data on adults, it can be seen that the literacy rate[6] in the world is still far beyond acceptable values, closer to 90% of the population older than 15 years of age. However, in spite of general data not being good enough, the less encouraging thing is that the literacy rate between men and women differs 5 percentage points, favoring the former. Undoubtedly, the worst data regarding female literacy correspond with regions from South and West Asia, and the Arab States, where female literacy rate is nearly over 50% and 60% respectively.

More developed countries' population from Northern and Western Europe, followed by Central Asia is the one offering by large the best literacy rates in any aspect. On the other hand, people from Sub-Saharan Africa features the worst literacy results as a whole.

---

[5] If the data regarding youth literacy rate, aged 15 to 24, is considered, the determining factor of literacy with respect to the use of ICT is much higher. Only two countries, Morocco and Pakistan, exceed 10 users per one hundred inhabitants, among all those countries whose youth literacy rate is below 80%. At the same time, the number of users is shooting up in those countries whose youth literacy rate is above 90%.

[6] For measurement purposes, UNESCO has long used the definition of literacy that relates to the ability to read and write, with understanding, a short simple statement related to one's daily life. A parallel definition, however, arose with UNESCO's introduction of the notion of functional literacy in 1978: a person is considered functionally literate if they can engage in activities, or effectively function, in his or her group and community. This definition also refers to the ability to continue to use reading, writing and calculation for personal and community development (UNESCO, 2008a).

Table 2. Adult and Youth Literacy, 2006

	Adults (15 years and older)		Youth (15 to 24 years)	
	Literacy rate	Illiterate population (000)	Literacy rate	Illiterate population (000)
	Male / Female	% Female	Male / Female	% Female
WORLD	83.6 88.3 / 78.9	776,164 64.3	88.9 91.2 / 86.5	130,537 59.4
Arab States	71.9 82.0 / 61.4	57,798 67.3	86.1 91.0 / 81.2	8,949 66.9
Central and Eastern Europe	97.4 98.9 / 96.2	8,235 80.0	98.8 99.2 / 98.4	774 67.2
Central Asia	98.6 99.0 / 98.2	784 67.6	99.5 99.4 / 99.6	82 43.0
East Asia and the Pacific	93.1 96.0 / 90.2	112,907 70.5	98.2 98.4 / 98.0	6,488 53.7
Latin America and the Caribbean	90.6 91.4 / 89.9	36,946 55.3	96.8 96.4 / 97.2	3,290 43.3
North America and Western Europe	99.1 99.3 / 98.9	5,682 61.2	99.5 99.5 / 99.5	495 52.4
South and West Asia	63.6 74.1 / 52.5	392,725 63.4	79.2 84.1 / 73.9	67,074 60.3
Sub-Saharan Africa	61.7 70.7 / 53.2	161,088 62.2	71.4 76.5 / 66.6	43,385 58.6

Source: Proper making from information of UNESCO (2008a).

The region of Latin America and the Caribbean is the one showing a lower female illiteracy rate with respect to population's total illiteracy rate. Therefore, the illiterate population, which is roughly 6 percentage points less than in North America and Western Europe, are women. These data, even more when it comes to the total population and not just young people, are promising for a region where several countries strive to get greater economic and social development.

The data regarding youth, aged 15 to 24, are generally parallel to adults'; they are more favorable, though, in all regions in terms of population's literacy and lower population's illiteracy rate. Nonetheless, it should be pointed out the fact that within illiterate population from Arab States the female rate is very similar between youth and adults; while as for the rest, to a lesser or large extent, the proportion between men and women with regard to population's illiteracy tends to equal. It's, therefore, the region where greater efforts should be made, beyond any cultural question, in order to promote female literacy. Furthermore, confirming and overcoming what has been said before, the region of Latin America and the Caribbean is the only one with a clearly greater male than female proportion of illiteracy population.

Figure 6 shows the relation between adult literacy and economic development in the countries of the world as a whole. The relation between adult literacy rate and GDPpc is clearly direct.

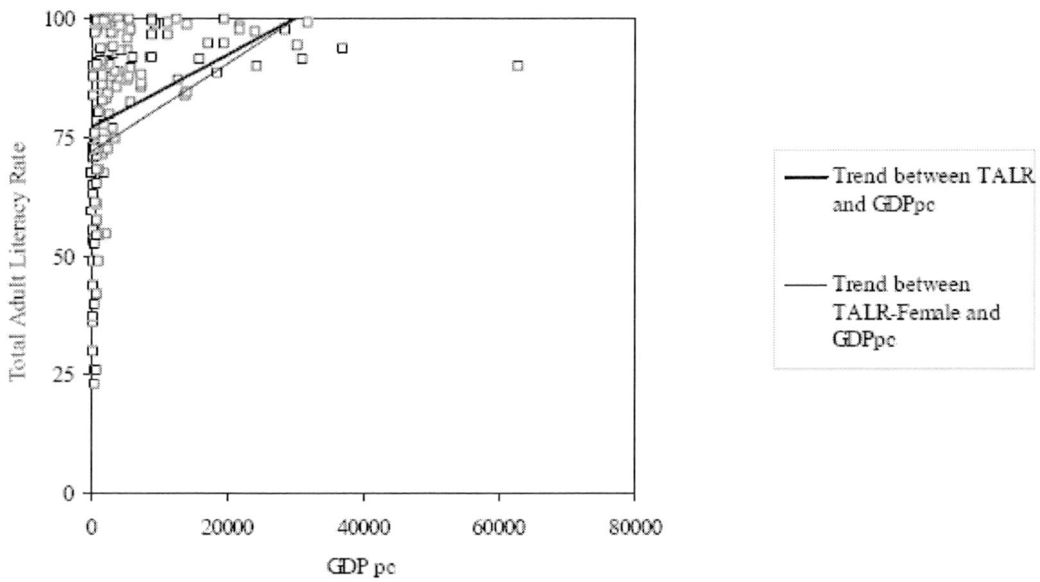

Source: Proper making from information of UNESCO (2008a) and ITU (2008).

Figure 6.

So, in spite of the fact that countries has an adult literacy rate above 80%; no country below this rate amounts to a per capita income of US$3,500. Moreover, only four countries (Oman, Saudi Arabia, Bahrain and the United Arab Emirates), all of them belonging to the geographic area of aforementioned Arab States, are above US$12,000 of GDPpc, whose population's total literacy rate is below 90%.

The relation between literacy and economic development is not only direct, but it can also be said that to reach high literacy rates within the population, at least above 90% jointly for both men and women, is necessary to subsequently get economic prosperity. However, taking into account that countries whose literacy rate is above 80% and GDPpc is still far from the more developed countries, it's clear that population's literacy itself is not enough to get higher rates of economic development.

In view of the trends shown in Figure 6, the efforts to improve population's literacy should be specially aimed at women. So, as it has been stated, in all regions of the world, female literacy rate is lower than male literacy rate; besides, the tendency to equal literacy rates in both groups is especially found in those countries of higher economic development. In other words, the worst female literacy rates and the greatest disparity with regard to the men's occur in those countries whose GDPpc is lower.

On the other hand, if the data regarding population, aged 15 to 24, are considered, the scene features some differences. As it's shown in Figure 7, literacy rates generally produce best youth data, and logically, the relation between literacy and economic development is still clearly direct. Population's education is, therefore, a need previous to economic development in a country.

Youth literacy rates in the world are more favorable than those relating to the total population, for both men and women. However promising this fact may be for the future, it is not the same with countries from the Sub-Saharan region in Africa; especially if it is considered what it has been previously stated about the female literacy rate in the Arab States.

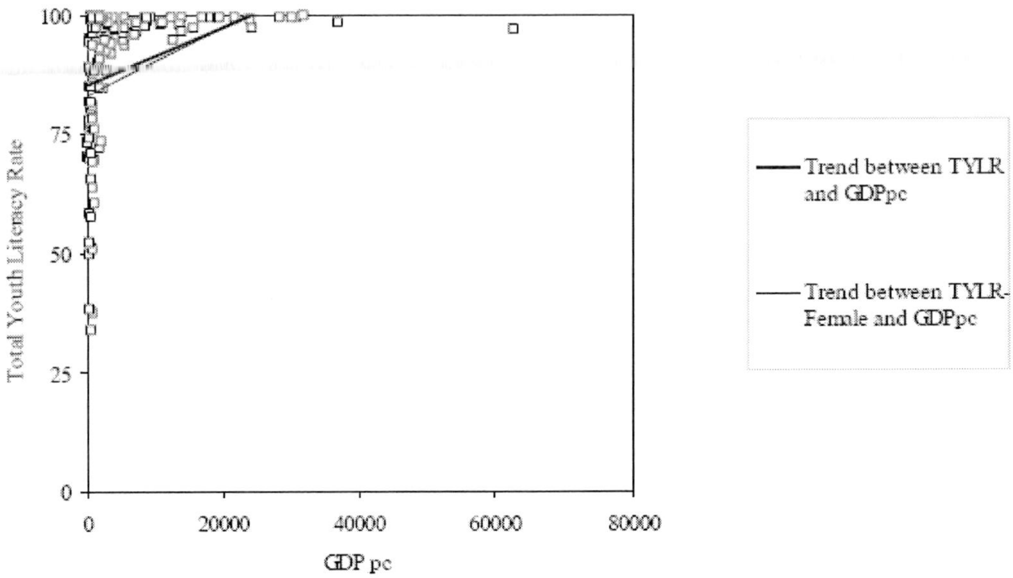

Source: Proper making from information of UNESCO (2008a) and ITU (2008).

Figure 7.

Hence, countries whose youth female literacy rate does not even reach 50% are listed and ordered from the lowest to the highest rate as follows: Afghanistan, Chad, Niger, Burkina Faso, Guinea, Mali, Ethiopia, Benin, Sierra Leone, Senegal, Mozambique and the Central African Republic.

According to the data on youth provided by UNESCO, almost three fifths of the countries in the world have a female literacy rate higher than men's. The importance of education, in general, and female population, in particular, on the development of countries is confirmed with the fact that this rate is clearer in those countries with high literacy rates and with an economic development above US$5,000; in addition to Latin American countries and the Caribbean, mostly showing high female literacy rates.

The link between education and economic development is beyond basic references concerning literacy rates. Population's training or, in other words, human capital training in a country is a productive investment, at least, similar to the one made in technology or industrial machinery. As a matter of fact, investment in physical capital and technology would not produce the desired results, if it were not kept in step with a qualified population in order to use and take advantage of these investments.

In economic terms, population's training is directly related to its own development. Therefore, investment made in each country in order to train its students is expected to have the very same relation with GDPpc. So, in Figure 8 it can be seen the data related to expenditure per student, in accordance with education attainment levels and GDPpc for OECD member countries.

At first sight, it can be easily noticed a certain proportion between expenditure per student and each country's economic development. Nonetheless, the link does not seem too clear with regard to expenditure per student in primary and secondary education. There are expenditure differences, but they are not so obvious between the wealthiest and least economically favored countries.

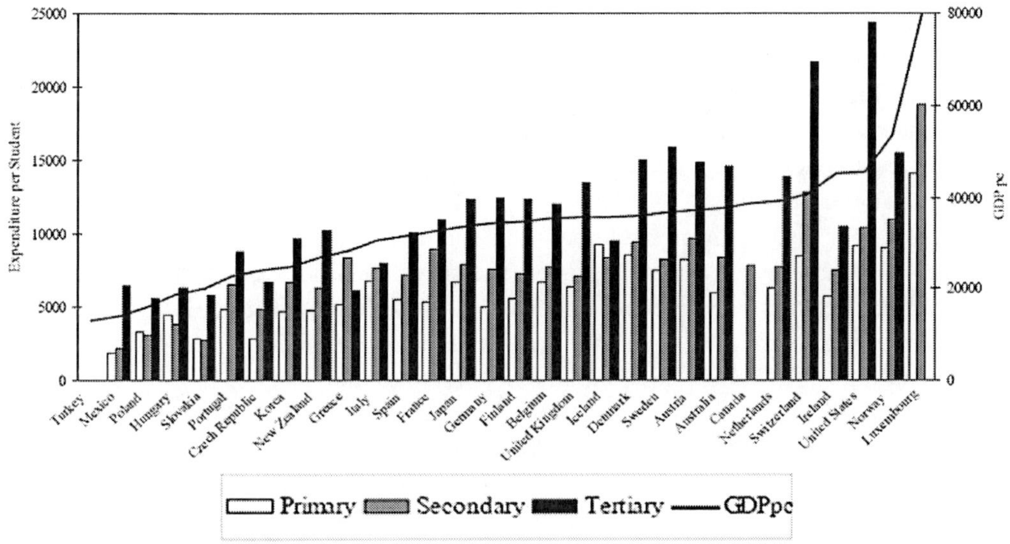

Source: Proper making from information of OECD (2009) and UNESCO (2008).

Figure 8. Expenditure per Student vs. GDP pc.

The more significant differences are found, though, in the expenditure volume per student in tertiary education. This type of expenditure shows a more direct relation to countries' development and, therefore, a greater influence on GDPpc. Historically, wealthiest countries are the ones spending more money in tertiary education. According to recent data for OECD, with the exception of Greece, all the countries spend more money per tertiary education[7] student than for those in primary and secondary education.

The examples of the United States, Switzerland or Sweden show that the fact that a country reaches a high economic development is not by chance, but the result of devoting for years considerable effort and economic resources to train the population, among other things. This is one of the ways that should be followed by those OECD member countries, aiming to increase their GDPpc in the medium term.

Beyond a context restricted to a group of countries, the United Nations Development Programme (UNDP) is the UN's global development network. The UNDP regards economic growth essential for human progress. As economic growth is not enough to reach the Millennium's Aims[8], other aspects related to development are considered. In that respect, the Human Development Index (HDI)[9] is contained in UNDP's Human Development Report. The HDI combines measures of life expectancy, standard of living (GDP per capita), and knowledge and education, as measured by the adult literacy rate and the combined primary, secondary, and tertiary gross enrollment ratio, determining the relative progress of a country.

---

[7] Categories established in accordance with the 'International Standard Classification of Education (ISCED 97)' (UNESCO, 2006a).

[8] See United Nations (2007) and (2008).

[9] The human development index (HDI) is a summary measure of human development. It measures the average achievements in a country in three basic dimensions of human development:

- A long and healthy life, as measured by life expectancy at birth.
- Knowledge, as measured by the adult literacy rate (with two-thirds weight) and the combined primary, secondary and tertiary gross enrolment ratio (with one-third weight).
- A decent standard of living, as measured by GDP per capita in purchasing power parity (PPP) terms in US dollars.

The differences in dimensions measuring the partial indexes making up the HDI tackle the possible existing relations among them with respect to education index. Accordingly, as it's shown in Figure 9, the logical relation between education index and GDP index is direct in accordance with the previous analyses conducted between the GDPpc itself as a measure of economic development and population's literacy rate as a basic reference of elementary education attainment level.

However, if a distinction is made between countries with a high education index[10] and those with a medium or low education index, the situation is not exactly the same. The drop in the trend line relating high education index to GDP index is positive, just like the drop in the line displaying the trend between the medium and low education index and the economic development indicator. Nonetheless, the line belonging to the group of those countries with a higher education index, which largely coincides with countries with a medium or high economic development, shows a sharper drop than the other one. In other words, the link between education and economic development is stronger in those countries whose education attainment level is higher. Therefore, it can be concluded that in countries whose adult literacy rate and whose number of students enrolled in different attainment levels are higher; there is a higher trend towards having a high economic development.

On the other hand, Figure 10 illustrates what happens if a long and healthy life is measured by life expectancy index at birth in relation to education index. As expected, in all cases, the relation between both indexes is direct.

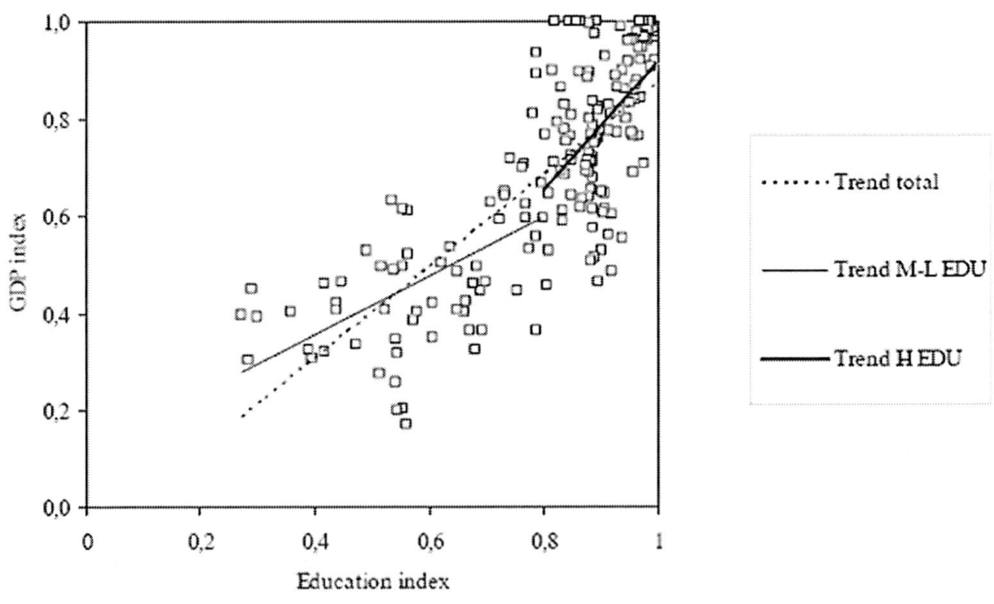

Source: Proper making from information of United Nations (2007).

Figure 9.

[10] The reference used to generally rank an index. An index of 0.8 (out of 1) or more is considered to be high; while the barrier between a medium and low index is at 0.5; a ranking very similar to the index used by Human Development Reports; eg.: United Nations (2007).

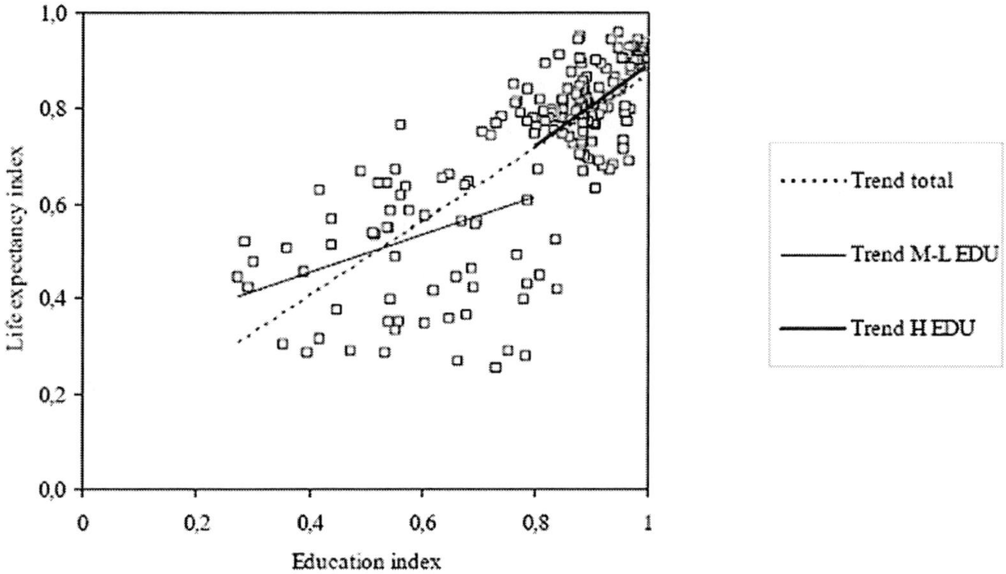

Source: Proper making from information of United Nations (2007).

Figure 10.

When making distinctions between countries with a high education index and those whose reference features a medium or low value, it's clear that there are differences, even though the relation is still positive. In other words, the higher the education attainment level is in a country's population, the higher the life expectancy at birth will be for the population in that country; however, this link is more likely to occur in countries with a better education development. In fact, the graph shows a distinct division between those countries with better prospects in life expectancy at birth, and with a high education index; and those countries with worse prospects in life expectancy at birth and medium and lower education index. To sum up, education can become not only the aim of development itself, but a way for the inhabitants of a country to reach a long and healthy life, as well as greater economic development.

4. European Union

In the European Union (EU), the importance of ICT and education for development is clear, especially since the so called Lisbon strategy[11] was set out by the European Council in the meeting held in the Portuguese capital in March, 2000, with the strategic aim of making Union's economy "the most dynamic and competitive knowledge-based economy in the world capable of sustainable economic growth with more and better jobs and greater social cohesion, and respect for the environment by 2010".

This strategy was based on three pillars:

[11] See European Council (2000).

- An economic pillar: to get a competitive economy stressing the need to adapt the information society's progress, and to make an effort in the field of research and development.
- A social pillar: to modernize the European social model through investment in human resources and fight against social exclusion, through investment in education and training, as well as an active policy for employment to lay the foundations for the knowledge economy.
- An environmental pillar[12]: the economic growth must be on a par with a sustainable use of natural resources.

To achieve its goal, the strategy devised in Lisbon has been reviewed throughout the years, and a series of quantitative aims related, among other aspects, to ICT and education has been established. Consequently, Table 3 reflects the scene of EU countries through some technological and educational variables.

The first column illustrates the population ratio, aged 20 to 24, having reached, at least, a non-compulsory level of secondary education. This is an educational variable which makes it possible to compare youth education attainment level in the EU; thus, the potential training of human capital in each country. In general, young Europeans' average training is highly qualified; although the average education attainment level has increased three percentage points since the enlargement of the EU, from 15 to 27 member states.

The countries whose youth rate has reached, at least, the level of non-compulsory secondary education is higher are precisely some of those joining the EU from 2004 on: Czech Republic, Poland, Slovakia and Slovenia. This fact is considerably significant, since there are three Southern European countries, Malta, Portugal and Spain, where young people are less interested in education. Hence, in general, young people from countries with lower development, and, particularly, young people coming from countries recently joining the growing competitiveness of the labour market in the EU are those who devote more time and effort to their own training through education. Comparatively, in countries with a settled economic development within the EU, young people either have little motivation to improve their opportunities in life, either lack appropriate incentives to devote more time to education.

On the other hand, columns in Table 3 containing indicators on ICT confirm a technological leadership in the EU, in compliance with the works conducted on the same topic[13]. So, the best six positioned countries in the European Union, regarding the use of ICT are the Northern EU countries of Denmark, Finland and Sweden; plus Ireland, Luxembourg and the Netherlands, whose Internet access data for households, and Public Administration access data for enterprises are noteworthy. Among countries with a lower level in these technologies are Bulgary, Greece and Romania.

Lastly, the e-commerce via the Internet features rather limited data in the framework of the European Union. Analyzing the data obtained in 2007, no country has shown a development in this kind of commerce, corresponding to the technological potential of the field. Thus, regarding e-commerce, only Ireland, the United Kingdom, Spain and Lithuania go beyond the barrier of 5%.

---

[12] This pillar was added in the European Council in 2001, held in Sweden.

[13] See González Sánchez and Fernández Jurado (2009) and González Sánchez (2005).

Table 3. European Union - Structural Indicators

	Youth education attainment level	Level of Internet access - households	E-government usage by enterprises	E-Commerce via Internet
	2007	2008	2008	2007
EU (27 countries)	78.1	60	68	4.2
EU (15 countries)	75.2	64	70	4.4
Austria	84.1	69	80	
Belgium	82.6	64	69	3.4
Bulgaria	83.3	25	58	0.5
Cyprus	85.8	43	65	0.6
Czech Republic	91.8	46	73	3.7
Denmark	70.8	82	90	
Estonia	80.9	58	77	
Finland	86.5	72	95	
France	82.4	62	73	
Germany	72.5	75	56	3.3
Greece	82.1	31	78	0.9
Hungary	84.0	48	60	2.4
Ireland	86.7	63	91	9.8
Italy	76.3	47	82	0.9
Latvia	80.2	53	55	
Lithuania	89.0	51	86	5.4
Luxembourg	70.9	80	90	
Malta	55.5	59	74	
Netherlands	76.2	86	85	
Poland	91.6	48	68	3.2
Portugal	53.4	46	75	
Romania	77.4	30	39	1.2
Slovakia	91.3	58	88	1.1
Slovenia	91.5	59	88	
Spain	61.1	51	64	6.2
Sweden	87.2	84	78	
United Kingdom	78.1	71	64	7.0

Source: Proper making from information of European Union (2008).

The ICT development in EU has been making steady progress since the implementation of Lisbon strategy. Nonetheless, the distance separating the EU from their main competitors, mainly the United States and Japan, is becoming increasingly worrying. Therefore, new and painstaking efforts should be made by different countries to make what it was set in Lisbon in 2000 come true.

CONCLUSION

Information and Communication Technologies and education have a clearly direct relation to economic development. More developed countries are precisely those where, by and large, the population's average education training and their use of ICT are widespread.

ICT are a key factor in the current economy. The fact of having or not having a basic technological infrastructure settles the basic differences between economies, and boosts a country's development potential. In this way, although they don't guarantee by themselves the economic prosperity, the greater access and use of ICT by the inhabitants of a country are a strong incentive for their economic development.

In the case of education, it may be said that it's a determining factor when it comes to explain some significant differences between developed countries and those which are less economically fortunate. Accordingly, the average training of a country's population doesn't justify the greater economic development of a country, since the lack of an appropriate basic training for the citizens is a burden to achieve economic and social advances for a country. The investment in education is, therefore, a basic tool to promote development for the present and future time.

All things considered, high education attainment and ICT levels are not enough to guarantee a fully developed economy. However, these are key factors to get and maintain an acceptable technological level. Thus, the lack of an appropriate technological level and average training within the population results in a more limited and poor economic development in most of the cases.

References

European Council (2000). Presidency Conclusions Lisbon European Council 23 and 24 March 2000. Lisbon, Portugal: European Council.

European Union (2008). Europe in figures: Eurostat yearbook 2008. Luxembourg: Office for Official Publications of the European Communities.

González Sánchez, V. M. and Fernández Jurado, Y (2009). Principales medidas de las Administraciones Públicas para fomentar el uso de las TIC en las empresas españolas. Economía Industrial, No. 370. 45-57.

González Sánchez, V. M. (2005). El papel de las TIC dentro del objetivo de Lisboa en la Unión Europea ampliada. Boletín Económico de ICE, No. 2832, 45-56.

ITU (2008). World Telecommunication / ICT Indicators Database 2008 (12th Edition). Geneva, Switzerland: International Telecommunication Union.

ITU (2006). World Telecommunication/ICT Development Report 2006: Measuring ICT for social and economic development. Geneva, Switzerland: International Telecommunication Union.

ITU (2003). World Telecommunication Development Report 2003: Access Indicators for the Information Society. Geneva, Switzerland: International Telecommunication Union.

OECD (2009). OECD Factbook 2009: Economic, Environmental and Social Statistics. Paris, France: OECD Publishing.

UNESCO (2008a). Global Education Digest 2008: Comparing Education Statistics across the World. Montreal, Canada: UNESCO Institute for Statistics.

UNESCO (2008b). International Literacy Statistics: A Review of Concepts, Methodology and Current Data. Montreal, Canada: UNESCO Institute for Statistics.

UNESCO (2006a). International Standard Classification of Education (ISCED 97). Montreal, Canada: UNESCO Institute for Statistics.

UNESCO (2006b). Report of the Ministerial Round Table on Education for All: 33rd Session of the General Conference. Paris, France: UNESCO Education Sector.

United Nations (2008). The Millennium Development Goals: Report 2008. New York, NY: United Nations.

United Nations (2007). Human Development Report 2007/2008. Fighting climate change: Human solidarity in a divided world. New York, NY: United Nations Development Programme.

World Bank (1998), World Development Report 1998-1999: Knowledge for Development. Washington, DC: The World Bank.

In: International Political Economy
Editors: M.A. Galindo Martin, E. Nissan ISBN: 978-1-60876-172-2

Chapter 13

THE IMPACT OF UNDOCUMENTED IMMIGRATION ON ID THEFT AND PROPERTY CRIME: A CASE STUDY FOR U.S.-MEXICO RELATIONS

Richard J. Cebula[1] and Mary Githens[2]
[1]Shirley and Philip Solomons Eminent Scholar,
Armstrong Atlantic State University, USA
[2] Armstrong Atlantic State University, USA

ABSTRACT

In the U.S., illegal immigration is a very controversial issue. One dimension of this controversy involves whether this illegal entry in the country leads to higher rates of crime. If a clear link between crime in the U.S. and illegal immigration is established, the argument for more border security and enforcement is established. Clearly, such policies could lead to political tensions between the U.S. and Mexico. That said, according to the Federal Trade Commission, identity theft constituted the most common consumer complaint in the U.S. in 2006. Using state-level data for the 50 states for 2005, we find, among other things, that the rate of reported identity theft per 100,000 population is directed related to the unemployment rate, the percent of the population residing in urban areas, and the extent of undocumented immigration. We also find investigate the impact of undocumented migration upon "property crime" in the forms of "robbery" and "burglary" per 100,000 population is directly impacted by undocumented migration, as well as the unemployment rate and the percent of the population living in urban areas.

1. INTRODUCTION: THE ISSUE OF IDENTITY THEFT AND THOSE OF ROBBERY AND BURGLARY

The issue of illegal immigration into the U.S. has been a serious political and economic issue for many years. Economic theory suggests that the massive inflows of illegal immigrants into the U.S. could have significant effects on U.S. labor markets in the form of both wages and employment. Furthermore, U.S. politics could be affected in the effort to either deport such immigrants or grant them refuge and potentially integrate them into either the Republican or Democratic parties. Moreover, to the extent that there is an effort to strengthen U.S.-Mexico border security, such a policy could lead to strained political relations between the two countries. An issue of potentially serious relevance to such strengthened border patrol and deportation policies is whether the influx of illegal immigrants through Mexico has significantly affected crime in the U.S.

The existence and extent of identity theft has been characterized as a "blight" on America's privacy and security landscape (Federal Trade Commission, 2007). There is little question but that cyber crime has grown dramatically in recent years (Swarns, 2006), and identity theft is its most common manifestation. Furthermore, Burger (2008) has estimated that in 2008 the averaged cost of an identity theft case to its victims and law enforcement was $31,000.

The conventional wisdom argues that when criminals illegally assume the identity of another individual ("ID theft"), they usually do so for financial/economic reasons (Cebula and Koch, 2008). More often than not, they intend to: (1) steal the victim's financial assets; or, (2) obtain goods and services under false pretenses, without paying; or (3) use the victim's identity as a cover for other illegal activities.

Michael Chertoff, the U.S. Homeland Security Director, argues that undocumented immigrants are among the major ID theft offenders (Swarns, 2006). Chertoff believes undocumented immigrants largely engage in ID theft so they can obtain some else's social security number, thus enabling them to hold a job, open bank accounts, and the like. Other hypotheses exist, however. Some theorize that ID theft is aided and abetted by the Internet, and there seems little doubt that some ID theft is accomplished by means of the Internet. The media, perhaps reflecting a desire to be politically correct, usually has focused upon this possibility. "Few Internet security watchers believe 2007 will be any brighter for the millions of fraud-weary consumers already struggling to stay abreast of new computer security threats and avoiding clever scams when banking, shopping, or just surfing online," wrote a *Washington Post* reporter (Krebs, 2006).

What we first propose to do in this study is to examine differences in ID theft rates across the 50 states. We make interstate differences in ID theft rates a function of variables prompted by economic theory such as the economic conditions within each state. More specifically, we consider oft-cited variables such as the urban vs. rural nature of the state, religious adherence, Internet access, economic conditions (such as unemployment), and, of course, the incidence of undocumented immigrants in a state. Subsequently, we shall also consider the role of undocumented migrants in two forms of property crime, more specifically, robbery and burglary.

To presage our results on the first of these three issues, we find that the states with the highest ID theft rates tend to be those that have the highest percentages of undocumented immigrants. Internet access, on the other hand, *negatively* impacts on the incidence of ID theft. This underscores the practical reality that while some of the most sophisticated instances of ID theft may involve the Internet, the massive majority of actual ID theft cases appears to involve simpler and more utilitarian motives---for example, undocumented immigrants stealing a social security number so that they can hold jobs in the U.S. and open bank accounts. We also find that the percentage of undocumented immigrants in a state is a highly significant predictor of the incidence of that state's ID theft. Having said that, we immediately stress that much more work needs to be done on this subject. Other factors also are shown to influence the incidence of identity theft.

In addition to identifying influences on the rate of ID theft, we also focus, using similar variables, determinants of both robbery and burglary. The consistent finding in all of the estimates is that in all cases, it appears that undocumented migrants play a significant explanatory role. The clear conclusion is to reconsider the securing of U.S. borders. The international political implications of such a policy could put a serious strain on U.S.-Mexico relations.

2. The Incidence and Reporting of Identity Theft

Title 18 USC 1028 of the Identity Theft and Assumption and Deterrence Act (1998) identifies an ID thief as someone who:

> ...knowingly transfers or uses, without lawful authority, any name or number that may be used, alone or in conjunction with any other information, to identify a specific individual with intent to commit, or to aid and abet, any unlawful activity that constitutes a violation of Federal law, or that constitutes a felony under any applicable State or local law.

One can see that this definition of ID theft is rather broad, perhaps purposely so, because ID theft has been a rapidly evolving concept. The law seemingly was designed to deal with unforeseen circumstances brought about by technological change. Consequently, what one authority regards as ID theft, another may not, sometimes because an act in question is not regarded as significant, and other times because an act is so new that it hasn't yet found a spot on enforcers' proverbial radar screens.

The Federal Trade Commission (2006) reported that state ID theft rates varied in 2005 from a low of 24.8 per 100,000 persons in North Dakota to a high of 156.9 per 100,000 persons in Arizona. The median states, Hawaii and Alaska, had rates of 63.5 and 63.4, respectively. California, with a 125.0 rate, ranked third among the states but had the largest total number of reported ID thefts (45,175) in 2005. Table 1 summarizes this information.

Some ID theft crimes go unreported or even unrecognized. One reason for this is that several forms of ID theft are not regarded as criminal acts, or at least fail to be treated as such. To the sometime applause of the public, members of the media occasionally assume false identities in order to pursue a story and, providing they do not attempt to obtain personal financial benefit, this variety of ID theft is not considered illegal in many states. Or, if it is, it frequently goes unprosecuted. Law enforcement authorities themselves sometimes assume false identities in order to capture alleged law violators and federal court dockets not infrequently feature cases in which one of the issues is alleged law breaking or deception by law enforcement agencies.

In still other cases, "pretexting" (assuming a false identity in order to obtain information) is at the heart of the matter. In 2006, the information technology giant Hewlett-Packard engaged in pretexting in 2006 in an attempt to obtain telephone records in an attempt to find a corporate leak. The Congress responded by approving a bill to criminalize pretexting aimed at obtaining someone's telephone records (Rogers and Mathews, 2006), but other forms of pretexting do not necessarily violate federal, state, or local laws.

Table 1. Identity Victims by State (per 100,000 Population)

Rank	State	Victims Per 100,000 People	Number of Victims	Rank	State	Victims Per 100,000 People	Number of Victims
	Arizona	56.9	9,320	26	Alaska	63.4	421
	Nevada	130.2	3,144	27	Louisiana	62.6	2,811
	California	125.0	45,175	28	Massachusetts	62.5	3,999
	Texas	116.5	26,624	29	Ohio	62.4	7,155
	Colorado	97.2	4,535	30	Minnesota	58.7	3,015
	Florida	95.8	17,048	31	Alabama	58.7	2,675
	Washington	92.4	5,810	32	Kansas	58.5	1,606
	New York	90.3	17,387	33	Arkansas	58.2	1,617
	Georgia	87.3	7,918	34	Rhode Island	58.2	626
10	Illinois	87.3	11,137	35	Tennessee	57.2	3,412
11	Maryland	86.6	4,848	36	So. Carolina	56.8	2,416
12	New Mex.	84.7	1,634	37	Nebraska	52.3	919
13	Oregon	87	2,973	38	Idaho	52.1	745
14	New Jersey	75.5	6,582	39	Wisconsin	50.3	2,782
15	Michigan	70.5	7,139	40	Mississippi	49.9	1,458
16	Delaware	69.1	583	41	New Hampshire	49.2	645
17	Virginia	68.2	5,183	42	Wyoming	44.0	224
18	Oklahoma	67.7	2,403	43	Kentucky	43.5	1,815
19	Missouri	67.6	3,920	44	Montana	42.5	398
20	Utah	67.5	1,668	45	West Virginia	37.3	677
21	No. Carolina	67.1	5,830	46	Maine	37.2	491
22	Indiana	67.0	4,201	47	Iowa	36.7	1,090
23	Connecticut	65.9	2,313	48	Vermont	32.3	201
24	Pennsylvania	63.6	7,908	49	South Dakota	30.0	233
25	Hawaii	63.5	810	50	North Dakota	24.8	158

Median: 63.4/63.5 Un-weighted Mean: 65.69.
Source: Federal Trade Commission (2006).

Yet, there are forms of pretexting that seldom result in any legal action. Individuals often assume false identities on web sites such as www.myspace.com and www.facebook.com by virtue of exaggerating their own virtues, or even blatantly lying about their essential characteristics (for example, a man telling a woman on myspace.com that he's 6'1" and a muscular 190 pounds rather than admitting that he's actually 5'1" and, 320 pounds). Such episodes may be frowned upon, but are seldom prosecuted unless they are accompanied by subsequent financial or sexual crimes.

The media frequently report large security breaches suffered by businesses and governmental agencies that apparently have exposed millions of individuals to potential ID theft (Swarns, 2006). A well-publicized example is the 2006 security breach at the U.S. Department of Veterans' Affairs, which resulted in lost personal data for an estimated 28.6 million veterans. Nor have the major credit card companies been exempt from security problems. In 2005, hackers penetrated the financial company Card Systems Solutions and stole personal data for more than 40 million Visa and MasterCard account holders. In the Veterans Affairs case, it appears this has not led to significant ID theft, whereas in the credit card case, the effects have not been revealed.

This leads naturally to a significant policy question. Should we regard these instances as ID theft because, in fact, individual identities were stolen, or focus instead only on those cases where the theft has recognizably led to criminal use of that ID? Actual Federal Trade Commission practice leans in the latter direction and therefore might be viewed as minimizing the actual occurrence of ID theft. Nevertheless, the Federal Trade Commission (2007) received almost 250,000 ID theft complaints in 2006.

The relevant point is the ID theft data published by the Federal Trade Commission report provide only a partial glimpse of ID theft and have obvious flaws (Newman and McNally, 2005). An act one individual or law enforcement officer regards as an actionable instance of ID theft may not be interpreted similarly by another individual or policeman. Hence, that act may go unreported. The Federal Trade Commission (2006) estimates that 61 percent of American ID theft victims do not notify a police department. Further, 32 percent of reported ID thefts were not discovered until a year after the theft occurred (Federal Trade Commission, 2006). By then, the metaphorical horse is gone from the barn.

Even so, the FTC data, which focus on credit card, phone and bank fraud as well as employment and government documents fraud in the U.S., now constitute the best information available. Perhaps more important, even if these data are only approximations of reality, they nonetheless are being used for purposes of resource allocation and public policy. Both the Department of Justice and the Federal Trade Commission pay attention to these data when they allocate law enforcement resources, and the media and elected officials usually treat these data as if they were handed down on tablets from Mount Sinai. Hence, it is important to know what these data tell us about the nature and sources of ID theft.

3. Previous Work on Identity Theft

Until very recently, the major source of information concerning empirical studies of the determinants of ID theft has been Newman and McNally (2005). In their review of the ID theft literature for the U.S. Department of Justice, the duo commented tersely that "...there are only a handful of studies that focus exclusively on identity theft, but they vary widely in quality and scope" (p. 11). In point of fact, analytical studies are scarce to *de facto* non-existent, whereas there have been many articles that either have discussed the increasing incidence of ID theft or have focused on the technological tricks thieves use to steal someone's ID. Nearly all studies eventually talk about the precautions that individuals and households might take in order to reduce their exposure. Smith and Lias (2005) and Smith (2005) are representative of this approach. These studies address the incidence of ID theft occurs, the usual ways in which it occurs, and what countermeasures individuals might take to reduce their vulnerability. Smith and Lias (2005), for example, surveyed 75 managerial employees in the Pittsburgh area, whereas Smith (2005) focused on a sample of 107 "working professionals" in the Pittsburgh metropolitan area to ascertain how they have dealt with potential or real ID theft. The Newman and McNally (2005) survey contains only a handful of other references to research studies, and these studies tend to rely heavily upon survey responses. Star Systems (2002) polled approximately 3,000 individuals via telephone; Gartner (2003) sampled 2,445 households; Harris Interactive 2003) focused on 3,462 adults; and the Federal Trade Commission (2003) conducted a randomized telephone survey of 4,057 individuals.

More recently, a survey by the Council of Better Business Bureaus and Javelin Strategy and Research (Johannes, 2006) relied upon 5,000 telephone interviews and in contrast to most other studies, interestingly concluded that the growth of ID theft has been tapered off. Nevertheless, the study concluded that 8.9 million American adults had been victimized by ID theft in 2005 and that the average financial loss per occurrence had risen to $6,383 (Johannes, 2006, p.1).

The commonality among these studies is their reliance upon a descriptive approach to the ID theft phenomenon. Like ornithologists cataloging birds, the authors of these studies describe the major varieties of ID theft and then proceed to outline precautions individuals can take in order to minimize their potential exposure to ID thieves. Thus, we are advised to choose complicated, not easy to understand, passwords on the Internet and to avoid supplying our social security numbers unless absolutely necessary and then never in an e-mail. These studies are not analytical and do not rigorously probe the determinants of ID theft. Thus, we are left to wonder which populations are the most likely to commit ID theft, as well as whether unemployment plays a role in ID theft, whether ID theft is an urban phenomenon, and how the Internet might be involved in ID theft.

The only published formal empirical studies to date to suggest (albeit in tentative terms) undocumented immigrants in the U.S. as major perpetrators of ID theft are those by Cebula, Koch, and Unemori (2007) and Cebula and Koch (2008). The more typical interpretation adopted by the media and found/espoused elsewhere, but one *not* based upon formal empirical analysis, is that well-educated American computer hackers and high technology thieves based in locations such as the Ukraine and the People's Republic of China are the parties guilty of ID theft (Krebs, 2006). It is possible that such malefactors are more significant in terms of the financial impact of each of their individual transgressions, but they are not so in terms of the absolute number of offenses.

We wish to emphasize that our results do not preclude such "foreign" parties from possible blame. However, in the case of foreign-based ID thieves, they are not directly included in our analysis since we examine the 50 U.S. states. We do not discount the fact that an American using the Internet to make a purchase can be duped by an Internet site that takes his money but does not deliver him the goods. Rather, the main point is that the incidence of such cases may be dwarfed by immigrant-related ID theft. Once the issue of ID theft has been fully considered, the focus shifts to the potential impact of undocumented immigration on property crime in the form of (1) robbery and (2) burglary.

4. A Simple Model of ID Theft

Whereas some data are available that quantify ID theft for metropolitan areas, in point of fact, the best political unit data available relate to the 50 states. Accordingly, our goal is to explain variations in the rate of ID theft, and subsequently, burglary and robbery, using state-level data. Hence, we estimate a reduced-from equation of the following form:

$$R_i = a + bX_{i,} + u_i \quad (1)$$

where:

R_i = rate of reported ID theft per 100,000
individuals during the year 2005 in state "*i*";
X_i = vector of state characteristics such as
population demographics, economic status, apparent religious commitment,
urban versus rural residence, education, Internet access; and
u_i = stochastic error term.
We adopt five categories of explanatory variables for each state:

- Economic conditions (UNEMPL, each state's unemployment rate in 2004)
- Urban/rural nature (URBAN, the percent of each state's population living in an urban area in 2000)
- Extent of religious affiliation (RELIGION, the percent of each state's population that identified itself as being Christian, 2000)
- Internet access (INTERNET, the percent of households in each state connected to the Internet, 2003)
- Incidence of undocumented immigrants (UNDOCIMM, the estimated percent of each state's population consisting of undocumented immigrants, as of March, 2005).

Data sources were, as follows: U.S. Census Bureau (2006, Tables 581, 27, 71, 1150); the Federal Trade Commission (2006, Table 329); and the Pew Hispanic Center (2006).

5. Empirical Results in ID Theft Determinants

The OLS (ordinary least squares) estimate, with White (1980) heteroskedasticity-corrected standard errors (and hence heteroskedasticity-corrected t-values), of the basic model is found in Regression 1 in Table 2. The ID Theft rate per 100,000 population is the dependent variable in the analysis. Except for the sign of the Internet access variable, the signs of the coefficients of the independent variables in Regression 1 correspond with reasonable *a priori* expectations. The sign on the coefficient of the undocumented immigrants variable is positive and highly significant (at the one percent level). This is hardly surprising, since only a cursory examination of Table 1 is necessary to see that the states with the largest incidence of ID theft also have the largest incidence of undocumented immigrants (see Arizona and California as good examples). Here, however, we have documented that relationship in a *ceteris paribus* context in which other relevant factors such as economic conditions, the extent of the states' urban population, religious adherence, and Internet access have been held constant in the estimating equation.

We cannot ascertain from the regressions in Table 2 whether the ID thefts perpetrated in states that have proportionately large numbers of undocumented immigrants are more or less *serious* in terms of their aggregate financial impact. It is reasonable to conclude, however, that the presence of undocumented immigrants in a state dramatically increases the incidence of ID theft in that state. Specifically, a one percent increase in undocumented aliens in a state generates an 8.778 unit increase in that state's rate of ID theft per 100,000 residents. This translates to a 13-14 percent increase in a representative state's ID theft rate. Thus, the ID theft response of a state to an increased proportion of undocumented aliens is highly elastic. That is, a representative state's ID theft rate responds very robustly to an increase in the proportion of undocumented immigrants in that state.

Table 2. Determinants of ID Theft, Burglary, and Robbery, 2005

Regression Coefficients, with t-Values in Parentheses			
Explanatory Variables	Regression 1	Regression 2	Regression 3
UNEMPL	4.141*** (3.56)	10.826** (2.29)	45.83** (2.04)
URBAN	0.4566*** (3.83)	--------	--------
RELIGION	-0.391*** (-4.15)	-0.866** (-2.15)	-4.105 (-1.59)
INTERNET	-0.758*** (-3.48)	-8.493*** (-6.76)	-20.509*** (-3.77)
UNDOCIMM	8.778*** (7.21)	15.22*** (8.90)	53.055*** (5.20)
MEDFAMINC	--------	0.0046*** (6.50)	-0.0033 (-1.04)
CONSTANT	49.03	215.75	1,850.59
R2	0.89	0.72	0.59
R2 (adj.)	0.88	0.68	0.55
F	73.87**	22.17***	12.83***

*** probability = 0.01; ** probability = 0 .05.

Notes: All regressions adopt the White (1980) heteroskedasticity adjustment (1980). The significance test for UNDOCIMM are two-tailed.

We also observe that the state unemployment rate apparently leads to higher state rates of ID theft. This coefficient, which cannot be regarded as surprising (the higher the unemployment rate, the greater the incentive to seek income from non-employment forms, including ID theft), is positive and statistically significant at the one percent level. Similarly, our finding that "urbanity"---highly concentrated urban populations in a state---is conducive to ID theft is consistent with intuition. This estimated coefficient is positive and statistically significant at the one percent level. It seems reasonable to assume that it is more difficult and perhaps less rewarding to commit ID theft in a rural situation since fewer people are accessible vis-à-vis a more urban setting. Moreover, "dumpster diving" is less likely to be a viable source of ID theft in rural areas than in urban areas.

It seems plausible to assume that those individuals who have strong religious beliefs and connections may be less likely to commit ID theft. Our proxy for these "moral" constraints is the percent of a state's adult population that declares itself to be Christian. We find that states with high religious adherence have lower rates of ID theft, holding other things constant. This estimated coefficient is negative and statistically significant at the one percent level also.

It is the negative sign on the Internet access coefficient that some might find confounding. *Ceteris paribus*, the negative coefficient suggests (albeit modestly in Regression 1) that increased Internet access diminishes ID theft. This finding conflicts with the views of some who regard ID theft as a fundamentally Internet-based phenomenon. The latter view appears to be false, at least as it applies to the incidence of ID theft, although it could still be true that Internet-based ID thefts involve the greatest dollar sums. These observations notwithstanding, since the coefficient on this variable is statistically significant at barely the ten percent level, it might useful to consider the results for this variable in the other estimates, where its statistical significance and β-coefficients are both greater.

State variations in the ID theft rate are much more sensitive to factors other than Internet access, especially the presence of undocumented aliens in a state. Indeed, if we hold economic conditions, urbanity, religion and other factors constant, then Internet access may well be a proxy for the relative sophistication of a state's residents in the use and protection of sensitive, private information. That is, if one had Internet access in one's homes, then one *might have been* less likely to place ourselves in situations where social security numbers or driver's licenses could be stolen. One also might have been more likely to erect Internet defenses against scams, "phishing," spy bots, and other techniques that might induce one to supply such information, willingly or unwillingly.

Regarding this estimate, there remain three further observations. First, the coefficient of determination is 0.89, so that the model explains nearly 90 percent of ID theft. Second, the F-statistic is statistically significant at far beyond the one percent level, attesting to the overall strength of the model. Third, these results are entirely consistent with those in Cebula and Koch (2008), who include law enforcement expenditures and educational attainment as arguments to explain ID theft.

6. Property Crime: Robbery and Burglary

This section of the study investigates whether undocumented migrants are associated with higher levels of robbery and burglary. The decision to commit such crimes is treated as being the result of a cost-benefit calculus. The model variables are very similar to those in the ID Theft investigation shown in Table 2; however, in place of the unemployment rate, median family income in 2004 is adopted (U.S. Census, 2006, Table 658). This substitution generates more robust results in the case of non-ID theft crimes, although the findings for the undocumented migration variable remain robust across all estimates. The Robbery variable is the number of robberies in 2004 per 100,000 population in each state, whereas the Burglary variable is the number of burglaries in 2004 per 100,000 population in each state. These data were obtained from the U.S. Department of Justice (2005, Table 5).

The results of the "robbery estimation" are provided in Regression 2, whereas that for "burglary" is found in Regression 3. In Regression 2, four of the five estimated coefficients exhibit the expected signs and are statistically significant at the five percent level; the estimated coefficient for one variable, that for median family income, has a *positive* sign and is statistically significant at far beyond the one percent level, even with a two-tailed test. The coefficient of determination is 0.72, so that the model explains nearly three-fourths of the variation in the robbery rate. Finally, the F-statistic is statistically significant at far beyond the one percent level.

The interpretation of the results is straightforward, even for the potentially anomalous case of median family income. First, the robbery rate is a decreasing function of the internet variable. Perhaps this attest once again to the possibility that this variable reflects savvy households who do not take the kinds of risks that raise the likelihood of being victimized by robbery.

The sign on the unemployment rate is statistically significant at the five percent level and positive—again—implying that when unemployment rates are higher, that the incentive to turn to crime, in this case, robbery, increases. The estimated coefficient on the religious affiliation variable is negative and significant at the five percent level, implying once again that religious affiliation implies a greater probability of not turning to crime. The positive and significant coefficient on the median family income variable has a different interpretation, namely, the higher the median family income the greater the potential gains from undertaking a robbery, i.e., the bigger the stakes (target for would-be criminals contemplating robbery as an income source). Finally, and most relevantly, the estimated coefficient on the undocumented migrant variable is positive and statistically significant at the one percent level even with a two-tailed test! Thus, it appears that the greater the percent of the population that consists of undocumented migrants, the greater the robbery rate. In particular, a one percent increase in undocumented immigrants implies a 15.22 unit increase in the robbery rate per 100,000 population in a state.

Finally, we come to Regression 3, which is the estimate for burglary. In this case, three of the five estimated coefficients exhibit the expected signs and are statistically significant at the five percent level or beyond. The coefficient of determination is 0.59, so that the model explains approximately three-fifths of the variation in the burglary rate. Finally, the f-statistic is statistically significant at the one percent level.

As shown in Regression 3 of Table 2, the unemployment rate coefficient is positive and statistically significant at the five percent level, implying that the higher the unemployment rate, the more appealing the act of burglary becomes as a source of income. Next, the greater extent of households have internet access, once again the less likely the incidence of being a victim of crime. In particular, the greater the greater the access to the internet, the lower the likelihood of being burglarized. Paralleling the discussion of ID Theft, this variable may reflect more sophisticated households that take more precautions to protect themselves, e.g., installing burglar alarms. Finally, the estimated coefficient for the undocumented migration variable is positive and statistically significant at far beyond the one percent level. Thus, once again, this factor proves to be an apparently large contributor to crime in the U.S. For example, a one percent increase in this variable induces a 53 unit increase in burglaries per 100,000 persons.

CONCLUSION

This study clearly is exploratory in character. The results are intriguing, but we would be wise to note the caveats dispensed by Friedman and Schwartz (1991), Christ (1993), and Tomek (1993), who have warned of the perils associated with strong policy conclusions based upon the statistical significance of coefficients in single regression equations. These economists stress that much more heed should be accorded to repetitive results that have been confirmed under appropriately rigorous testing circumstances. Results that emanate from a single study, however strong, must be regarded as preliminary. That said, the results here are extensions of prior studies by Cebula and Koch (2008) and Cebula, Koch, and Unemori (2007) that yield entirely compatible results!

We state the obvious when we point out that that state-level ID theft data necessarily yield limited conclusions. The same is true of robbery and burglary data. We need to perform more work at the level of metropolitan areas, cities, and individuals in order to reach stronger conclusions. Furthermore, there is the danger of falling prey to the ecological fallacy, that is, to inferring individual conclusions from group data. Here, this means that we can make statements about state-level data and variables, but not necessarily about individuals. We cannot unequivocally conclude that undocumented immigrants are a major cause of ID theft, robberies, and burglaries; however, we *can* state that a clear pattern exists in which those states that have relatively more undocumented immigrants do have much higher rates of ID theft, robbery, and burglary.

That said, it does appear that a strong statistical relationship exists between the presence of undocumented immigrants and the ID theft rate, as well as robbery and burglary. Michael Chertoff, the nation's Director of Homeland Security, surmised that undocumented immigrants have been heavily involved in ID theft (Chertoff, 2006). At this point, his speculations appear to be well worth further investigation. Furthermore, perhaps a significant proportion of ID theft could be eliminated if attention were paid to ways and means by which undocumented immigrants illegally both acquire and then utilize personnel ID information belonging to legal residents of the United States.

In any case, illegal immigration into the U.S. remains a serious political and economic issue. A concern of potentially serious relevance to this issue and hence to strengthened border patrol and deportation policies is whether this influx of illegal immigrants through Mexico has significantly affected crime in the U.S. The findings in this study appear to strongly support the latter perspective. To the degree that these results become increasingly recognized, the impetus to curb border crossings will likely increase, i.e., it is probable that there will be a renewed effort to strengthen U.S.-Mexico border security. Of course, such a policy could lead to strained political relations between these two countries.

REFERENCES

Burger, A. K. (2008). The Cost of ID Theft, Part I: Beyond Dollars and Cents, *E-Commerce Times,* February 5. twww.ccommercetimes.com/story/61515.html?welcome =1202389102.

Cebula, R.J., and Koch, J.V. (2008). The Impact of Undocumented Migration on ID Theft in the United States, *The Open Economics Journal*, 1, 37-46.

Cebula, R., Koch, J.V., and Unemori, M. (2007). An Empirical Analysis of Identity Theft Determinants in the U.S., *Review of Business Research*, 7, 1-8.

Christ, C. (1995). Assessing Applied Econometric Results, *Federal Reserve Bank of St. Louis Review,* 75, 71-94.

Federal Trade Commission. (2007). *Consumer Fraud and Identity Theft Complaint Data.* http://www.consumer.gov/sentinel.

Federal Trade Commission. (2006). *Identity Theft Victim Complaint Data: Figures and Trends, January 1-December 31, 2005*. Washington, D.C.: Federal Trade Commission

Friedman, M., and Schwartz, A.J. (1991). Alternative Approaches to Analyzing Economic Data, *American Economic Review*, 81, 39-49.

Identity Theft and Assumption and Deterrence Act. (2008).

Johannes, R. (2006). *The 2006 Identity Fraud Survey.* Pleasanton, CA: Council of Better Business Bureaus and Javelin Strategy and Research.

Krebs, B. (2006). Cyber Crime Hits the Big Time in 2006. *Washington Post Online.* www.washingtonpost.com/wp-dyn/content/article/2006/12/22, December 22.

Newman, G.R., and M. M. McNally, M. M. (2005). *Identity Theft Literature Review.* Washington, D.C.: U.S. Department of Justice.

Pew Hispanic Center. (2006). Estimates of the Unauthorized Migrant Population. http://pewhispanic.org/files/factsheets/17.pdf

Rogers, D. and Mathews, R.G. (2006). Congress Approves Bill to Criminalize 'Pretexting'. *Wall Street Journal*, 258, December 11, A6.

Schneir, B. (2007). Solving Identity Theft. Forbes.com. www.forbes.com/2007/01/ 19/identity-theft-security-tech-security-cz_bs_0122identity, March 29.

Smith, A.D. (2005). Identity Theft as a Threat to CRM and E-Commerce, *Electronic Government: An International Journal*, 2, 219-46.

Smith, A.D., and Lias, A.R.. (2005). Identity Theft and E-Fraud as Critical CRM Concerns, *International Journal of Enterprise Information Systems*, 1, 17-36.

Star Systems. (2002). *Identity Theft and Security Concerns: 2002 Consumer Survey.* www.star.com/pdf/STARIDTheft.pdf.

Swarns, R.L. (2006). Illegal Immigrants at Center of New ID Theft Crackdown. *New York Times*, 156, December 14, A26.

Tomek, W.G. (1993). Confirmation and Replication in Empirical Econometrics: A Step Toward Improved Scholarship, *American Journal of Agricultural Economics*, 75, October, 6-14.

U.S. Census Bureau. (2006). *Statistical Abstract of the United States, 2006.* Washington, D.C.: U.S. Government Printing Office.

U.S. Department of Justice. (2006). *Crime in the United States, 2005*. Washington, D.C.: U.S. Government Printing Office.

Wall Street Journal Online. (2007). www.wsj.com/public/article/PR-CO-20070112-904029, January 12.

White, H. (1980). A Heteroskedasticity-Consistent Covariance Matrix Estimator and a Direct Test for Heteroskedasticity, *Econometrica*, 48, May, 817-38.

In: International Political Economy
Editors: M.A. Galindo Martin, E. Nissan
ISBN: 978-1-60876-172-2

Chapter 14

RELIGIOUS DIVERSITY AND CORRUPTION: CROSS COUNTRY EVIDENCE

Oguzhan C. Dincer and James E. Payne
Illinois State University, USA

ABSTRACT

Using recently developed indices of fractionalization and polarization, we investigate the effects of religious diversity on corruption across countries. We find a linear and positive relationship between religious polarization and corruption and an inverse U-shaped relationship between religious fractionalization and corruption, and thus the corruption maximizing level of religious fractionalization. According to our results, a 1 standard deviation increase in polarization index causes the corruption index to increase by 0.17 standard deviations which is almost 3 times larger than the effects of some of the control variables such as openness and education on corruption. All else constant, corruption is maximized when the fractionalization index is equal to 0.57 which falls well within the range of observed values.

1. INTRODUCTION

Corruption is one of the most serious problems that every country has to deal with today. Although it has been around for a very long time, we still have not uncovered all of the factors making corruption in one country more prevalent than another. Although, corruption in a country is affected by several factors, most of the studies focus only on economic factors such as per capita GDP or openness. In our opinion, demographic factors such as ethnic and religious diversity are as important as economic factors. For instance, ethnic diversity is likely to cause politicians to act along ethnic lines and hence cause corruption to increase. Indeed, several studies have found a positive relationship between ethnic fractionalization and corruption.[1] According to van den Berghe (1987) and Vanhanen (1999), the members of an

[1] See Treisman (2000), Alesina et al. (2003) and Glaeser and Saks (2006).

ethnic group display ethnocentric behavior by favoring their group members over non-members. As long as different ethnic groups exist in a country and as long as politicians allocate resources towards backers of their own ethnicity, the members of ethnic groups are likely to continue to support the politicians of their own ethnic groups, even if they are known to be corrupt.[2]

However, in our opinion, religious diversity is perhaps as important as ethnic diversity in explaining corruption. For example, according to Vanhanen (1999), the tendency to favor one's own group members does not only include ethnic groups but also includes religious groups. Nevertheless, the effects of religious diversity on corruption have not drawn a lot of attention in the literature. To our knowledge there are only a few studies investigating the relationship between religious diversity on corruption. Using cross-country data, Alesina et al. (2003), for instance, found a positive relationship between religious fractionalization and corruption. In this study, we investigate the effects of religious diversity on corruption by using data for 105 countries.[3] Although our study parallels Alesina et al. (2003), we do find an interesting set of relationships between two different measures of religious diversity and corruption which are quite different from their findings. Specifically, we find a linear and positive relationship between religious polarization and corruption and an inverse U-shaped relationship between religious fractionalization and corruption, and thus the corruption maximizing level of religious fractionalization. Our results confirm the findings by Dincer (2008) in the case of U.S. states.

Section 2 presents and summarizes the data on religious diversity and corruption, as well as on the respective control variables. Section 3 discusses our findings regarding the effects of religious diversity on corruption while Section 4 provides a check on the robustness of the results. Section 5 concludes.

2. DATA

As mentioned in the introduction, the analysis of the relationship between religious diversity and corruption encompasses a cross-section of 105 countries. There are two competing indices frequently used in empirical studies: the fractionalization index (*FI*) and polarization index (*PI*).[4] In our study we use both of these indices to measure religious diversity across countries. *FI*, which gives us the probability that two randomly selected individuals in a country belong to two different religious groups, is calculated as follows:

$$FI_i = 1 - \sum_{j=1}^{J} n_{ij}^2 \tag{1}$$

where n is the population share of group j in country i. It increases with the number of groups and reaches a maximum if every individual in a country belongs to a different religious group.

[2] Glaeser and Saks (2006)

[3] The list of countries with the data on polarization, fractionalization, and corruption indices are given in Table 1.

[4] Alesina et al. (2003), for example, use both fractionalization and polarization indices to investigate the relationship between diversity and growth.

On the other hand, *PI* measures the distance of any distribution of religious groups from the situation that leads to the maximum ethnocentric behavior. *PI* is calculated as

$$PI_i = 1 - \sum_{j=1}^{J} \left(\frac{0.5 - n_{ij}}{0.5} \right)^2 n_{ij} \tag{2}$$

In contrast to FI, PI reaches a maximum when there are two religious groups of equal size in a country.[5] In our study, we use the religious polarization and fractionalization indices calculated by Montalvo and Reynal-Querol (2005) based on the data from *L'etat Des Religions Dans Le Monde* and *The Statesman's Yearbook* for the year 1987. Their calculations include the following religious groups: Judaism, Christianity, Islam, Buddhism, Hinduism, Taoism, Confucianism, Chinese Religions, Bahaism, Synretic Cults, Animist Religions, Other Religions, and No Religion. Taking the polarization index first, Africa is the most religiously polarized region with average PI of 0.70. OECD countries, on average, are the least polarized religiously. OECD average of PI is 0.14. Turning to the fractionalization index, Africa and Southeast Asia are the most religiously fractionalized regions. The average FI is 0.41 in both regions. Not surprisingly, the least fractionalized countries are the OECD countries with an average FI of 0.09.

Figure 1, taken from of Montalvo and Reynal-Querol (2005), shows FI and PI as functions of the number of groups (assumed of equal size).

Figure 2 shows the relationship we find between *PI* and *FI,* respectively for 135 countries.[6] For low levels of fractionalization, *PI* and *FI* are positively and highly correlated. For medium levels of fractionalization, the correlation is zero, and for high levels of fractionalization it is negative. It is not surprising, then, to observe that the relationship between fractionalization and corruption and the relationship between polarization and corruption are rather different and that is exactly what we find.

In addition to measures of religious diversity, the measurement of corruption is vital to our analysis. While it is not possible to measure corruption directly, it is possible to measure the perceptions of corruption. Subjective corruption indices based on perceptions of corruption developed by several institutions such as *International Country Risk Guide* (ICRG), *Business Environment Risk Intelligence* (BERI), and *Transparency International* (TI) are available. However, in this study, we use the *World Bank Corruption Index* for the year 2000 developed by Kaufmann, Kraay, and Zoido-Lobaton (2002). For simplicity and ease of exposition, we rescale the index to take a value -2.5 for the least corrupt, and +2.5 for the most corrupt. Again, Africa is the most corrupt region with an average corruption index of 0.66 while the OECD is the least corrupt with an average corruption index of -1.53.

Besides our measurement of religious diversity as a determinant of corruption, we include a set of control variables in our regressions to minimize the potential for omitted variable bias. First, following La Porta et al. (1999) and Treisman (2000), we control for the legal system in the country using a dummy variable *Common Law*.

[5] In a country with three religious groups distributed with percentages 45, 45 and 10, the polarization index is higher than with the percentages 33.3, 33.3 and 33.3 or with 90, 10, 0. See Montalvo and Reynal-Querol (2005) for a detailed discussion.

[6] Figure 2 displays data for 135 countries of which 30 countries were excluded from the empirical analysis due to the unavailability of data for many of the control variables.

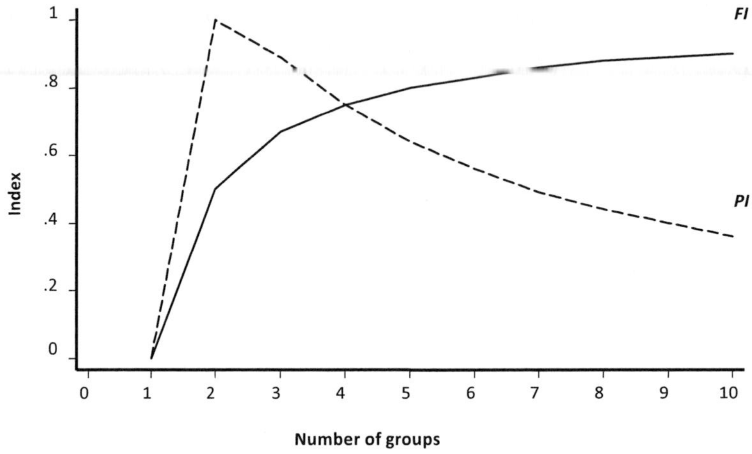

Figure 1. Polarization and Fractionalization.

According to La Porta et al. (1999) and Treisman (2000), legal systems differ in their degree of protection of private individuals from corrupt public officials. Both studies have found lower corruption in countries with common law systems. Second, Ades and Di Tella (1999) assert that restrictions on international trade create opportunities for corruption. In other words, they suggest that openness to international trade lowers corruption. We measure openness (*Openness*) as the share of exports and imports in gross domestic product using data from the *Penn World Tables*. Third, both Ades and Di Tella (1999) and Treisman (2000) make the case that it is likely that natural resource abundance creates corruption opportunities for public officials who allocate rights to exploit these resources. Their results reveal a positive relationship between the share of fuels, minerals, and metals in total exports and corruption. Thus, we incorporate the share of fuels, minerals, and metals in total exports in our analysis (*Resource*) using data from the World Bank. Fourth, Treisman (2000) argues that a federal structure is likely to lower corruption by creating competition between different levels of government at both the local and federal. On the other hand, it is also likely that corruption is higher at the local level due to the frequent contact between the private individuals and the public officials. Treisman (2000) found a positive relationship between federalism and corruption. We control for the governmental structure using a dummy variable (*Federal*). Fifth, Glaeser and Saks (2006) present evidence to suggest that private individuals with more education are more willing to monitor public officials and to take action when they engage in corruption via their voting behavior. To this end we measure education as the share of population aged 25 and above with a secondary school degree (*Education*). Finally, we include the level of economic development as measured by per real capita GDP (*GDP*) using data from the *Penn World Tables*. As countries get richer they have more resources to fight corruption as evident by the negative relationship between per capita GDP and corruption found in the previously cited studies.[7] All of our control variables are for the year 1990. Summary statistics for diversity and corruption indices as well as for the respective control variables are given in Table 1 while pair-wise correlations are shown in Table 2.

[7] We also include a region dummy (*MENA*) for the countries in the Middle East and North Africa.

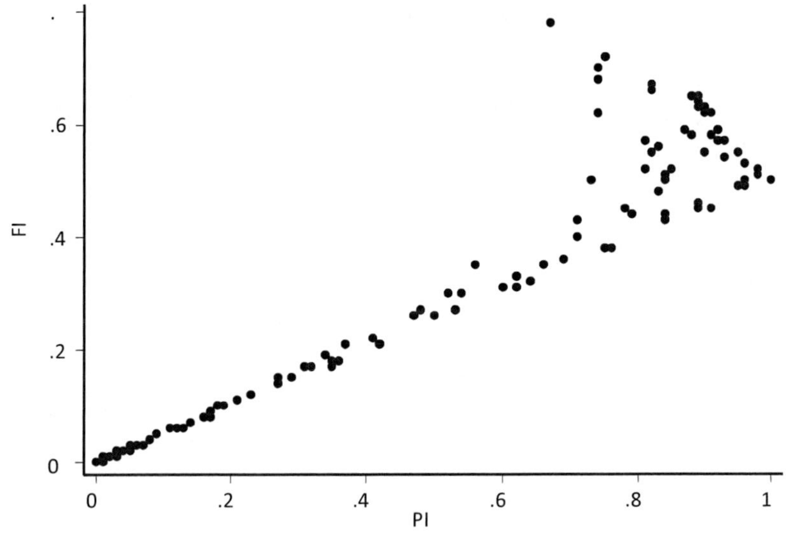

Figure 2. Religious Pofilarization and Religious Fractionalization.

3. MODEL AND RESULTS

A. Polarization and Corruption

With respect to religious polarization and corruption, our model takes the form

$$Corruption_i = \beta_0 + \beta_1 PI_i + \beta_2 X_i + \varepsilon_i \quad (3)$$

where $Corruption_i$ represents the corruption index in country i, PI_i represents the religious polarization index in country i, and X_i represents the set of control variables that affect corruption as well as the region dummies (*Education*, *GDP*, *Openness*, *Common Law*, *Natural Resource*, *Federal*, and *MENA*). The results of the ordinary least squares (OLS) estimation are presented in the first column of Table 3. The estimated coefficient of *PI* is positive and significant at the 1 percent level, indicating a strong positive relationship between religious polarization and corruption. As the results given in Table 3 suggest, a 1 standard deviation increase in polarization index causes the corruption index to increase by 0.17 standard deviations which is almost 3 times larger than the effects of openness and education on corruption.

Table 1. List of Countries

Country	PI	FI	Corruption
Afghanistan	0.96	0.49	1.91
Algeria	0.03	0.02	0.76
Angola	0.91	0.45	1.49

Table 1 (Continued)

Country	PI	FI	Corruption
Argentina	0.18	0.1	0.29
Australia	0.04	0.02	-1.96
Austria	0.05	0.03	-1.93
Bahamas, The	0.06	0.03	-1.39
Bahrain	0.93	0.54	-0.69
Bangladesh	0.5	0.26	0.94
Barbados	0.37	0.21	-1.39
Belgium	0.07	0.03	-1.55
Benin	0.82	0.55	0.61
Bolivia	0.96	0.53	0.54
Botswana	1	0.5	-0.74
Brazil	0.62	0.33	-0.04
Burundi	0.95	0.49	1.14
Cameroon	0.89	0.65	1.09
Canada	0.16	0.08	-2.02
Cape Verde	0	0	-0.18
Central African Republic	0.9	0.55	1.3
Chad	0.9	0.63	0.88
Chile	0.27	0.15	-1.45
China	0.82	0.67	0.28
Colombia	0.31	0.17	0.59
Comoros	0.01	0.01	1.1
Congo, Dem. Rep.	0.84	0.43	1.6
Congo, Rep.	0.66	0.35	1.01
Costa Rica	0.08	0.04	-0.87
Cote d'Ivoire	0.89	0.65	0.52
Cyprus	0.62	0.31	-0.79
Denmark	0.01	0.01	-2.18
Dominica	0.01	0	-0.44
Dominican Republic	1	0.5	0.4
Country	PI	FI	Corruption
Ecuador	0.6	0.31	0.86
Egypt, Arab Rep.	0.36	0.18	0.38

Country	PI	FI	Corruption
El Salvador	0.14	0.07	0.43
Ethiopia	0.91	0.62	0.46
Fiji	0.93	0.57	-0.15
Finland	0.01	0	-2.34
France	0.19	0.1	-1.5
Gabon	0.53	0.27	0.59
Gambia, The	0.48	0.27	0.4
Germany	0.12	0.06	-2
Ghana	0.88	0.58	0.25
Greece	0.06	0.03	-0.73
Grenada	0.04	0.02	-0.61
Guatemala	0.76	0.38	0.56
Guinea	0.84	0.44	0.79
Guinea-Bissau	0.91	0.58	0.88
Guyana	0.87	0.59	0.38
Haiti	0.75	0.38	1.44
Honduras	0.27	0.14	0.72
Hong Kong, China	0.74	0.7	-1.19
Hungary	0.04	0.02	-0.69
Iceland	0.03	0.01	-2.21
India	0.56	0.35	0.38
Indonesia	0.82	0.66	0.97
Iran, Islamic Rep.	0.35	0.18	0.51
Iraq	0.95	0.55	1.46
Ireland	0.01	0	-1.59
Israel	0.54	0.3	-0.98
Italy	0.01	0	-0.98
Jamaica	0.29	0.15	0.25
Japan	0.81	0.57	-1.35
Jordan	0.35	0.17	-0.04
Kenya	0.83	0.48	0.98
Korea, Rep.	0.67	0.78	-0.19
Kuwait	0.78	0.45	-1.04
Lesotho	0.64	0.32	0.19

Table 1 (Continued)

Country	PI	FI	Corruption
Liberia	0.89	0.64	1.66
Luxembourg	0.03	0.01	-2.05
Madagascar	0.98	0.52	0.06
Malawi	0.82	0.55	0.44
Malaysia	0.74	0.68	-0.36
Mali	0.62	0.33	0.64
Malta	0	0	-0.83
Mauritania	0.02	0.01	0.19
Mauritius	0.89	0.63	-0.43
Mexico	0.16	0.08	0.37
Morocco	0.08	0.04	-0.06
Mozambique	0.83	0.56	0.69
Nepal	0.34	0.19	0.43
Netherlands	0.09	0.05	-2.18
New Zealand	0.04	0.02	-2.16
Nicaragua	0.27	0.14	0.93
Niger	0.42	0.21	0.97
Nigeria	0.84	0.5	1.17
Norway	0.01	0	-2.14
Oman	0.29	0.15	-0.83
Pakistan	0.71	0.4	0.76
Panama	0.52	0.3	0.37
Papua New Guinea	0.13	0.06	0.79
Paraguay	0.12	0.06	1.3
Peru	0.89	0.46	0.33
Philippines	0.21	0.11	0.53
Poland	0	0	-0.51
Portugal	0	0	-1.24
Rwanda	0.71	0.43	0.72
Samoa	0.07	0.03	0.03
Saudi Arabia	0.11	0.06	-0.5
Senegal	0.32	0.17	0.27

Country	PI	FI	Corruption
Seychelles	0.05	0.02	-0.61
Sierra Leone	0.92	0.57	0.93
Singapore	0.74	0.62	-2.2
Solomon Islands	0.17	0.08	0.98
Somalia	0.01	0	1.75
South Africa	0.79	0.44	-0.56
Spain	0	0	-1.43
Sri Lanka	0.73	0.5	0.18
St. Lucia	0.09	0.05	-0.47
St. Vincent and the Grenadines	0.12	0.06	-0.09
Sudan	0.71	0.43	0.9
Suriname	0.75	0.72	-0.42
Swaziland	0.69	0.36	0.19
Sweden	0.02	0.01	-2.23
Switzerland	0.03	0.02	-2.13
Syrian Arab Republic	0.41	0.22	0.61
Taiwan, China	0.92	0.59	-0.77
Tanzania	0.88	0.65	1.08
Thailand	0.27	0.14	0.2
Togo	0.9	0.62	0.64
Tonga	0.06	0.03	0.59
Trinidad and Tobago	0.81	0.52	-0.14
Tunisia	0.04	0.02	-0.14
Turkey	0.02	0.01	0.2
Uganda	0.85	0.52	0.97
United Arab Emirates	0.84	0.51	-0.83
United Kingdom	0.14	0.07	-2.13
United States	0.47	0.26	-1.77
Uruguay	0.17	0.09	-0.68
Vanuatu	0.64	0.32	0.85
Venezuela	0.23	0.12	0.67
Yemen, Rep.	0.98	0.51	0.66
Zambia	0.89	0.45	0.9
Zimbabwe	0.96	0.5	0.96

Table 2. Summary Statistics

	Mean	Std. Dev.	Min	Max
Corruption	0.07	1.08	-1.91	3.34
PI	0.47	0.36	0	1
FI	0.29	0.24	0	0.78
GDP	6475.89	6441.84	399.22	25670.57
Education	10.51	9.47	0.4	46.4
Openness	74.13	49.17	6.59	358.11
Resource	0.28	0.45	0	1
Common	0.23	0.42	0	1
Federal	0.12	0.32	0	1

Table 3. Pairwise Correlations

	Corruption	PI	FI	GDP	Education	Openness	Resource	Common Law	Federal
Corruption	1.00								
PI	0.65	1.00							
FI	0.44	0.95	1.00						
GDP	-0.90	-0.47	-0.39	1.00					
Education	-0.71	-0.37	-0.25	0.76	1.00				
Openness	-0.24	0.09	0.16	0.21	0.14	1.00			
Resurce	0.33	0.18	0.14	-0.23	-0.16	0.00	1.00		
Common Law	-0.17	0.19	0.20	0.11	0.03	0.16	-0.07	1.00	
Federal	-0.25	-0.24	-0.21	0.33	0.20	-0.15	-0.15	0.11	1.00

B. Fractionalization and Corruption

As mentioned earlier, the religious fractionalization index increases with the number of groups. On the other hand, according to Montalvo and Reynal-Querol (2005), ethnic and religious fractionalization do not necessarily increase ethnocentric behavior: we are, in fact, less likely to observe ethnocentric behavior in highly homogeneous and highly heterogeneous countries. Increases in diversity, after some point, decrease the effect of an individual ethnic or religious group on corruption. If this is indeed the case, we should see an inverse-U shaped relationship between the religious fractionalization and the corruption which should yield a corruption maximizing level of fractionalization. To capture the presence of such a relationship we modify our basic model as follows:

$$Corruption_i = \beta_0 + \beta_1 FI_i + \beta_2 FI_i^2 + \beta_3 X_i + \varepsilon_i \quad (4)$$

Including *FI* and FI^2 together in the model is, in fact, related conceptually to the polarization effect. Indeed, if there is an inverse-U shaped relationship between *FI* and *Corruption*, it means that the higher the polarization, the higher the corruption.

The results of the OLS estimation are given in the second column of Table 4. The estimated coefficient of *FI* is positive and FI^2 is negative and they are both significant at the 1 percent level.[8] This does indicate an inverse-U shaped relationship between the religious

[8] *FI* and FI^2 are jointly significant at the 1 percent level as well.

fractionalization index and the corruption index. All else constant, the corruption is maximized when *FI* = 0.57 which falls well within the range of observed values of FI (0.00; 0.78). *FI* would equal 0.50 if there were two equal religious groups in a country. In other words, according to our results, corruption is maximized when there are two equal ethnic or religious groups in a country. It makes perfect sense because, as mentioned earlier, *PI* reaches a maximum when there are two equal religious groups in a country. Indeed, we do find a positive relationship between religious polarization and corruption. Our results concerning the effects of the control variables on corruption are consistent with earlier studies. The estimated coefficients for *Education*, *GDP*, *Openness*, *Common Law*, *Resource,* and *Federal* are statistically significant in both models. We find that increases in per capita GDP decreases corruption. The higher the level of education in a country, the lower is the corruption. Furthermore, the more open the country is to international trade the lower is the corruption.

As the share of fuels, minerals, and metals in total exports increases, corruption increases. Finally, while corruption is lower in countries with common law systems, it is higher in countries with a federal governmental structure. Finally, corruption is higher in the Middle Eastern and North African countries.[9]

Table 4. OLS Estimation: Religious Diversity and Corruption

	Corruption	Corruption
PI	0.58 (0.14)***	
FI		1.89 (0.74)***
FI^2		-1.65 (1.11)*
GDP (100^2)	-1.29 (0.10)***	-1.27 (0.10)***
Education	-0.007 (0.005)*	-0.008 (0.006)*
Openness	-0.001 (0.001)*	-0.002 (0.001)**
Resource	0.29 (0.09)***	0.29 (0.09)***
Common Law	-0.29 (0.08)***	-0.31 (0.08)***
Federal	0.23 (0.11)**	0.21 (0.11)**
MENA	0.15 (0.09)*	0.15 (0.10)*
N	105	105
R-squared	0.87	0.88

Standard errors in parentheses. All tests are one-tailed.
* significant at 10%; ** significant at 5%; *** significant at 1%.

[9] Initially, we did include other regional dummy variables in our regressions. Nevertheless, since they were never significant we decided to keep only one regional dummy *MENA*.

4. Robustness of the Results

The main robustness issue is the presence of outliers. To address this issue, we employ Hadi's (1992, 1994) and Grubbs' (1969) methodologies. Neither methodology identifies any outliers in our estimations. Second, in order to get a more detailed picture of the relationship between polarization and fractionalization indices and corruption, we estimate the model using kernel regression. Kernel regression is simply a non-parametric data driven regression technique that determines the shape of the relationship between the dependent variable, corruption, and the independent variables, in this case, religious polarization and fractionalization. Figures 3 and 4 present the results of the kernel regression of corruption on religious polarization and fractionalization, respectively.[11]

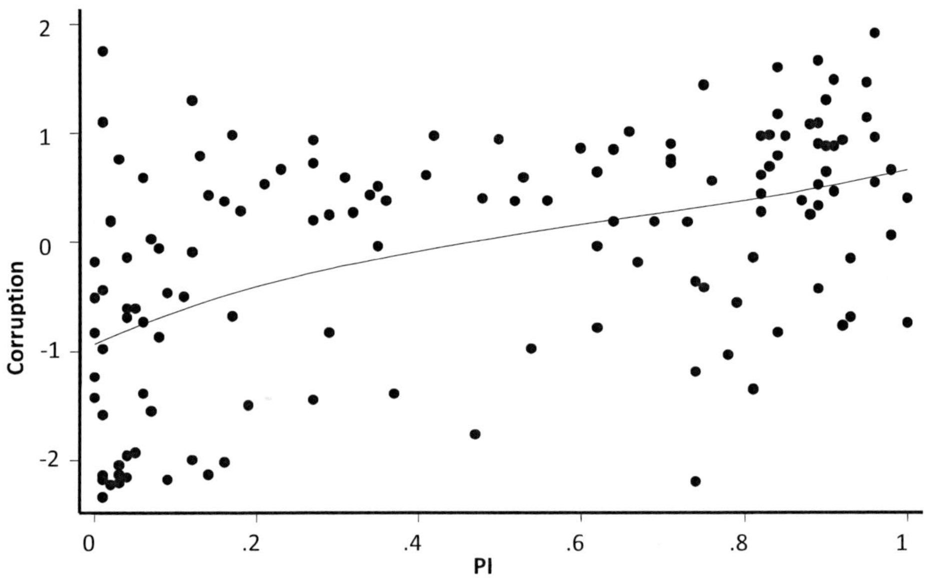

Figure 3. Kernel Regression: Corruption and Religious Polarization.

The results of the kernel regression also confirm the positive relationship between polarization and corruption and the inverse U-shaped relationship between fractionalization and corruption.

Concluding Remarks

There are quite a few studies in the literature investigating the possible causes of corruption across countries. In this study, we add a new dimension by investigating whether or not religious diversity affects corruption and second how it does so. To measure religious diversity, we use both polarization and fractionalization indices. Most of the studies in the literature have treated these two indices as two rival indices and conducted their investigation

[11] A Gaussian kernel with a half bandwidth of 25 percent is used. The results are not particularly sensitive to the choice of the kernel. Epanechnikov kernel, for example, yields very similar results.

accordingly. They have assumed a linear relationship between polarization and corruption as well as a linear relationship between fractionalization and corruption. This is not a realistic assumption considering that for low levels of fractionalization, the polarization and fractionalization indices are positive and highly correlated; for medium levels of fractionalization, the correlation is zero; and for high levels of fractionalization, the correlation is negative. In other words, it is more realistic to assume a linear relationship between polarization and corruption and a non-linear relationship between fractionalization and corruption. Indeed, when we use the polarization index as our measure of diversity, we do find a positive and linear relationship between religious diversity and corruption and when we use the fractionalization index, we find an inverse-U-shaped relationship between religious diversity and corruption.

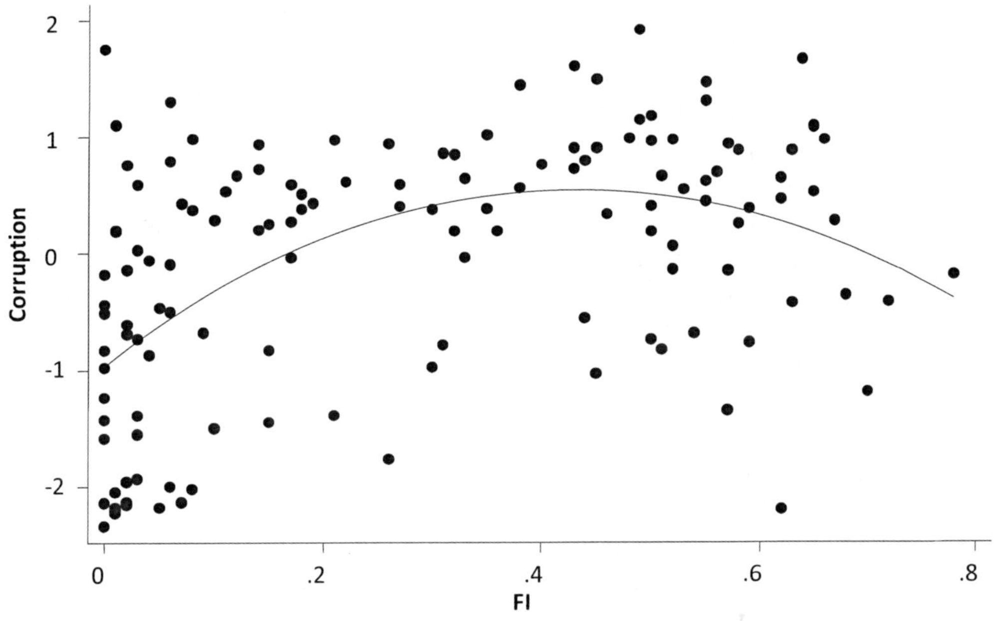

Figure 4. Kernel Regression: Corruption and Religious Fractionalization.

According to our estimations, religious diversity *per se* explains almost 25% of the variation in corruption across countries. This percentage increases to almost 90% when control variables are included in the analysis. A 1 standard deviation increase in religious polarization index causes corruption index to increase by 0.17 standard deviations which is almost 3 times bigger than the effects of openness and education on corruption. All else constant, the corruption index is maximized when the fractionalization index is equal to 0.57.

There are, of course, many questions not answered by our study and a number of paths are available for future research. Treisman (2000), for example, found a negative relationship between the share of Protestants in a country's population and corruption. It may be worthwhile to investigate if the effect of Protestantism on corruption changes depending on the level of religious diversity in a country.

REFERENCES

Ades, A. and Di Tella, R. (1999). "Rents, Competition and Corruption." *American Economic Review, 89, 982-994.*

Alesina, A., Devleeschauwer, A., Easterly, W., Kurlat, S. and Wacziarg, R. (2003). "Fractionalization." *Journal of Economic Growth*, 8, 155-194.

Berghe, P. L. van den (1987). The Ethnic Phenomenon. Westport. CT: Praeger.

Dincer O. C. (2008). "Ethnic and Religious Diversity and Corruption." *Economics Letters*, 99, 98-102.

Glaeser, E. L. and Saks, R. E. (2006). "Corruption in America." *Journal of Public Economics*, 90, 1053-1072.

Grubbs, F (1969). "Procedures for Detecting Outlying Observations in Samples." *Technometrics*, 11, 1-21.

Hadi, A. S. (1992). "Identifying Multiple Outliers in Multivariate Data." *Journal of the Royal Statistical Society*, *Series* (*B*), 54, 761–771.

Hadi, A. S. (1994). "A Modification of a Method for the Detection of Outliers in Multivariate Samples." *Journal of the Royal Statistical Society*, *Series* (*B*), 56, 393–396.

Kaufmann, D., Kraay, A. and Zoido-Lobaton, P (2002). "Governance Matters II: Updated Indicators for 2000/01." World Bank Policy Research Working Paper 2772.

La Porta, R., Lopez-de-Silanes, F., Shleifer, A. andVishny, R.W. (1999). "The Quality of Government." *Journal of Law, Economics and Organization*, 15, 222–279.

Montalvo, J. G. and Reynal-Querol, M. (2005). "Ethnic Diversity and Economic Development." *Journal of Development Economics*, 76, 293-323.

Treisman, D. (2000). "The Causes of Corruption: A Cross-National Study." *Journal of Public Economics*, 76, 399-457.

Vanhanen, T. (1999). "Domestic Ethnic Conflict and Ethnic Nepotism." *Journal of Peace Research*, 36, 55-73.

In: International Political Economy
Editors: M.A. Galindo Martin, E. Nissan
ISBN: 978-1-60876-172-2

Chapter 15

SOCIAL MARKET ECONOMY AND WELFARE STATE TOWARDS THE FORMATION OF A NEW CYBERECONOMY

José-Manuel Saiz-Álvarez
Nebrija University, Spain

ABSTRACT

The recent economic and financial crisis has led to questions about the appropriateness of State intervention in the economy and the need for greater regulation. This has increased State intervention, characteristic of the European Ordoliberal model, and clashes with the U.S. Neoliberal model. In this chapter the benefits of a greater EU-style State intervention are stated, and how ICTs can contribute to the development of Latin American and Central and Eastern European countries.

1. INTRODUCTION

Globalization is changing paradigms among corporations, a process accelerated in the first decade of the XXI Century. From an internal corporate view based on mere profit maximization, newly-born firms and technologically advanced ones interact to maximize the number of customers whose decisions are being taken into account. In fact, we are verifying this firm's philosophical change, as it is stated that it is better for corporations to "stop listening to your customers and start interacting with them" (Shiffman, 2008: p. 21).

This greater interaction between businesses and customers also exists in politics among politicians and citizens. This is positive, not only to ensure a greater flow of information to maximize the levels of social and economic welfare among countries, but also to achieve social and economic changes as a whole.

Consumers are transforming their attitudes and decisions from passive (net receiving) to active (net giving), as they increasingly influence the market resulting in a higher influence in the market. This fact is increasingly important, mainly when economic and financial crises arise, as attitudes and psychological variables are vital for corporations to compete, and even to survive.

In this economic structural change, the Information and Communication Technologies (ICTs), mainly the Internet, have a key role to play. We need to think of the Web as a living entity, where hundreds of millions of Internet users freely interact in a 365x24x7 scheme. In the midst of a great change from the static and plain one-to-one consumer influence in a word-of-mouth axis, Internet users in the XXI century will interact in social networks linked worldwide, conceived as social capital (Saiz-Álvarez, 2009), so viral marketing and political power in the Net can emerge. This type of marketing will change what has been established from the XX century back to the beginning of the Industrial Revolution.

ICTs are reinventing the usual marketing practices based on a direct relationship between sellers and buyer-consumers. In this relationship, publicity has a key role to play, as it interacts between them, and can be directed to guide a consumer's decisions as a whole.

On the other hand, from an economic policy perspective, the European Union (EU) follows the Ordoliberal model characterized by an active State intervention in the economy. This has favored the Central and Eastern European Countries accession to the EU on May 1, 2004. So, Ordoliberalism is based on combining free market and State interventionism to achieve Pareto efficiency for a society as a whole[1]. Although it is possible to have Pareto efficiency without allocative efficiency by shifting resources in the economy, a gain in benefit to one individual could be greater than the loss in benefit to another individual, as stated in the Kaldor-Hicks efficiency, so before such a shift, the market is not allocatively efficient, but might be Pareto efficient. State regulation, according to ordoliberals, must foster competition and should be directed to avoid the creation of monopolies and oligopolies, while separating economic objectives from political ones.

The objective of this chapter is to analyze how ordoliberalism can contribute to manage the triple-C (Economic crisis, Financial Crisis, and Credibility in the Economic Policy) by combining State interventionism, when necessary, and a free market based on active consumers. The US-based financial crisis has recently shown, according to many thinkers, that classical US neoliberalism must be more flexible, while permitting State interventionism to regulate markets when necessary to avoid further financial and commercial disequilibria.

2. Ordoliberalism and the Freiburg School

The triple-C, that is now hitting the economic structures worldwide, has provoked in the actual members of the European Union (EU-27)[2] a reaffirmation in Ordoliberalism (German neoliberalism) by combining State interventionism and free market (social market economy) (*Soziale Marktwirtschaft*). Far from the term "socialism", Ordoliberalism stresses on combining free market and social welfare not only to help the wealthy, but also to care for all citizens as a whole that compete in a market economy. Ordoliberalism defends, but limits, State interventionism, so it is generally higher in depth in the EU if compared to the US. Ordoliberalism, in fact, is at least responsible from three economic miracles in Europe:

[1] Ordoliberalism has been separated from neoclassical liberalism after Röpke (1946, 1999) and Rüstow (1950) where laissez-faire capitalism has been criticized.

[2] It is expected that by 2020 the EU will be formed by 33 members.

Germany[3] and Austria in the 1950s (*Wirtschaftswunder*), and in Spain in the 1960 and mid-1980 decades (*Milagro económico español*).

One of the key premises to apply Ordoliberalism is the existence of the so-called Welfare State[4] based on citizen's rights to enjoy higher, and more equitable, living standards. Born after the Second World War, the Welfare State is criticized by right-wing libertarians who argue that removing money through legal mechanisms from the working citizens to non-working ones is argued to diminish economic inactivity, and to be theft of the person's property and/or labor and a violation of his property rights.

Despite these critics, mainly arisen from British and French economists, the chief proponents of Ordoliberal theory include German scholars and politicians who design the economic and political model that has been widespread throughout the European countries as a whole.

Being the founder of the Freiburg School, Walter Eucken (1891–1950) was accompanied by Franz Böhm (1895–1977), Hans Grossmann-Doerth[5] (1894–1944), Leonhard Miksch (1901–1950), Alfred Müller-Armack[6] (1901–1978), Wilhelm Röpke (1899–1966), Alexander Rüstow (1885–1963), and Friedrich A. von Hayek (1899–1992).

Economics must be fully understood only when social, political and psychological factors are included as stated by Röpke (1946), a well-grounded Welfare State believer, who points out that free enterprise depends on sociological, moral, and cultural factors for its maintenance and survival, as the "sphere of the market, of competition, of the system where supply and demand move prices and thereby govern production, may be regarded and defended only as part of a wider general order encompassing ethics, law, the natural conditions of life and happiness, the state, politics, and power" (Röpke, 1999: p. 90). Social market economy is based in three cornerstones: freedom, social equity and a sound and well-grounded Christian Social Ethics.

Streit (2006) defends Neoliberalism from attacks done by left-wing politicians arguing that these attacks reveals little knowledge of the European history of ideas and even less knowledge of the workings of a market system, particularly of competition in the case of globalization, and Neoliberal economic and social policies have been designed to serve vested interests over decades, reflecting now the ailment of a rent-seeking society.

From an economic point of view, the EU-27 is an amalgam of very diverse nations with different political, social and economic structures. The strong cultural, historical, linguistic, economic and social development of all Europe enriches his legacy to humanity. The legacy continues over time, as the continent is unified, and is affecting the people inhabiting it.

One of the biggest differences between the European and the US Neoliberal models is the strong role of the State in the European economy. Intervention that is made from four levels

---

3 Ludwig Erhard, as Minister of Finance in the Konrad Adenauer's Government from 1949 to 1963, is widely recognized as the father of the German economic miracle. While in Germany, economic growth was based on private investment, in Austria the economic growth was based on nationalization of industries and efficiency in labor practices.

4 Outside Europe, there are also Welfare States in Middle Eastern countries (Bahrain, Brunei, Kuwait, Saudi Arabia, Oman, Qatar, and United Arab Emirates) and in Latin America (Uruguay).

5 He argued that a strong State is needed to support social and economic welfare. Close with Eucken, Grossmann-Doerth is considered to be the co-founder of the Ordoliberalism School.

6 He coined the term "Social market economy" during a discussion in a meeting at Hamburg University in 21-22 June 1946. Contrary to all his colleagues who were members of the Freiburg School, Müller-Armack belonged to the Cologne School.

simultaneously: local, regional, national and European, are similar to the Welfare state interventionism as a solid and sustainable social and economic model.

3. Ordoliberalism: Limit Intervention with Supervised Competition

The recent crisis in the U.S. financial system originating from junk mortgages, with the consequent impact on the real economy, has brought into the EU doubts about the goodness of the US Neoliberalism. Over the past few months, critical voices have called into question not only the kindness of the free market, but also the regulatory role of supervisors and the State.

One of the strongest criticisms has been given as a result of the insufficient regulation and monitoring carried out by central banks. Is it good and desirable to have greater regulation? Is the European model better in this regard? What has been learned after the accession of the members of Central and Eastern Europe, former communist countries into the Soviet orbit, into the European Union?

To answer these questions, it is important to take into account the role played by central banks. Central banks are frequently used by their governments as: (1) Instruments for a monetary policy for reducing inflation; and (2) Lenders of last resort to prevent and contain financial disruptions. Perceiving this role — and avoiding inflationary pressures — two conditions must be fulfilled: (1) Technically the banks must be tied to the central bank; (2) Institutionally the central bank needs political autonomy in pursuing exclusively assigned objectives, especially price stability (Görgens and Ruckriegel, 2007).

According to the EU model, mainly based on the European common currency unit, central banks have a tight supervision and regulation role that is strengthened by a net of 15 institutions. The largest existing regulation in Europe in both economic and finance sectors has diminished the impact of a financial crisis in Europe, except Iceland and the United Kingdom, as these two countries have operated with junk mortgages following the US model.

This stronger EU regulation, compared to the US, is complemented with a tight control, interpretation and application of competition rules (Mestmäcker, 2008), trying to avoid illegal practices, for example, trust, illegal mergers, market-and-price sharing agreements, and abuse of dominant position. This control is done from the European Commission, as "competition policy is vital to avoid that smaller players are not the victims of larger competitors, who simply abuse their dominant position, or who get preferential access to state aid. Competition policy is essential to make sure that there is a level playing field and that all national markets are open for all competitors, whatever their size" (Kroes, 2009).

The most crucial task for the liberalization of network industries is the control of the incumbent's and former monopolist's market power. In theory, this can be effected either through *ex ante* regulation by a special agency, which focuses on a limited number of industries, or through *ex post* control by general competition authorities. Haucap and Uhde (2008) show that such a simple dichotomization, neither captures the complexity of the problem, nor the diversity of possible institutional arrangements. Any recommendation on the institutional design of the regulatory framework should depend on how competition has developed in the past what can be expected for the future. However, the consistency of competition law across sectors may suffer, and the regulator may be more prone to regulatory capture than a competition authority. Therefore, they argue that any sector-specific *ex post* control should be accompanied by a sunset clause to guarantee the transition into general competition law. *Ex post* regulation can, however, facilitate a faster exit from sector-specific regulation by climbing down the so-called ladder of remedies.

The company's profit maximization, often with the best competitive position achieved in the sector, aims to benefit stakeholders, especially shareholders, thus ensuring stable business growth rates. A company in continuous growth and with increased opportunities for merging processes, risks becoming an oligopoly in the short term, and a monopoly in the medium-and-long term. So consumers are harmed in the medium-and-long term. That is why, it is essential that Government intervention, except in certain extreme situations but always on a limited basis, must ensure businesses not to reach a position of market dominance detrimental to free competition that can distort market signals as a result of the monopoly power of corporations. EU regulation and supervision are generally good and desirable in certain situations, so it is generally accepted in Europe.

Some of the features of the European ordoliberalism unsuccessfully have tried to be applied into Latin American countries. The reasons for this failure can be found in a multitude of social, economic and political reasons, which must be included the following: (1) Absence of a middle class large enough to sustain a Welfare State similar to the one existing in Europe. This deficiency is supplied by State interventionism, that is more intensive and profound than it would be economically desirable, making many countries in Latin America to be converted into subsistence economies dependent on State financial aid, at regional or local levels, in order to survive; (2) Lack of a progressive tax system (opposite to neocons who defend a regressive tax system), which prevents the occurrence of a redistribution of income from wealthier taxpayers to the poor to guarantee social justice; (3) The close relationship between economic and political interests, generating corruption that benefits oligarchies only; (4) The emergence of subsistence economies characterized by exporting low-added value services and goods; (5) Absence of economic locomotives (i.e., Germany and France in the EU) that can impulse the Latin American region as a whole; (6) The existence of strong external-and-internal debts that impede economic growth and social justice; and (7) The avoidance of capital to invest, close with, in some countries, the generation of black money illegally transferred abroad.

International development and co-operation policies try to achieve two goals simultaneously: poverty alleviation and democratization. Using a rational choice approach to non-democratic regimes, Pies and Wockenfuss (2008) argue that there is a trade-off between these two goals when development policies are applied to, or within, dictatorships. In any such cases, more poverty alleviation means less democratization, and this fact can be resolved only if co-operation accelerates development.

The higher levels of growth, wealth creation and economic-and-social welfare, the better the EU Welfare State will be, and the less political and economic corruption we shall have. Besides, the Welfare State is empowering democratic processes in Europe, especially in the "new Europe" nations (Slovakia, Slovenia, Estonia, Hungary, Latvia, Lithuania, Poland and Czech Republic). So, the strong partnership between government and enterprises is the creation of a widespread crowding-in effects that largely outweigh crowding-out effects resulting, in many cases, in a positive State intervention.

4. GLOBALIZATION, ICT AND VIRAL MARKETING

Faced with these problems and imbalances in Latin American countries, a new economic paradigm can emerge to allow these nations to escape from poverty and underdevelopment. For decades there have been a number of growth strategies, in which the technology was not conceived as a solution.

The intense use of ICTs to avoid underdevelopment, as well as good training programs in which universities have a key role to play, constitutes a new economic paradigm to give economic value to enterprises based on intellectual capital (as a sum of human capital, relational capital and structural capital). Paradigm strictly focused on the common good (Figure 1).

One of the main forces of the Latin America countries, as in BRIC (Brazil, Russia, India and China) is given by population. Latin American's population pyramids are distinctly pyramidal, unlike of the oldest countries in the world wherein the distribution of the population is in the form of an inverted pyramid, if the population is very old, or in the form of a piggy bank, if the mature population (30-55 years) overwhelms others.

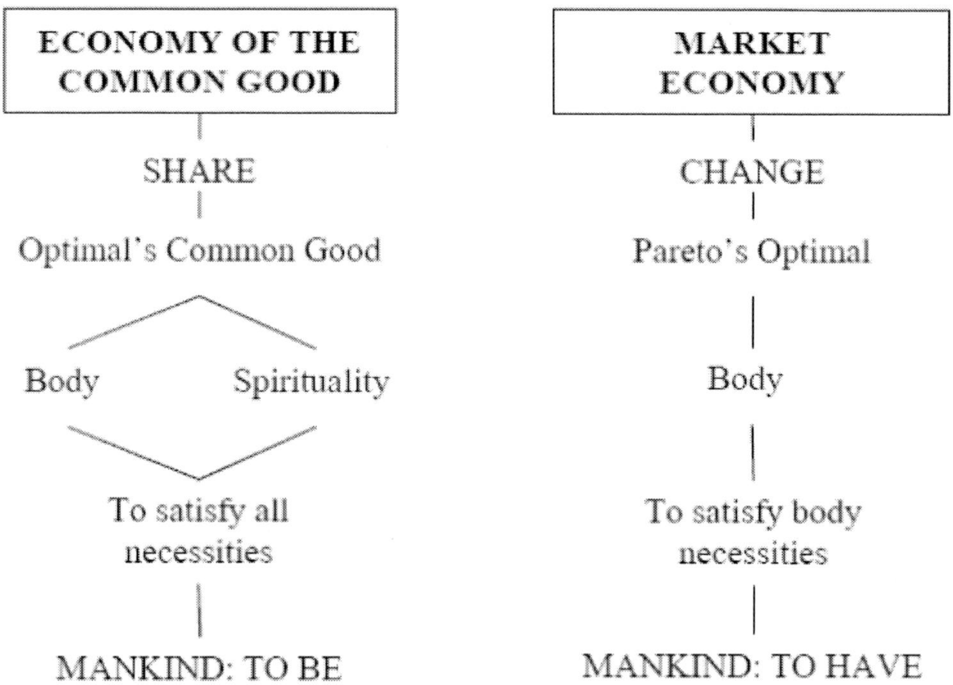

Source: Saiz-Alvarez (2004a, p. 120).

Figure 1. Economy of the Common Good.

The proper technical and vocational education towards the population aiming to combat corruption, the achieving of a fair distribution of wealth, the relief of debt and the improvement of transport and communications, will make Latin America a more prosperous and socially just countries. And in order to achieve this double goal, both desirable from ethics and social justice, ICT have a crucial role to play, not only to train people in remote and outlying villages, but also to change consumer habits, as in First World countries where populations seek comfort, price and quality of products and services they buy. That is why a reinvention of the marketing in Latin America, like what is happening in Central and Eastern Europe and in some regions in India, is necessary and good for companies, regardless of their geographical location, so they can achieve higher sustainable profit and growth.

4.1. Viral Marketing as a Reinvention of Marketing

Viral marketing can be defined as the use of ICTs as an active tool for marketing in interaction with consumers, whose decisions are based on a Word-of-mouth and social networks (mainly Facebook, Xing, Hi5, LinkedIn, Tuenti and Ciao) strengthen by friendship, family relations, loyalty and firms and clients' reputation. Viral marketing is much powerful than a traditional marketing, as it seeks "to increase awareness or adoption of a product by taking advantage of the relationship network among consumers, that is, awareness or adoption spreads from consumer to consumer" (Hill, Provost and Volinsky, 2008, p. 2) by recommending them (Kautz *et al*, 1997) based on reputation.

Viral marketing has received a series of names, as it has been called *word-of-mouth marketing, diffusion of innovation, buzz marketing* and *network marketing*. Although some seminal research works have been published to clearly distinguish among these types of marketing, we can conclude that all of them are so well-interconnected that there is no a large difference among them[7]. As a result, viral marketing can be threefold be achieved (Hill, Provost and Volinsky, 2008, p. 5):

a) *Implicit advocacy*. Implicit or conspicuous advocacy is getting more important as a strategy of part of viral marketing. Firms commonly capitalize on influential individuals, as journalists, athletes and actors, to sell their products as a sign of distinction and success.
b) *Explicit advocacy*. It happens when consumers (real or potential) can become oral advocates of large known products. In this case, publicity campaigns can reinforce the selling of these products that can be sold worldwide.
c) *Network targeting*. In some occasions firms can be even more interested in selling their products to a selected group of consumers, as part of the marketing process of the product. In this case, products are, in general, highly-priced and not largely produced.

Although these three ways can be combined, viral marketing is characterized by joining network targeting and implicit advocacy. Nevertheless, this new type of marketing mainly benefits to large corporations, most of them multinationals, as their products are widely known by consumers. As a result, it is expected the establishment of strategic alliances among firms to keep them in pace of leadership.

When explicit advocacy is strong, product value tends to augment, as well as price as demand increases. Satisfied consumers are the best tool for marketing in a Word-for-mouth bases, as psychological variables play a key role in the selling process, as sharing information about a product in a social network, for example, can destroy the firm's selling objective for

[7] In Orzan and Orzan (2007) differences between Word-of-Mouth Marketing and Viral Marketing are studied.

the year or the season. In this sense, Internet is playing a key role as hundreds of millions of citizens interact everyday.

4.2. Viral marketing, Information and Leadership

Viral marketing is directly connected to real-time information. In effect, good news about a product not only affects to future (and present) consumers, but also to, even the financial stability of the firm, as shares, for example, can be negative or positively affected. As viral marketing affects to consumer's preferences and values, as well as the product diffusion, it finally affects to the firm's EBITDA (*Earnings before Interests, Taxes, Depreciation and Amortization*) and directly connected to it, to stakeholders and, above all, stockholders.

Consumer decision making comes about as an attempt to solve consumer problems and desires (Hawkins *et al*, 2004). In this sense, consumers' needs can be fully satisfied, and even new market niches can be achieved. Viral marketing can be, as a result, a low-cost tool for competition to achieve higher economic results for corporations that will benefit the stakeholders as a whole, and mainly shareholders.

The speed of product diffusion depends to some extent on the speed of product adoption, and predicts the number of users that will adopt an innovation (Saiz-Alvarez and García-Ochoa, 2008). This number is estimated taking into account the joint influence of marketing viral, publicity and market potential, but not taking into account the product life cycle, as in Moore (1999), or the multiproduct life cycle, as in Saiz-Alvarez (2004b). Product diffusion is connected to price, technology, and consumption effects (bandwagon, snob and novelty effects). Excepting less-developed countries, Internet has boosted competition worldwide. As a result, they must use ICTs to reduce the gap between consumers and the firm. As new technologies arise, viral marketing spreads throughout the Net, and competition increases, as consumers have a lot of virtual places to buy and to satisfy their needs.

In this viral marketing, consumer's value is important. As it is subjective, only qualitative techniques can be used to analyze it, and firms are obliged to augment the number of products to achieve consumers with specific and specialized needs. As these needs are positively fulfilled, consumers' values will be higher thanks to a well-conceived firm's viral marketing policy. Hill, Provost and Volinsky (2008) note that telecommunication networks present a natural test bed for viral marketing models, as: (1) viral-marketed consumers, those who have previously communicated with a person who subscribes to the service, respond 3-5 times greater than non-viral marketed consumers; (2) modeling attributes constructed from the consumer network can ameliorate target marketing; and (3) new consumers can be attracted due to advocacy (e.g., word-of-mouth) using viral marketing. As stated by Huberman, Romero and Wu (2008) scarcity of attention and the daily rhythms of life and work makes people default to interacting with those few that matter and that reciprocate their attention, that is, mainly a set of friends and followers.

4.3. The Importance of Word-of-Mouth

Word-of mouth can be defined as a type of spontaneous communication, mainly used in small social networks (family, friends and coworkers), that gives information to members of the net to guide consumer decisions towards certain products. The larger the network is, the more effective is the word-of-mouth. But this information will only be effective if it is credible by listeners and followers.

One of the main strengths of the word-of-mouth is that the information is credible, as social networks were the information is shared are small. A positive word-of-mouth positively affects to firm's goodwill and shares and stock options' prices if the corporation is valued in the Stock Markets. Besides, publicity costs tend to diminish while corporate image increases its value among consumers.

Information transmitted by word-of-mouth is different from information transmitted in an impersonal way (Koenig, 1985), as in the former the source is identifiable while in the latter is not (Mauri, 2002). As a result, information in the former case is transmitted more quickly and it is considered conveyable.

Word-of-mouth can be examined from a multiple-fold perspective (Mauri, 2002: p. 4): (a) *Address*, that is, word-of-mouth positive or negative; (b) *Intensity*, measured by the number of contacts; (c) *Speed,* relationship between number of contacts and time; (d) *Persistence*, duration of time; (e) *Importance,* consumers' decisions role, variable according to products and subjects; and (f) *Credibility*, depending on the social net work strength.

Depending on these variables, a given ICTs and highly-valued technological changes, a new labor market can be created (Saiz-Álvarez, 2004a) where interactive consumers share information, so Internet will be fundamental for success. Modern-and-highly capital valued firms will be able to lead this process wherein intellectual capital, formed by human capital, structural capital and relational capital, has a key role to play.

5. A New Economy, a New Society

The New Economy is defined by "a greater use of science by industry; the proliferation of academic disciplines; the diffusion of a series of critical inventions; the rise of big business; and the growth of retailing" (Goldin, 2001). This New Economy, born from speculation, competition and free markets, has expanded rapidly around the world thanks to globalization. Hence the New Economy acts as a soft power that shapes and transforms slowly, but steadily, societies and economies that are distant from the main financial and commercial world.

This transformation is especially acute in former communist countries in both Asia and Europe, where there was no separation between political power and economic incentives that the economic inefficiency, political corruption and social inequality. The exchange of information obtained from ICTs has accelerated this process of transformation, which has placed these countries in the main financial flows, trade and economic world. Consequently, ICTs are changing the economic, social and entrepreneurial structures. We are witnessing the birth of a Postindustrial Technological Cybersociety (PTC) (Saiz-Alvarez, 2008) where the technology unites borders, reduces social differences, helps people and businesses to create and wider market niches, lowers operating costs, and gives greater economic and technical efficiency.

Seen from this perspective, ICTs constitute a golden opportunity to regain lost ground, enabling a better adaptation to consumers. Thus, in a globalized environment, ICTs allow "designing and delivering superior customer value propels organizations to market leadership positions in highly competitive global markets" (Johnson and Weinstein, 2004: p. 2). This New Economy based on the intercom and new technologies can compete simultaneously with first-and-second order advantages, provided that in this second case the Unit labor costs are low, as in Latin America and the countries of Central and Eastern Europe.

The political, economic and social structural changes of Central and Eastern European countries after the fall of the Berlin Wall on November 9, 1989, and thus allow the change from a communist system to a free market, has led to study the transfer or return of property rights to the rightful owners who were expropriated or evicted from their homes decades ago. According to Wegehenkel and Walterscheid (2008) after the collapse of socialist regimes with a command economy, there was a burst of decentralization but this movement has been recently reversed. Only those countries with decentralized economic systems will be able to create economic welfare ethically based on social justice.

What role is playing the State in these countries of "New Europe"? What role should play in America? In my opinion, only when State intervention is limited, it will be economically effective. Berthold and Koch (2008) state that public debt can be conceived as a negative external effect caused by politicians trying to reduce the costs of their political offer in gaining advantages in the political competition. An increasing public debt must be limited in order to achieve higher economic growth rates.

When the public deficit is used to manage politically the votes of citizens, it is simultaneously a cause of greater political corruption and the rise of populism. Therefore, we must secure the benefits in terms of flexibility in resource allocation and prices on offer, so "policymakers must reinforce their external strategy of liberalization with an internal strategy that gives the State substantial responsibility in building physical and human capital and mediating social conflicts" (Rodrik, 1999).

Conclusion

ICTs are changing the economic and social development of countries, which is especially evident in the "New Europe", and can be a model for initiating structural economic transformation processes in other regions, especially in Latin America. One of the key factors of success for achieving this change is given by the formation of experienced intellectual capital in each country, as well as developing new marketing channels, including viral marketing.

Along with these policy changes initiated in the private sector, it is essential to foster a process of constant adjustment and supervision by public authorities to ensure transparency and good practices of the free market. Recent economic and financial crises, accelerated due to a lack of good regulation and supervision, has generated criticism towards the U.S. Neoliberal model, while in the EU, as Ordoliberalism prevails, free market is mixed with State intervention. This is an Ordoliberal model that is the foundation of the so-called Welfare State.

Therefore, given the benefits of the EU Ordoliberalism, it is foreseeable that this crisis has laid the groundwork for increasing the level of supervision and regulation by public authorities towards the private sector, as is done in Europe. We are thus witnessing the birth of a new cybersociety characterized by economic globalization, the transfer of millions of data and information in real time, and the intensive use of ICTs and competition worldwide. This is the new society of the XXI century where foreign languages, specialization, formation and professional experience are the keystones for success.

REFERENCES

Balan, C. (2007). Foundations of Strategic Marketing based on Measuring Client's Value (written in Romanian, *Fundamentarea Strategiei de marketing pe baza masurani valorii clientilor*), *Revista de Marketing Online*, *1* (3), Bucarest (Romania): Academy of Economic Studies, School of Marketing, 65-75.

Berthold, N. and Koch, D. (2008). "The Impossibility of Balanced Budgets", *ORDO - Jahrbuch für die Ordnung von Wirtschaft und Gesellschaft* (in English: *ORDO - The Annual Review of Economic and Social Systems*), *59*, 39 – 62.

Del Arco, J. (2004). *Ethics for the Web Society* (written in Spanish, *Ética para la Sociedad Red*). Madrid: Dykinson.

Goldin, C. (2007). The New Economy, Technology, and Learning Outcome Assessments. *Educause Quarterly*, *3*, 6-8.

Hawkins, D.I. et al. (2004). *Consumer behavior: building marketing strategy*, Boston: McGraw-Hill Irwin.

Huberman, B.A.; Romero, D.M. and Wu, F. (2008). Social Networks that matter: Twitter under the Microscope [On-line serial] *First Monday*, *14* (1), Chicago, Ill.: University of Illinois.

Görgens, E. and Ruckriegel, K. (2007). Central banks between government power and stability interest, *ORDO - Jahrbuch für die Ordnung von Wirtschaft und Gesellschaft* (in English: *ORDO - The Annual Review of Economic and Social Systems*), *58*, 17 – 32.

Haucap, J. and Uhde, A. (2008). Regulation and Competition Law in Liberalized Network Industries as Seen form a New Institutional Economics Perspective, *ORDO - Jahrbuch für die Ordnung von Wirtschaft und Gesellschaft* (in English: *ORDO - The Annual Review of Economic and Social Systems*), *59*, 237 – 262.

Hill, S.; Provost, F. and Volinsky, C. (2008). Viral Marketing: Identifying likely adopters via consumer networks, *New York University Working Papers*, 2451/14128, October.

Kautz, H. et al. (1997). Referral web: Combining social networks and collaborative filtering, *Communications on the Acm*, *40*, (3), 63-65.

Johnson, W.C. and Weinstein, A. (2005). *Superior Customer Value in the New Economy. Concepts and Cases*, 2nd Ed. Nueva York: CRC Press.

Koenig, F. (2002). *Rumor in the Market Place: The Social Psychology of Commercial Hearsay*. Dover: Auburn House Publishing Co.

Kowitz, R. (1998). *Alfred Müller-Armack. Economic Policy as a Vocation. A Legal History of the Social Market Economy and Political Workings of University Teachers*. (written in German, *Alfred Müller-Armack. Wirtschaftspolitik als Berufung. Zur Entstehungsgeschichte der Sozialen Marktwirtschaft und dem politischen Wirken des Hochschullehrers*), Cologne.

Kroes, N. (2009). How competition policy benefits SMEs. In: *Craft and SME Convention of UEAPME* (European Association of Craft, Small and Medium-sized Enterprises) at European Economic and Social Committee, Brussels, 27th April.

Mauri, A.G. (2002). The Quality of Firm's Output as Factual Communication: The Role of Word-of-Mouth [On-line serial] (written in Italian, *Le prestazioni dell'impresa come comunicazione 'di fatto' e il ruolo del passaparola*), *Sinergie*, vol. 59, pp. 1-13. [Available at SSRN: http://ssrn.com/abstract=740207]

Mestmäcker, E-J. (2008). Freedom of Competition and Efficiency of Firms, *ORDO - Jahrbuch für die Ordnung von Wirtschaft und Gesellschaft* (in English: *ORDO - The Annual Review of Economic and Social Systems*), *59*, 185 – 208.

Orzan, M. and Orzan, G. (2007). Word-of-Mouth Marketing *vs* Marketing Viral (written in Romanian, *Word-of-Gura de Marketing vs Marketing virale*). *Revista de Marketing Online*, *1*, (3), Bucarest (Romania): Academy of Economic Studies, School of Marketing, 76-80.

Pies, I. and Wockenfuß, C. (2008). Poverty Reduction versus Democracy Promotion? How to Overcome the Trade-Off in Development Cooperation, *ORDO - Jahrbuch für die Ordnung von Wirtschaft und Gesellschaft* (in English: *ORDO - The Annual Review of Economic and Social Systems*), 59, 405 – 439.

Rodrik, D. (1999). *The New Global Economy and developing Countries: Making Openness Work*. Policy Essay, 24. Washington, D.C.: Overseas Development Council.

Röpke, W. (1999). *A Humane Economy: The Social Framework of the Free Market*, 4d ed., Wilmington, DE: ISI Books (1st ed. (1946) in German, *Civitas Humana. Grundfragen der Gesellschafts-und Wirtschaftsreform* (Fundamental Questions of Social and Economic Reform), Zürich: Rents).

Rüstow, A. (1950). *The Failure of Economic Liberalism* (written in German, *Das Versagen des Wirtschaftsliberalismus*), Metropolis.

Saiz-Álvarez, J.M. (2009). Group Cyber-entrepreneurships and Virtual Social Networks in the Postindustrial Technological Cybersociety (PTC) (written in Spanish, *Ciberemprendedores grupales y redes sociales virtuales en la Cibersociedad Tecnológica Postindustrial* (CTP)), *ICADE*, *76*, January-April, Madrid (Spain): Pontifical University of Comillas, 83-93.

Saiz-Álvarez, J.M. (2008)(*Coord.*). *Economic Integration and Social Development: reflections on the challenges of XXI Century* (written in Spanish, *Integración Económica y Desarrollo Social: reflexiones ante los retos del siglo XXI*). Madrid (Spain): FIEC.

Saiz-Álvarez, J.M. (2004a). *Keys for a New Labor Market* (written in Spanish, *Claves para un nuevo mercado de trabajo*). Alicante (Spain): ECU.

Saiz-Álvarez, J.M. (2004b). *Audiovisual Economy* (written in Spanish, *Economía Audiovisual*). Buenos Aires (Argentina): Libros en Red.

Saiz-Álvarez, J.M. and García-Ochoa, M. (2008): *Business Innovation and Economic Globalization* (written in Spanish, *Innovación empresarial y globalización económica*). 2nd Ed. Madrid (Spain): FIEC.

Schmidt, A. (2008). Order Economic Concepts of Competition: Competition Policy between Economic Freedom and Efficiency, *ORDO - Jahrbuch für die Ordnung von Wirtschaft und Gesellschaft* (in English: *ORDO - The Annual Review of Economic and Social Systems*, *59*, 209–236.

Streit, M.E. (2006). Neoliberalism – a questionable system of ideas?, *ORDO - Jahrbuch für die Ordnung von Wirtschaft und Gesellschaft* (in English: *ORDO - The Annual Review of Economic and Social Systems*), *57*, 91–98.

Wegehenkel, L. and Walterscheid, H. (2008). The Structure of Property Rights and the Evolution of Economic Systems–Path Dependences Leading Towards Centralization? *ORDO - Jahrbuch für die Ordnung von Wirtschaft und Gesellschaft* (in English: *ORDO - The Annual Review of Economic and Social Systems*), *59*, 313 – 341.

INDEX

B

C

F

G

H

I

J

K

L

N

O

P

Q

R

S

T

U

V

W

Y

Z